Coastal Navigation

&

Q&A MANUAL

by

Jackie and Noel Parry

Published in Australia 2018 by SisterShip Training Pty Ltd, Jackie Parry. NSW Australia

www.sistershiptraining.com

Copyright ©SisterShip Training Pty Ltd / ©Jackie Parry

All rights reserved. Without limiting the rights under copyright above, no part of this publication may be reproduced, stored in or introduced into a retrieval system or transmitted in any form or by any means (electronic, mechanical, photocopying, recording, or otherwise), without prior written permission of the owner/Publisher.

National Library of Australia data:

Jackie Parry, 2018, Coastal Navigation

ISBN: 978-0-6451815-4-8

In Partnership with RTO 20665 – The Learning Professionals – ABN 87 281 145 065

SisterShip Training Pty Ltd – ABN 99 635 698 896 – is an authorised Nominated Representative of The Learning Professionals – ABN 87 281 145 065 – RTO 20665 – and is approved by NSW Maritime to provide practical boat training and/or knowledge testing for the NSW general boat driving licence and PWC driving licence.

Why Choose Us

Our philosophy
"There is no such thing as a silly question"
and
"Be an encourager there are far too many critics in the world already".

With over 60 years combined, international experience, we will share all our experience with you, gained from traversing over 80,000 nautical miles.

- Trained local NSW Marine Police
- Taught commercial maritime tickets at TAFE
- Ex-Marine Rescue Skippers
- Circumnavigated the world one-and-a-half times (we've circumnavigated Tahiti too!)
- Award winning Skippers (joint top student Master 5, top student MED3)
- Award winning authors
- Written pilot books
- Written best-selling memoirs (on our travels)
- Written manuals on: Navigation, Weather, and created a useful Log Book (Shop Nautical)
- Host a popular Podcast Show: Turning your Cruising Dreams into Reality
- Professional maritime trainers for 10 years
- Taught/sailed/worked on a variety of boats all over the world
- Utilised a wide variety of marine equipment (VHF/HF/MF, Navigation systems, radar)
- AIS, GPS, plotters, Weather, etc), all over the world
- Partnered with a Registered Training Organisation and we conform to National Training Standards
- Everyone is treated equally and fairly
- Documented safety system – we look after your personal details
- Competitive pricing

We love all things boating, and we are super proud to watch many of our students turn into great skippers!
One of our team has even set a blue-water sailing record!

Don't take our word for it, read the testimonials on our website
www.sistershiptraining.com

SHOP NAUTICAL
WWW.SISTERSHIPTRAINING.COM

BY THE SAME AUTHOR, AVAILABLE FROM: WWW.SISTERSHIPTRAINING.COM/SHOPNAUTICAL

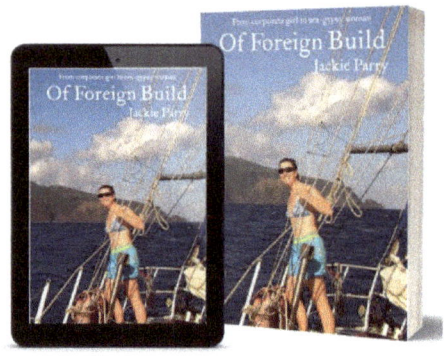

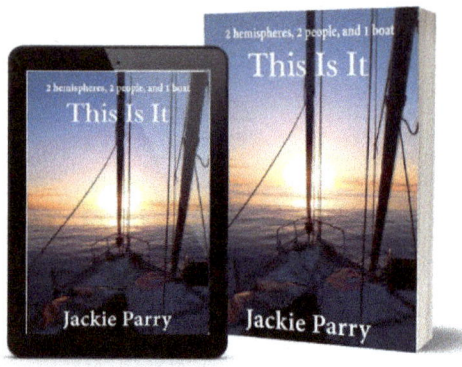

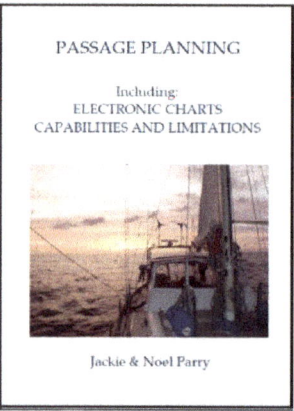
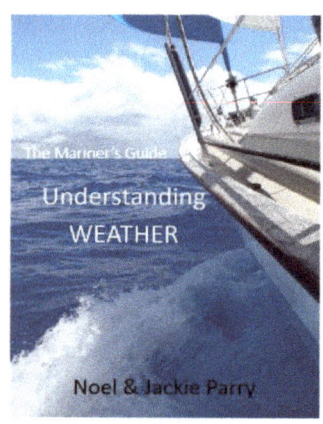

Contents

Why Choose Us 3
Our philosophy 3
INTRODUCTION 10
SECTION ONE 11
    WHERE ON EARTH ARE WE? 11
        What do the Co-ordinates Mean? 11
        Latitude 11
        How are the Angles Measured? 12
        Longitude (Meridians) 13
        How are the Angles Measured? 14
        The Great Circle 14
    LATITUDE AND LONGITUDE 15
        Degrees, Minutes, and Seconds – Decimalise Example 15
        Exercise 1 and 2 – Time Calculations on page 1 Questions and Answers booklet 15
        Answers 1 and 2 – Time Calculations on page 31 Questions and Answers booklet ...15
    DISTANCE 16
        Nautical Mile/One Minute of Latitude 16
    DIRECTION 17
        The Degree 17
    SPEED DISTANCE TIME 19
        Formula and Calculations 19
        Speed, Distance, Time – Example 1 19
        Speed, Distance, Time – Example 2 20
        Speed, Distance, Time – Example 3 20
        Speed, Distance, Time – Example 4 21
        Exercise 3 – Speed, Distance, Time on page 2 Questions and Answers Booklet 21
        Answers 3 – Speed, Distance, Time on page 32 Questions and Answers Booklet 21
    CHARTS 21
        Purpose 21
        It answers the question, *"Where am I?"* 21
        Features 21
        Chart Errors 25
        Example 1 – Chart Errors: 26
        Example 2 – Chart Errors: 26
        Zone of Confidence (ZOC) Are your chart depths and seafloor features accurate? ...26
        Possible errors in depths 28

Defining Positions 28

SYMBOLS AND ABBREVIATIONS 29

Exercise 4 – Chart Symbols page 6 in Questions and Answers Booklet 29

Answers 4 – Chart Symbols page 38 in Questions and Answers Booklet 29

CHART WORK 30

Navigation Equipment 30

Equipment List 31

Position: Correct Chart Work & Symbols 32

PLOTTING BY LATITUDE AND LONGITUDE 33

How to Plot Your Position 33

Exercise 5 – Position Practice page 9 in Questions and Answers Booklet 40

Answers 5 – Position Practice page 41 in Questions and Answers Booklet 40

POSITION FIXING BY BEARING AND DISTANCE 41

Distance 41

Measuring Over Large Distances 43

Exercise 6 – Distance page 9 in Questions and Answers Booklet 46

Answers 6 – Distance page 41 in Questions and Answers Booklet 46

BEARINGS 47

Direction 47

True Bearings 48

Finding your Course 49

Direction and Bearings 49

Reciprocal Course 51

Exercise 7 – Direction/Bearings page 9 in Questions and Answers Booklet 56

Answers 7– Direction/Bearings page 41 in Questions and Answers Booklet 56

SECTION SUMMARY 56

SECTION TWO 57

THE COMPASS – TRUE TO COMPASS AND COMPASS TO TRUE 57

Compass 57

True North and Magnetic North 57

Cardinal points and steering 57

Points of a compass 57

True chart work 57

True to Compass (or Compass to True) 58

Variation 58

Example - Variation: 58

More Variation Examples 59

Converting True to Compass and Compass to True 61

Example – Compass to True	62
DEVIATION	63
Calculating Deviation	63
Example Deviation Card	64
Example: Calculating Deviation	65
TOTAL ERROR	67
Example – total error	67
BEARINGS	67
Hand-Bearing Compass	67
Exercise 8–Compass to True and True to Compass page 10 in Questions and Answers Booklet	68
Answers 8–Compass to True and True to Compass page 42 in Questions and Answers Booklet	68
THREE BEARING FIX	68
Example – Three Bearing Fix:	68
Cocked Hat	72
Exercise 9: Three Bearing Fix page 14 in Questions and Answers Booklet	75
Answers 9: Three Bearing Fix page 44 in Questions and Answers Booklet	75
POSITION BY BEARING AND DISTANCE	75
Exercise 10– Radar Range Fix page 14 in Questions and Answers Booklet	77
Answers 10– Radar Range Fix page 44 in Questions and Answers Booklet	77
Additional Notes on Radar Use	78
Relative Bearings	78
Bearings Illustrated	79
Additional Notes for Radar Settings	80
Example for Relative Bearing Calculations	81
Exercise 11 – Bearings page 14 in Questions and Answers Booklet	81
Answers 11 – Bearings page 44 in Questions and Answers Booklet	81
SECTION SUMMARY	81
SECTION 3	82
DEDUCED RECKONING (DR) AND ESTIMATED POSITION (EP)	82
Position - DR	82
Example – Deduced Reckoning	82
POSITION – ESTIMATED POSITION (EP)	83
Exercise 12 – Position - DR and EP page 18 in Questions and Answers Booklet	83
Answers 12 – Position - DR and EP page 46 in Questions and Answers Booklet	83
POSITION - RUNNING FIX	84
Exercise 13 – Position - Running Fix page 19 in Questions and Answers Booklet	85

Answers 13 – Position - Running Fix page 46 in Questions and Answers Booklet	85
DOUBLE THE ANGLE OFF THE BOW	85
The Isosceles Triangle - how does it help us?	88
Exercise 14 – Position - Double the Angle off the Bow page 19 in Questions and Answers Booklet	88
Answers 14 – Position - Double the Angle off the Bow page 47 in Questions and Answers Booklet	88
THE TRANSIT BEARING	89
Exercise 15 – Position - Transits page 19 in Questions and Answers Booklet	90
Answers 15 – Position - Transits page 47 in Questions and Answers Booklet	90
SET AND DRIFT	90
Counteracting Set and Drift	90
Exercise 16 – Position – Three Bearing Fix with Set and Drift page 20 in Questions and Answers Booklet	93
Answers 16 – Position – Three Bearing Fix with Set and Drift page 47 in Questions and Answers Booklet	93
LEEWAY	94
Exercise 17 – Leeway page 21 in Questions and Answers Booklet	96
Answers 17 – Leeway page 49 in Questions and Answers Booklet	96
Terminology Reminder	97
SECTION SUMMARY	98
FURTHER INFORMATION	99
Publications	99
SALIENT POINT LATITUDES - CHART NO. AUS 252	101
EXERCISE 1: TIME CALCULATIONS	1
EXERCISE 2: TIME CALCULATIONS	1
EXERCISE 3: SPEED, DISTANCE, TIME	2
EXERCISE 4: CHART SYMBOLS	6
EXERCISE 5: POSITION PRACTICE	9
EXERCISE 6: DISTANCE	9
EXERCISE 7 DIRECTION	9
EXERCISE 9: THREE BEARING FIX	14
EXERCISE 10: RADAR RANGE FIX	14
EXERCISE 11: BEARINGS	14
EXERCISE 12: POSITION – DR and EP	18
EXERCISE 13: POSITION – RUNNING FIX	19
EXERCISE 14: POSITION – DOUBLE THE ANGLE OFF THE BOW	19
EXERCISE 15: POSITION – TRANSITS	19
EXERCISE 16: POSITION – THREE BEARING FIX WITH SET AND DRIFT	20

EXERCISE 17: LEEWAY	21
REVISION	22
Answers Section	30
EXERCISE 1: TIME CALCULATIONS – ANSWERS	31
EXERCISE 2: TIME CALCULATIONS – ANSWERS	31
EXERCISE 3: SPEED, DISTANCE, TIME – ANSWERS	32
EXERCISE 4: CHART SYMBOLS EXERCISE 4 - ANSWERS	38
EXERCISE 5: POSITION PRACTICE - ANSWERS	41
EXERCISE 6: DISTANCE - ANSWERS	41
EXERCISE 7: DIRECTION/BEARINGS - ANSWERS	41
EXERCISE 8: COMPASS TO TRUE AND TRUE TO COMPASS - ANSWERS	42
EXERCISE 9: THREE BEARING FIX – ANSWER	44
EXERCISE 10: RADAR RANGE FIX - ANSWER	44
EXERCISE 11: BEARINGS - ANSWER	44
EXERCISE 12: DR AND EP - ANSWERS	46
EXERCISE 13: RUNNING FIX - ANSWER	46
EXERCISE 14: POSITION – DOUBLE THE ANGLE OFF THE BOW - ANSWERS	47
EXERCISE 15: POSITION – TRANSIT BEARINGS - ANSWERS	47
EXERCISE 16: POSITION – THREE BEARING FIX WITH SET AND DRIFT - ANSWERS	47
EXERCISE 17: POSITION – LEEWAY – ANSWERS	49
REVISION - ANSWERS	50
SALIENT POINTS	56

INTRODUCTION

Where on Earth are we?

But more importantly, what does that mean?

Navigation is basically the art of determining where you are and what direction and distance you must go.

Therefore, we must learn to find out where we are and what that means for us. We do this by understanding the nautical chart, plotting our position, and laying off direction in degrees and distance in nautical miles.

The 'what does this mean?' part is about how you get to where you want to go safely.

Where is your safe water? At all times, you should know this in preparation for an emergency. For example, to avoid flotsam. With a radical course change to port will you remain in enough depth? Or would starboard be a safer option?

We can't prepare for every eventuality at sea, but the prudent mariner plans as best they can with what's at hand.

Therefore, we must know about latitude and longitude to plot our position and know we are safe. To reach port before dark we must know how to measure distance and calculate the time it will take. To ensure we are avoiding those reefs we must learn how to plot a course and find direction.

We will introduce each one of these elements prior to learning our first formulae to calculate speed, distance, and time – which are extremely useful tools.

Then we'll take an in-depth look at the chart, how every word, letter, notation and number is relevant, important, and useful. We'll interpret the key areas that are paramount for our safety.

That learning foundation will underpin the next element, the practical side of plotting, fixing positions, measuring distance taking bearings, converting True to Compass and Compass to True and all that comes with the joy of navigating.

A note of caution SisterShip Training can only provide information and advice, it is up to you to ensure you have understood and can carry out your navigation correctly.

Congratulations, with this manual you've taken a positive step forward to being safer on the water.

Fair winds,
Jackie and Noel

Note: Whilst every effort has been made to ensure the accuracy of the information contained in this manual, no guarantee can be given that all errors and omissions have been excluded. Should any misprints or discrepancies be discovered in our work we shall be glad if students will be good enough to notify us.

SECTION ONE
WHERE ON EARTH ARE WE?

What do the Co-ordinates Mean?

To find an exact position on Earth we must have two coordinates: Latitude and Longitude.

Latitude and longitude are the lines that are drawn on charts (and maps). It is standard practice (and easier) to decimalise the minutes in order to use formulas for navigation.

Latitude

The equator: An imaginary line on a chart or map which perfectly bisects the Earth midway between the two poles. It is halfway between the North Pole and the South Pole.

The equator is the line of the 0° latitude and therefore the starting point for measuring latitude.

All lines on the Earth's surface which run parallel to the equator are called Parallels of Latitude. Depending on which side of the equator they lie, they are named North or South.

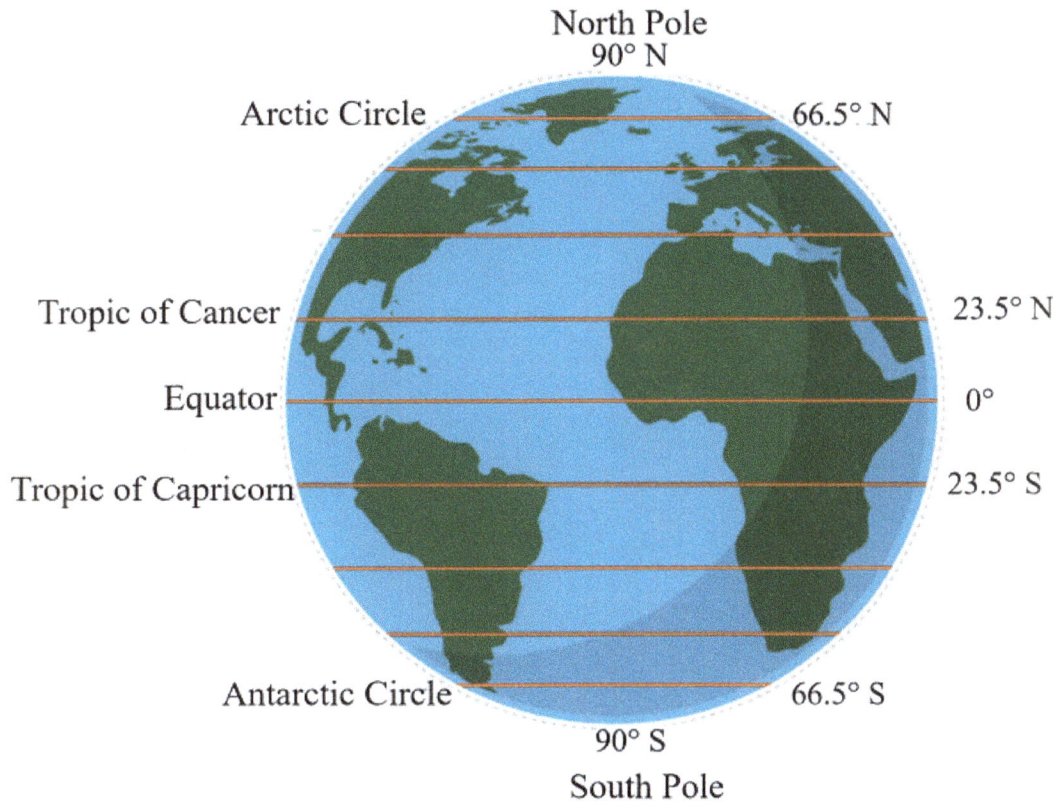

The image shows the lines of latitude (they are parallel to the equator). Of course, the lines follow the curve of the Earth, even though they appear straight on this diagram.

Above the equator (0°) the latitudes are north, and below they are south.

The Tropic of Cancer and The Tropic of Capricorn are used in this image as the example, they are at 23.5° north and south respectively.

You can see that latitude is measured from 0° to 90° north or south.

TIP: If you read or write a latitude measurement that is more than 90°, you instantly know there is an error somewhere.

How are the Angles Measured?
Latitude is measured by the angle at the Earth's centre between the place in question and the equator.

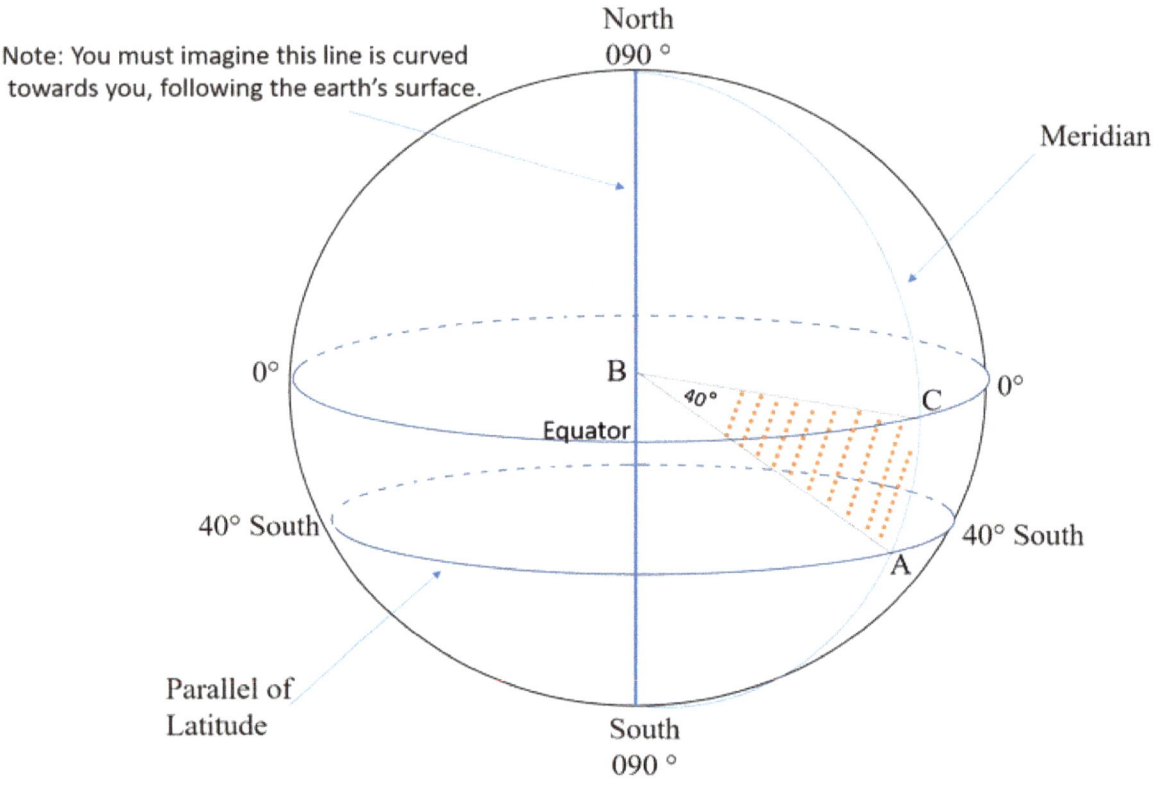

This image shows:
- The equator is at 0°
- The latitude of the North Pole is 90°N
- The latitude of the South Pole is 90°S

The latitude of every point between must be either:
- Measured in degrees north from 0° (Equator) to 90°N, or
- Measured in degrees south from 0° (Equator) to 90S°
- This image shows the latitude line at 40° south
- Study the shaded area marked A, B, and C. This shows how the measurement is calculated.
- B is the centre of the Earth
- C is the Equator
- A is the 40° line of latitude

You do not need to worry about finding the angle, as nautical charts provide the degrees of the angle. However, it is important to understand how latitude (and longitude) is found.

Longitude (Meridians)

The imaginary line drawn from the North Pole extending to the South Pole and running through Greenwich is the Prime Meridian.

Just as the Equator divides the north and south hemispheres, the Prime Meridian divides the globe into east and west hemispheres.

All lines on the Earth's surface which run north to south as per the Prime Meridian are called Meridians of Longitude. Depending on which side of the Prime Meridian they lie, they are named east or west.

Longitude is the distance east or west of the Prime Meridian measured in degrees.

000° is the prime meridian (through Greenwich).

The longitude of every point between must either be:

- Measured in degrees East from 000° to 180°, or
- Measured in degrees West from 000° to 180°

The Meridian at 180° (180th meridian or antemeridian) east or west of the Prime Meridian divides the Earth into eastern and western hemispheres. (This is also used for the basis for the international date line, the line does not run straight though, it zigzags to avoid political and country borders. It also moves to avoid cutting some countries in half).

That's a lot of words – a diagram is easier.

TIP: If you come across a longitude written that is more than 180°, you will instantly recognise that there is an error somewhere.

Two opposite sides of the Earth

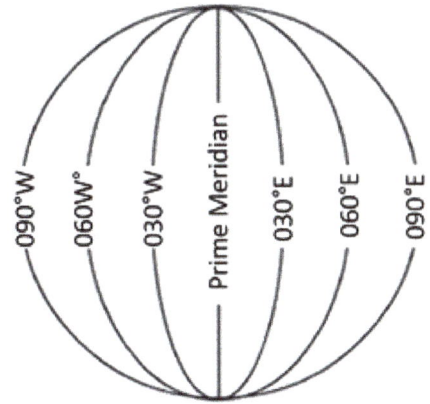
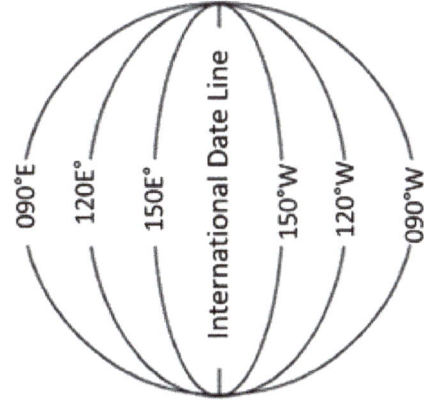

Prime Meridian = 000°
One side of the Earth showing lines of Longitude 30° apart

International dateline = 180°
The other side of the Earth showing lines of Longitude 30° apart

Longitude is measured by the angle at the Earth's centre between the place in question and the prime meridian and is always between 0° and 180°, east or west.

©Jackie Parry

How are the Angles Measured?

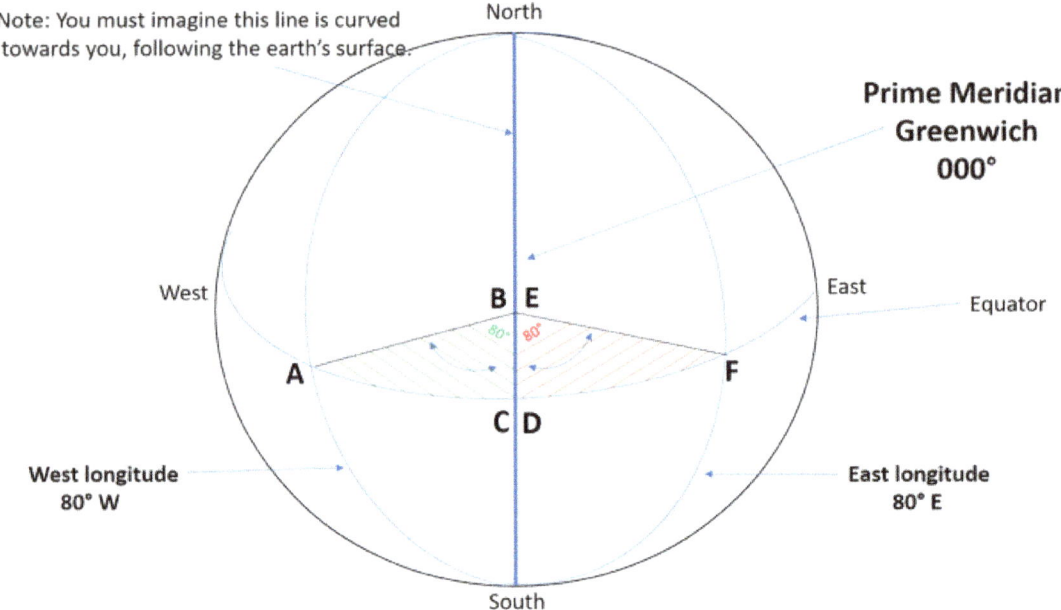

The green shaded area depicts the angle measured from the centre of the Earth to the Prime Meridian to the longitude line west (in this example, measured at 080°W)

B is the centre of the Earth
C is the Prime Meridian
A is the 080°W line of longitude

The orange shaded area depicts the angle measured from the centre of the Earth to the Prime Meridian to the longitude line east (in this example, measured at 80° E)

The Great Circle

The Great Circle is the largest circle that can be drawn around the Earth's sphere. When cutting a sphere exactly in half you have cut along one of its great circles.

All Meridians are great circles.

The Equator is a great circle (i.e. cutting the Earth in half). Great circles are useful in planning routes as it depicts the shortest pathway between two points on the Earth's surface (noticeable over long distances).

The Great Circle route follows the curvature of the Earth making it a shorter route (noticeable when doing greater distances) than a straight line drawn on a Mercator chart.

©Jackie Parry   www.sistershiptraining.com

LATITUDE AND LONGITUDE

Writing latitude and longitude correctly is extremely important. The next person on watch must be able to read and understand what you have written on the chart and in the log book.

Latitude should always be written first (in some areas in the USA longitude is written first, latitude first is more widely accepted):

E.g.   00° 36' 12" S   080° 25' 42" W

Written above shows: degrees (°), minutes (') and seconds (").

There are sixty minutes in a degree and sixty seconds in a minute.

You can instantly spot an error if the minutes (') or seconds (") are sixty or higher. The highest number of minutes that can be used is fifty-nine: e.g. 1   00° 59' 12"

00° 61' 12" is incorrect and should be: 01° 01' 12"

E.g. 2   001° = sixty minutes
00° 62' is written incorrectly and should be written as 01° 02'

Just like a clock we have 60 seconds to the minute, 60 minutes to the degree and 360 degrees to the circle. This means that we can now express angles down to a very small measurement, e.g. 76°35'36". This can also be expressed as 76°35.6'. Here, we have decimalised the seconds. This method is the most common when using angular measure. To do this we divide the number of seconds by 60.

EXAMPLE: 36 seconds =   36 / 60 = 0.6 minutes

                6 seconds = 0.1   36 seconds = 0.6
                12 seconds = 0.2   42 seconds = 0.7
                18 seconds = 0.3   48 seconds = 0.8
                24 seconds = 0.4   54 seconds = 0.9
                30 seconds = 0.5   60 seconds = 1

Degrees, Minutes, and Seconds – Decimalise Example

Example 1: Show 30 seconds as a decimal of a minute
Method: divide seconds by 60
30 / 60 = 0.5 minutes

To convert decimal minutes back to seconds, multiply the decimal by 60
0.5 x 60 = 30 seconds

Example 2: Convert 40 seconds to a decimal of a minute
Method: Divide 40 seconds by 60
40 / 60 = 0.66 or 0.7 minutes

Exercise 1 and 2 – Time Calculations on page 1 Questions and Answers booklet
Answers 1 and 2 – Time Calculations on page 31 Questions and Answers booklet

DISTANCE
Nautical Mile/One Minute of Latitude

We know that we measure in degrees (°), minutes (') and seconds (") or decimals of a minute.
One minute of latitude is equal to one nautical mile (1,852 metres or 1.852 kilometres).

TIP: You MUST measure distance from the latitude scale adjacent to the area you are working in on a chart, NEVER from the longitude scale. The Mercator projection used in constructing the chart creates a distorting elongation of the longitude scale.

As well as defining our position in latitude and longitude, our location may be given in relation to a known geographical position, for example: "8 nautical miles south east of Greenwell Point harbour entrance."

TIP: When relaying a position, it is good practice – and clearer on the radio – to say each number individually, e.g.

151° 21.12' E

"One-five-one degrees, two-one decimal one-two minutes east."

Distance on the earth is expressed in nautical miles, and is the spatial separation of two points.

Summary

Place the pencil compass points (or dividers) on the distance to measure.

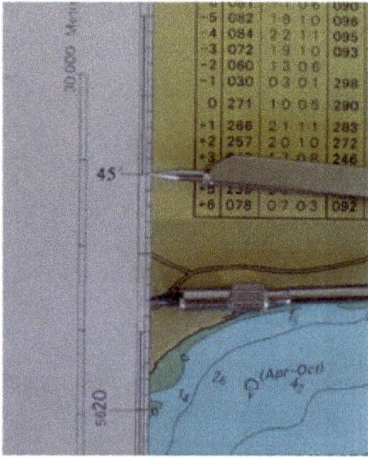

Measure the distance on the latitude scale adjacent to the area you measured

DIRECTION
Direction is expressed in the angular difference in degrees from one position to another.

The Degree
In navigation, angular measurement or direction is recorded and viewed in degrees.

One degree = 60 minutes of arc.
One minute = 60 seconds of arc.

Parts of a minute can be expressed in seconds, e.g. 30 seconds, or as a decimal of that minute, e.g. 0.5 minutes.

It is important to go back to basics with understanding degrees, especially as we later move forward into True and Compass calculations.

Cardinal Points

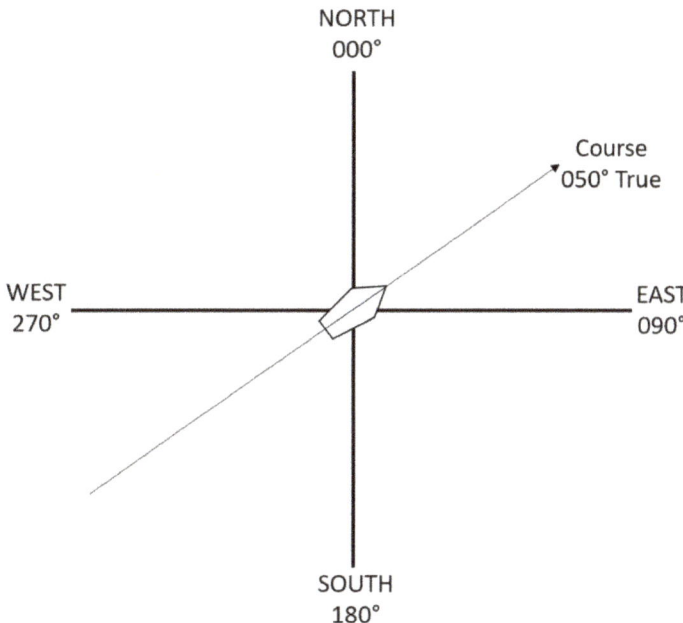

Start at 000° and move clockwise to 090°, continue clockwise to 180°, 270° and then 360°, which is also 000°, that is important to remember.

These four points are the cardinal points and are in TRUE direction.

A True bearing uses the direction toward the geographic north pole as a reference point.

Direction is usually measured from north to the ship's head.

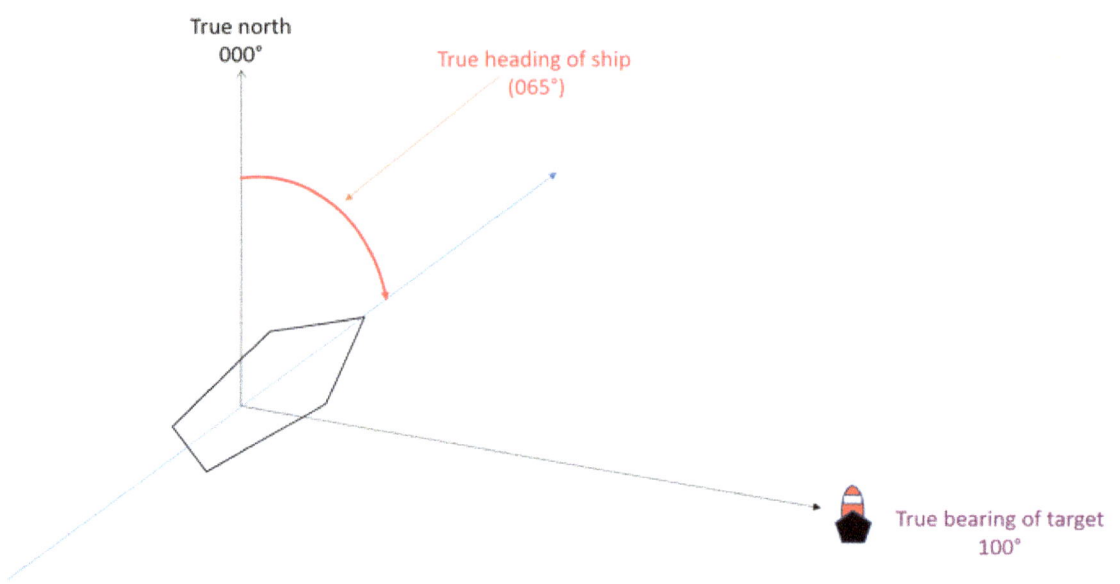

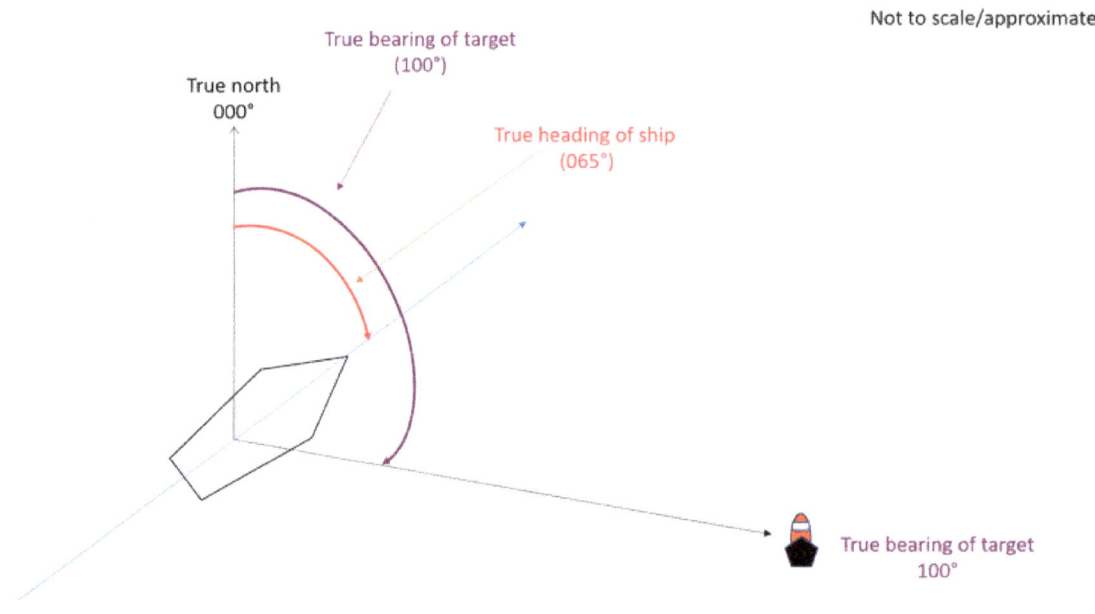

SPEED DISTANCE TIME

There's an easy formula for Speed, Distance, and Time.

In marine navigation:
- Speed is referred to as knots and relates to distance over time, e.g. one nautical mile per hour
- We travel distance in nautical miles.
- The nautical mile equals one minute of latitude on the Mercator chart (degrees of latitude are 60 minutes apart).
- Time is measured over 24 hours, e.g. 1500 hours equals 3 pm.
- Time is expressed as hours, minutes and seconds. The seconds can be expressed as decimals of a minute.

Formula and Calculations

D= Distance, S= Speed, T= Time.

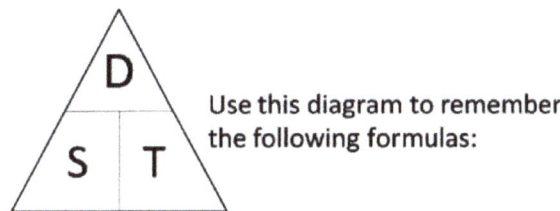

Use this diagram to remember the following formulas:

$$D = S \times T$$
$$S = D / T$$
$$T = D / S$$

These formulae allow us to calculate the third element if two of the three are already known (speed, distance or time).

TIP: Don't forget the answer will be decimalised so you must convert the decimal figure back into minutes for your log book/other crew.

Speed, Distance, Time – Example 1

How long does it take to travel 5 nautical miles at a speed of 10 knots?

TIP: Write out every stage of the calculation to avoid mistakes.

The question requires an answer in time and provides the speed and distance.
Using the formula write out what you know:

Time   =   D/S

Time   =   5nm /10kts   =   0.5 of an hour

Turn the decimalised minutes into actual minutes

0.5 is half an hour, i.e. 30 minutes. You calculate this by:
0.5 (decimal of an hour) x 60 = 30 minutes

Answer: It will take 30 minutes to travel 5 nautical miles at the speed of 10 knots.

©Jackie Parry   www.sistershiptraining.com

Speed, Distance, Time – Example 2

You've been travelling for 8 hours 42 minutes at 13 knots. How many nautical miles have you covered?

Solution: write down what you know. Time = 8 hours 42 minutes, speed = 13 knots

TIP: Convert the minutes to decimal first. The number of minutes divided by 60 = the number of minutes expressed as a decimal of an hour.

42 / 60 = 0.7, therefore the time = 8.7 hours.

Apply the formula

D = S x T =
D = 13 knots x 8.7 hours = 113.1 Nautical Miles

TIP: Calculate an approximate figure, in your head, to enable you to instantly recognise if there is an error. Take the example above, 8 hours 42 minutes is close to 9 hours.

If you travel for 9 hours at 10 knots that's 90 nautical miles. You are travelling faster at 13 knots so you know it is going to be over 90 nm.

Answer: You have travelled 113.1 nm at 13 knots for 8 hours 42 minutes.

Speed, Distance, Time – Example 3

You may want to calculate how long it is going to take to reach port – to know if you can make it prior to dark, for instance.

There are 28 nautical miles to go. Your speed is 5.7 knots, how long will it take to get there?

Time = Distance / Speed
Time = 28nm / 5.7 knots
Time = 4.91 hrs

We need to convert this to a time we can recognise.

TIP: We already know there are five sixes in 30 (we almost have 30 nm to go and we are doing almost 6 knots), so we know the answer is going to be around 5 hours.

Convert the decimalised time back to hours and minutes:

.91 hrs x 60 = 54.6   Our answer is 4 hours 55 minutes (round up)

Answer: It will take 4 hours and 55 minutes to reach port with 28 nm to go at a speed of 5.7 knots.

©Jackie Parry

Speed, Distance, Time – Example 4

If you must reach port in the example above, in, say, 4 hours, we can determine the speed required to achieve that goal and reach port prior to dark.

Referring to our memory triangle we can see that:

Speed required = D / T
= 28 / 4
= 7 knots

Answer: To reach port in 4 hours, the speed required is 7 knots.

Exercise 3 – Speed, Distance, Time on page 2 Questions and Answers Booklet
Answers 3 – Speed, Distance, Time on page 32 Questions and Answers Booklet

CHARTS

Purpose
A nautical chart provides necessary information to promote safe and efficient navigation.

Taking a fix by visual bearings, for example, can be used directly or as a back-up/check on the vessel's position via GPS.

It answers the question, *"Where am I?"*
But maybe, more importantly, we should ask, *"What does that mean?"* Am I near rocks? Am I safe? That's the number one priority and that's why paper charts are so important.

Features
A chart will show the depth of water by soundings and depth contours, shoreline, topographic features, nature of the bottom, tidal streams, magnetic variation etc., for the area, as well as:

- Authority: The publisher that is responsible for the chart. E.g. NOAA, British Admiralty, Australian Hydrographic Service.

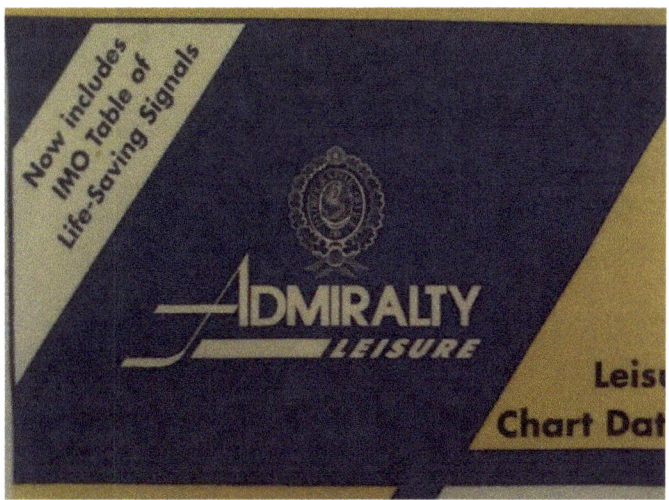

- Printing Date/Publication: Usually in the centre bottom margin, includes new editions and large corrections.

- Title: Provides the description of the area covered, e.g. Outer approaches to the Solent.

- Markers/Buoys/Cardinal markers – Refer to book/chart BA5011 (now NP5011).

- Seabed symbols.

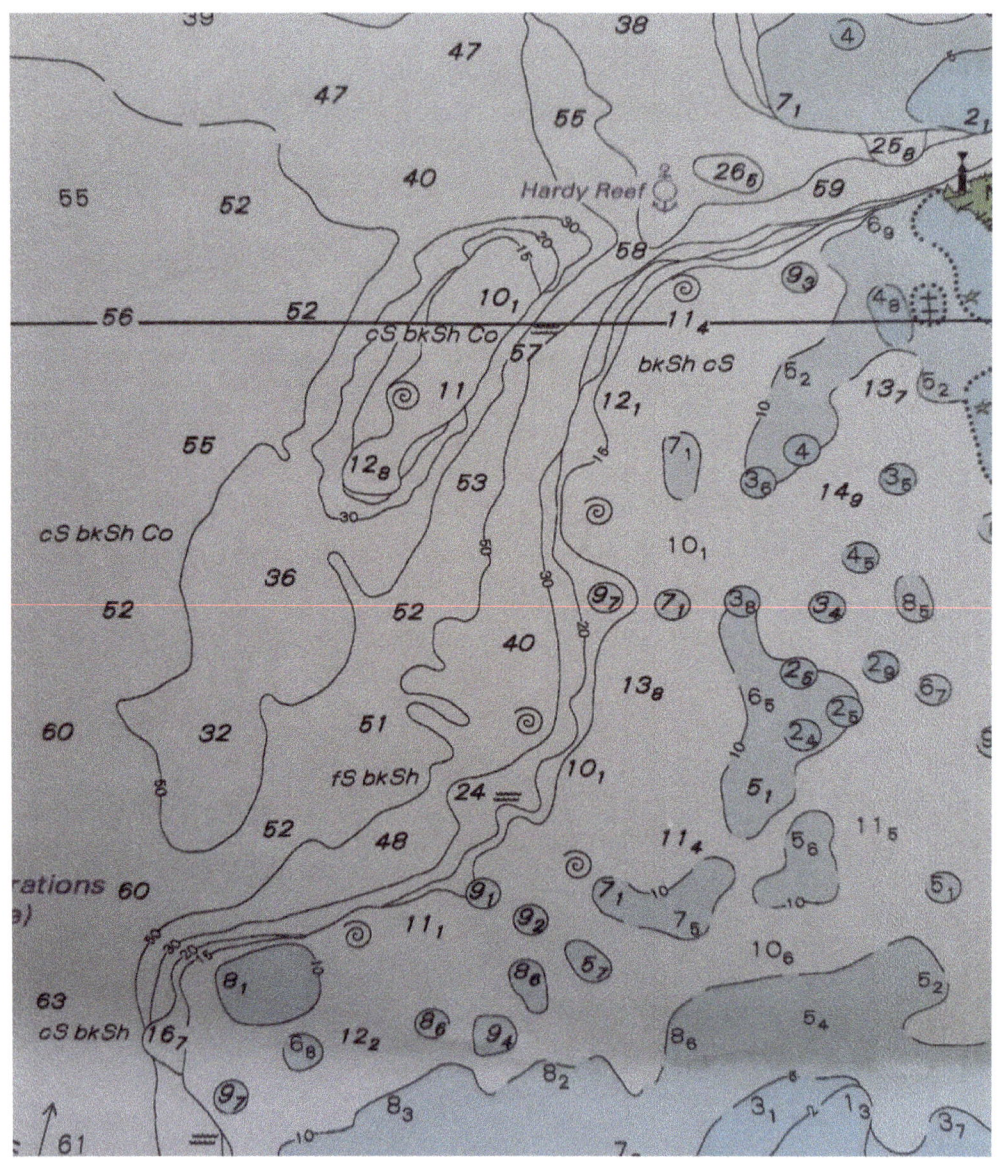

- Landmarks: Radio masts, churches, etc.

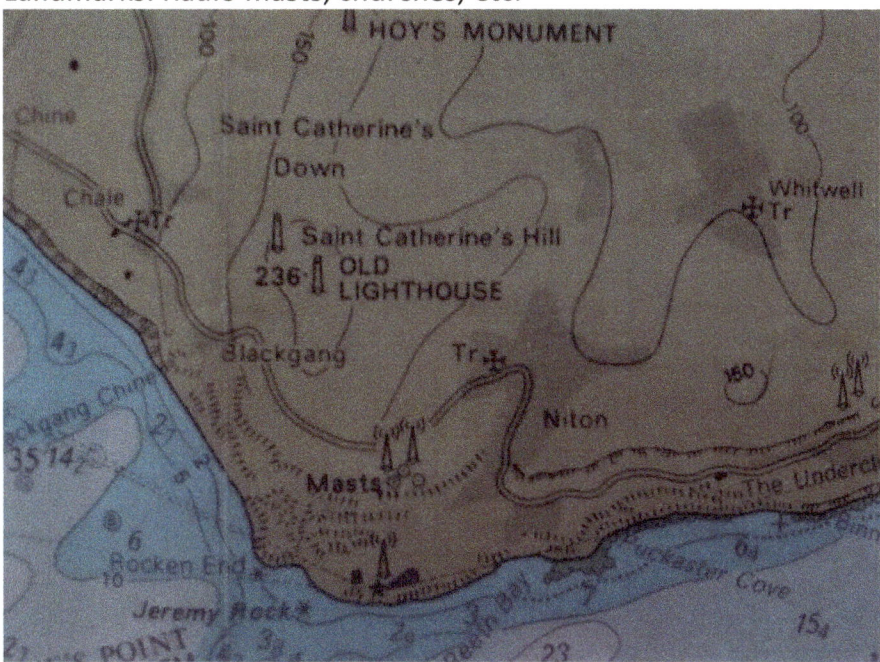

- Compass Rose: Used for laying off your course or bearings.

- Magnetic Variation: On the Compass Rose showing the angle between True North and Magnetic North (varies in place and time).

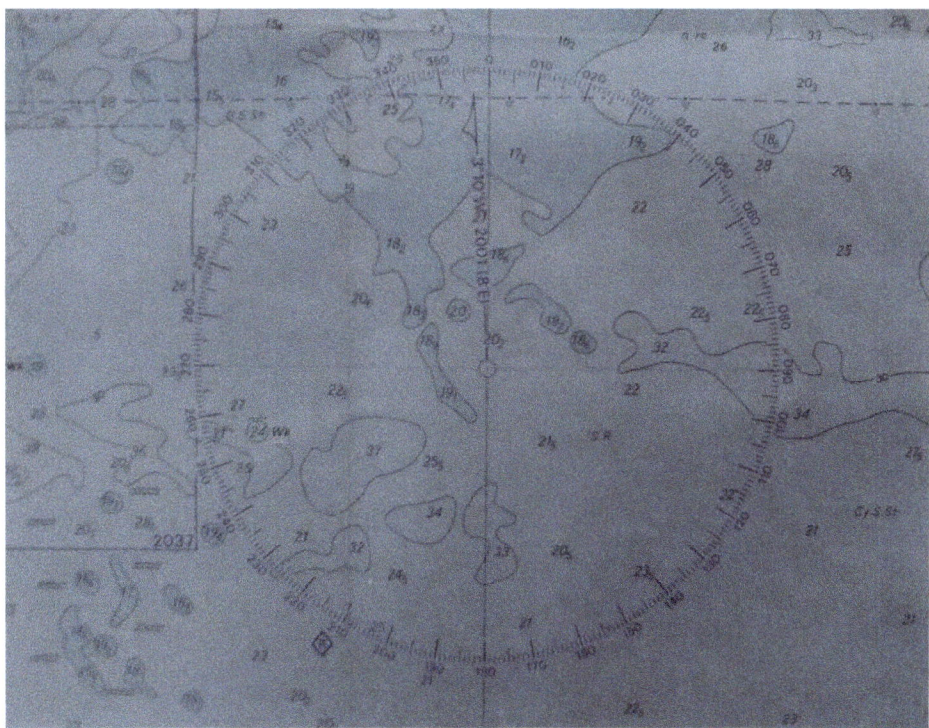

- Depths: reduced to Chart Datum, which means they use the datum of the Lowest Astronomical Tide (LAT). The Lowest Astronomical Tide is the lowest levels which can be predicted to occur under average meteorological conditions.

Note: LAT is not the lowest level that may be reached as storm surges may cause considerably lower levels to occur.

Soundings and drying heights: Soundings are given below Chart Datum; Drying heights are given above Chart Datum. See image below:

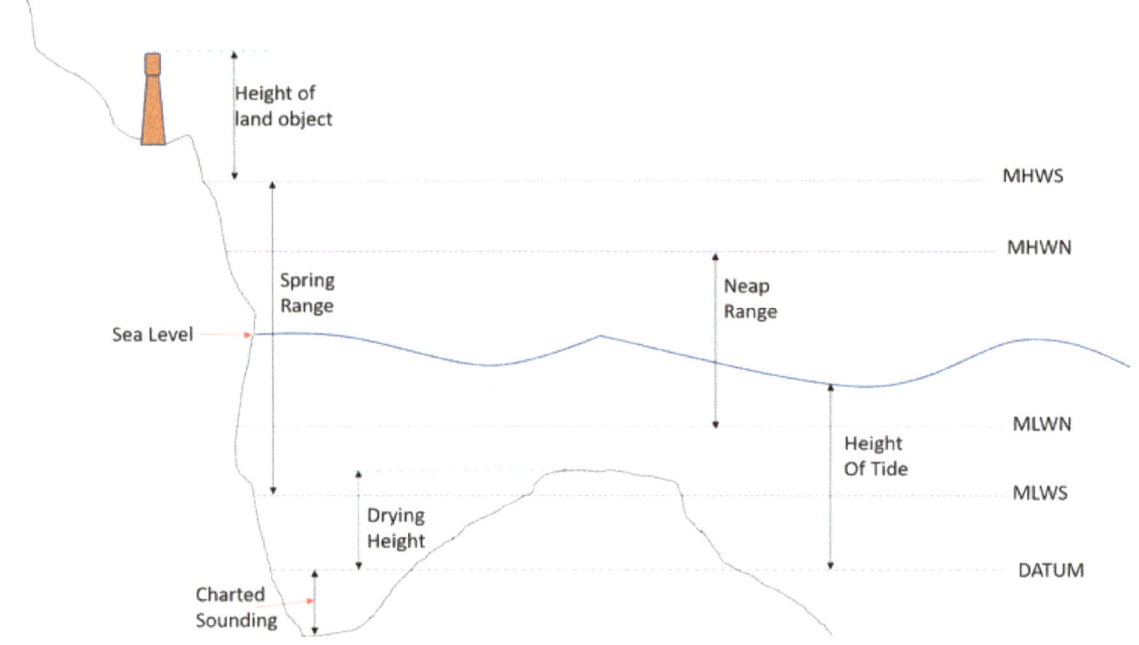

MHWS – Mean High Water Spring MHWN – Mean High Water Neap
MLWN – Mean Low Water Neap MLWS – Mean Low Water Spring

- Small Corrections: Placed in the lower left margin as the chart is amended via Notices to Mariners (Australia – issued fortnightly). Provisional and temporary notices must only be entered with pencil. Officially a magenta coloured pen is used for permanent corrections. Ensure you purchase a pen that does not feather or bleed on the chart, or fade. (PaperMate InkJoy 550 RT 1.0M is a good option).

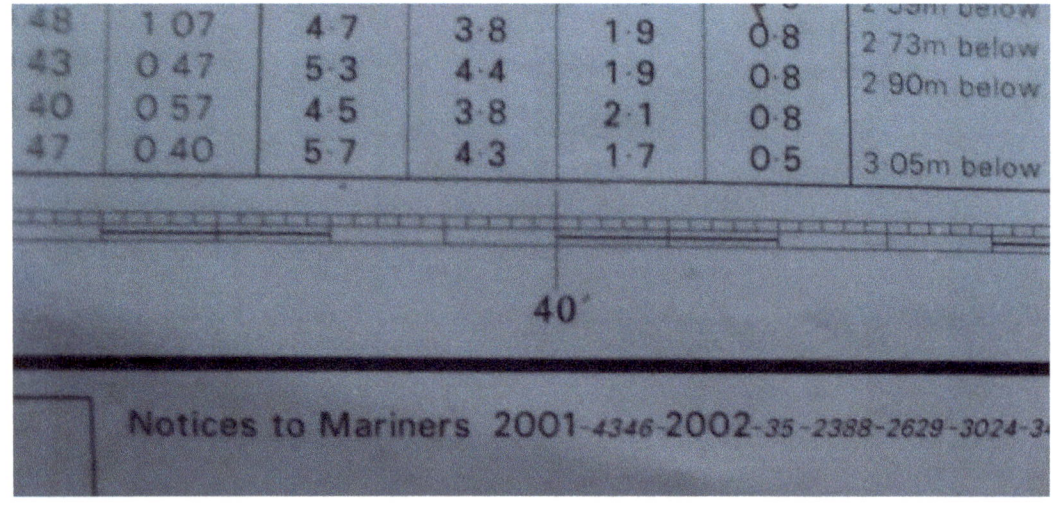

TIP: Before purchase you should ensure that the chart is corrected to the latest Notices to Mariners (or the regular document issued by your country's relevant authority).

©Jackie Parry

Scale: World Charts have the smallest scale (showing the largest area), for planning ocean routes, and studying ocean currents and magnetic variation. (Large scale charts – small area (e.g. harbours)).

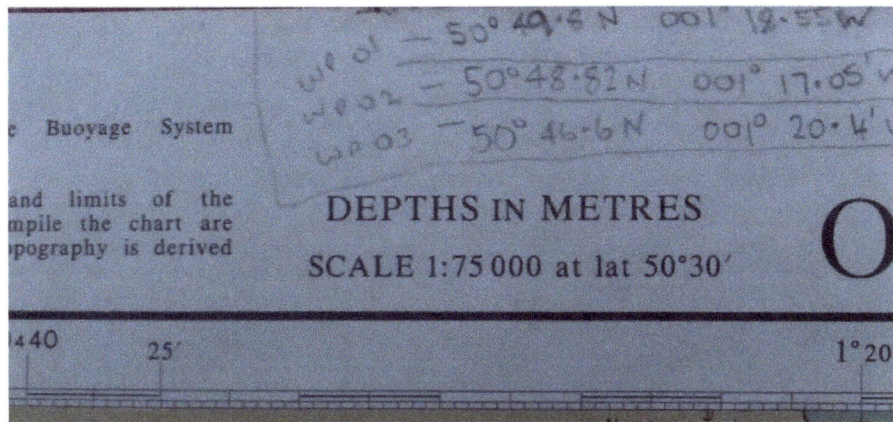

- Ocean Charts are typically 1:10,000,000, these are for planning and position fixing on off-shore ocean passages, e.g. Pacific Ocean.
- General Charts are typically 1:1,000,000 and used for coastal navigation.
- Coastal Charts are typically 1:150,000 and used for inshore navigation.
- Plan Charts are typically 1:75,000 with insets of 1:37,500 and provide greater detail of harbours and rivers.

The Legend: Located, most often, over land, i.e. on the chart where no essential navigation information will be obscured.
It will show:
- Area Depicted
- Survey Dates
- Units of Sounding – Fathoms or Metres or Feet
- Notes on Heights
- Natural Scale
- Projection – Mercator or Gnomonic (we use Mercator, Gnomonic is a perspective projection in which part of a spherical surface is projected from the centre of the sphere onto a plane surface tangential to the sphere's surface, is useful for Great Circle sailing.
- Tidal Information
- Caution Notes
- Depth Contours/Isobaths: Lines that connect showing the same depth.
- Zone of Confidence (ZOC)

Chart Errors

If you are plotting on older charts you may find that the GPS co-ordinates put you on an island! In this case, the GPS is more accurate than the chart. All positions will need to be offset by the amount given in the title of the chart. Every modern chart will have a note stating whether the GPS co-ordinates can be plotted directly or an offset is to be followed. This is a good example that shows you must check all the information provided on the chart, very carefully. Much older charts, prior to GPS, may have no information at all regarding GPS derived co-ordinates.

Note: A GPS chart plotter may still require offset corrections as it may be based on inaccurate charts.

Example 1 – Chart Errors:

Chart AUS 252 Whitsunday Group. Under the chart title it states:

SATELLITE DERIVED POSITIONS
Positions obtained from the Global Positioning System (GPS) in the WGS 1984 Datum can be plotted directly onto this chart.

Example 2 – Chart Errors:

Chart AUS 802 Cape Liptrap to Cliffy Island, (on older charts) states:

Positions are related to the Australian Geodetic Datum (1966)
(see SATELLITE DERIVED POSITIONS Note).

Next to title it states:

SATELLITE DERIVED POSITIONS
Positions obtained from the Global Positioning System (GPS) in the WGS 1984 Datum must be moved 0.09 minutes SOUTHWARD and 0.08 minutes WESTWARD to agree with this chart.

Making the corrections: In the case of chart AUS 802 the correction would be as follows:

GPS (WGS 1984) position	39° 00.00' S	146° 15.00' E
	+ 0.09' S	- 0.08' W
	---------------	----------------
	39° 00.09' S	146° 14.92' E

Corrections vary: Some South Pacific Island charts will note corrections that can be over one nautical mile out!

Zone of Confidence (ZOC) Are your chart depths and seafloor features accurate?

Seventy percent of the earth is covered with water. Hydrographic offices around the world conduct regular surveys, but the task is ongoing and has been for a long, long time.

The method of conducting these surveys has, of course, changed over the years. At the start, they were completed with lead lines by hand and single beam echo sounders. Later came the wire-drag method, with the obstruction detected with the wire stretching. The modern technique uses SONAR multi-beam waves to record the depths. This data is processed with other data, e.g. tides.

It's worth remembering that a hydrographic surveyor can only physically see the parts that rise above the sea surface. For the rest, the surveyor puts their confidence in their systems.

The major shipping routes has priority for surveying which means that mariners must have the skills to interpret the quality indicators that should be on every official chart.

The Zone of Confidence (ZOC) has replaced the Reliability Diagram (aka Source Diagrams).

Older charts may still have the Reliability Diagram which requires knowledge of past and present hydrographic surveying practices to fully understand. This is why the ZOC was developed by the Australian Hydrographic Office, and is now in use worldwide.

ZOC categories warn mariners which parts of the chart are based on good or poor information and which areas should be navigated with caution.

Chart AUS252

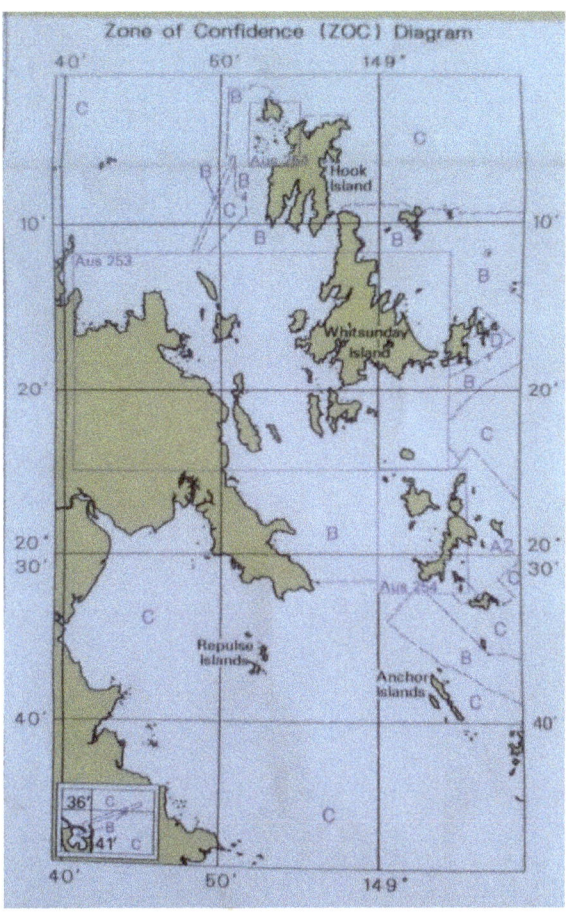

ZOC CATEGORIES
(For details see Seafarers Handbook for Australian Waters AHP 20)

ZOC	POSITION ACCURACY	DEPTH ACCURACY	SEAFLOOR COVERAGE
A1	±5m	=0·50m + 1%d	Significant seafloor features detected
A2	±20m	=1·00m + 2%d	Significant seafloor features detected
B	±50m	=1·00m + 2%d	Uncharted features hazardous to surface navigation are not expected but may exist
C	±500m	=2·00m + 5%d	Depth anomalies may be expected
D	Worse than ZOC C	Worse than ZOC C	Large depth anomalies may be expected
U	Unassessed - The quality of the bathymetric data has yet to be assessed.		

Possible errors in depths

When a depth is measured during a survey, there can be two errors to this depth.

The depth itself may not be accurate.
The position at which this depth is marked may not be accurate.

You must apply the maximum possible errors wherever required.

Nothing replaces a proper look out, following The International Regulations for Preventing Collisions at Sea (COL REGS), and approaching a port by day. Give shallow areas of a questionable sounding a wider berth. And use every available resource and skill you have. You're the Skipper you're responsible.

Resource: The Australian Hydrographic Office
http://www.hydro.gov.au/prodserv/important-info/important-info.htm

Defining Positions

Chart positions are defined by latitude and longitude or bearing and distance.
The **Latitude** scale is on the sides of the chart and used for distance measurements.

One minute of latitude is equal to 1 nautical mile. It also defines the position north or south of the equator.

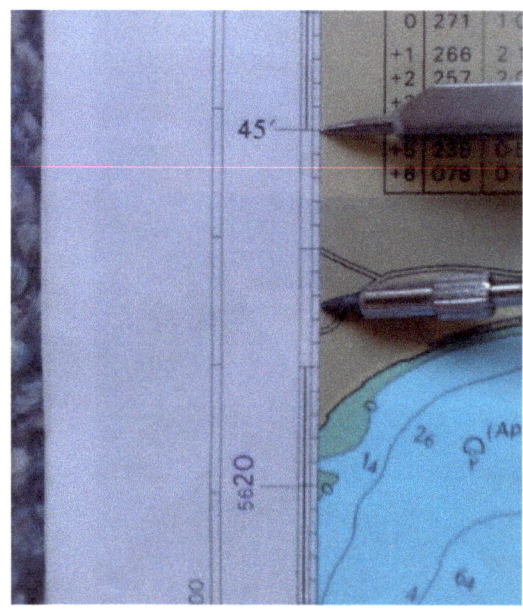

Latitude Scale

The **Longitude** scale is across the top and bottom of the chart and defines the position east or west of Greenwich.

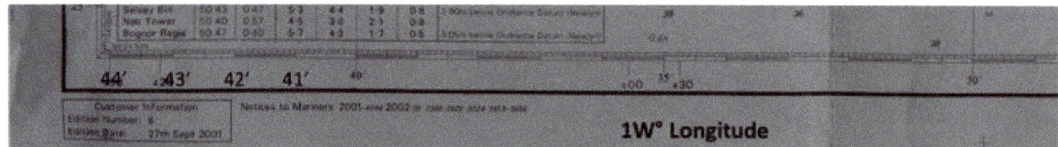

To define position by bearing and distance we use the compass rose, and the latitude scale.

©Jackie Parry www.sistershiptraining.com

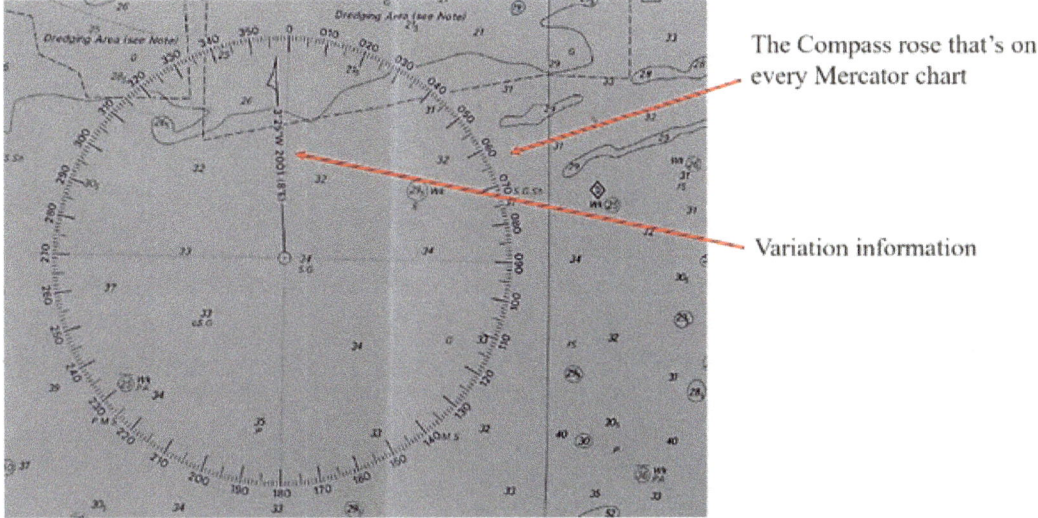

SYMBOLS AND ABBREVIATIONS

Every line and symbol on a chart is relevant. Each one is explained in the book NP5011 Symbols and Abbreviations book.

There are certain symbols and abbreviations that you must be able to recognise without reference to NP5011, e.g.

- Rocks, Wrecks and Obstructions
- IALA Buoys and Beacons
- Light Characteristics
- Areas of limitations
- Water depths
- Nature of the bottom

The International Association of Marine Aids to Navigation and Lighthouse Authorities (IALA), previously known as International Association of Lighthouse Authorities is an Intergovernmental organisation founded in 1957 to collect and provide nautical expertise and advice.

Exercise 4 – Chart Symbols page 6 in Questions and Answers Booklet
Answers 4 – Chart Symbols page 38 in Questions and Answers Booklet

CHART WORK

Navigation Equipment

Protractors & Parallel Rulers
The Chart Protractor (e.g. Bi-Rola or the Portland Course Plotter) is recommended, as opposed to (or in addition to) parallel rules. By placing the ruler anywhere on the chart and rotating the protractor to line up north and along your chart latitude or longitude lines, a bearing can be read off easily.

In the diagram below, the top ruler is the Chart Protractor. Parallel rules are a good tool, but when 'walking' them across a chart it is easy to slip and slide, especially on a moving boat.

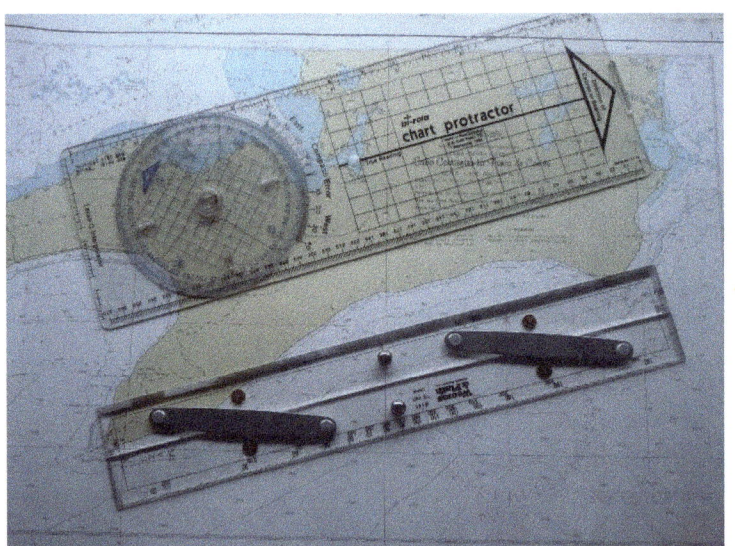

 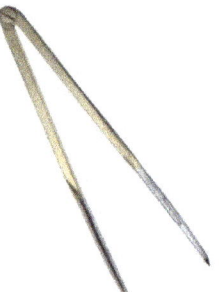

Single-hand dividers **Straight dividers**

Dividers are excellent for measuring distances accurately, of course you can use a simple pencil compass to do the same job. However, for larger distances the dividers (pictured above) open out wider enabling the navigator to measure longer distances.

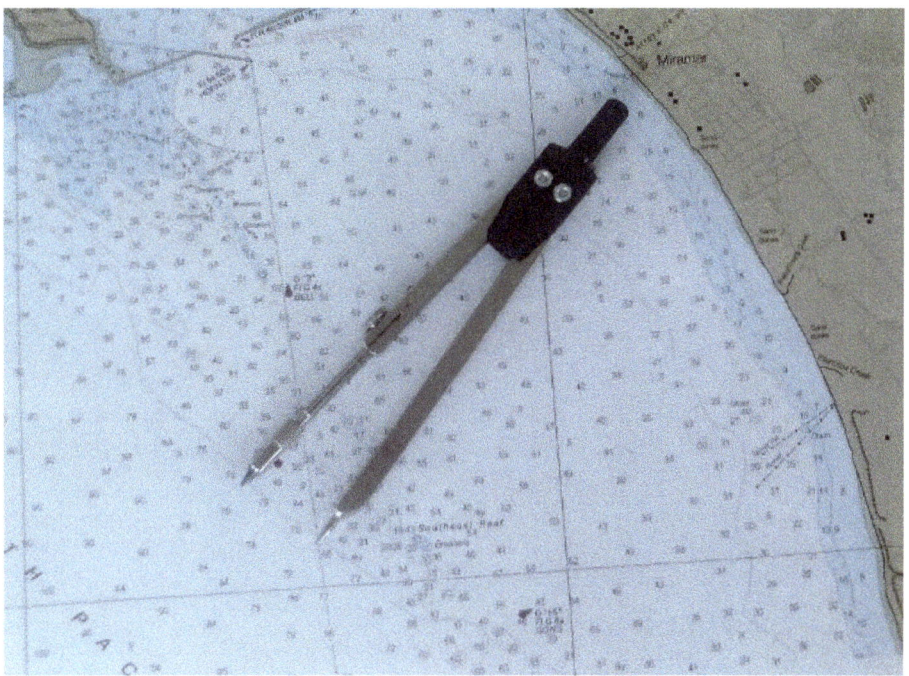

Pencil compass
A pencil compass is necessary for drawing arcs during navigation.

Equipment List
- 2B pencils
- Soft eraser
- Dividers
- Pencil Compass
- Parallel Ruler or Bi-Rola Ruler

Onboard, in addition to the above, you will need:
- Compass to take bearings (handheld and ship's)
- Accurate clock
- Sounding device
- Calculator (double check your calculations)
- Notepad

TIP: Electronic equipment are aids to navigation and require back-up as per the equipment listed above, plus your knowledge on how to use the equipment correctly and navigate. The skipper is responsible for everything and everyone on board.

Position: Correct Chart Work & Symbols

On the chart, use the following symbols so everyone understands the workings.

Symbol	
Compass Bearing (for a fix)	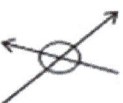
Radar Ranges (for a fix)	
Transferred position line)	
Transferred radar range	
Course To Steer (CTS)	
Course Made Good (CMG) ie course we are making good	
Set and Drift of current	
Wind (from where it blows, In the direction is blows to)	

©Jackie Parry

PLOTTING BY LATITUDE AND LONGITUDE
How to Plot Your Position

Plot 20° 43.5' S   149° 04.4' E on AUS252 at 1000 hrs

Study the Lat/Long scales.
Find the approximate area you are plotting within.

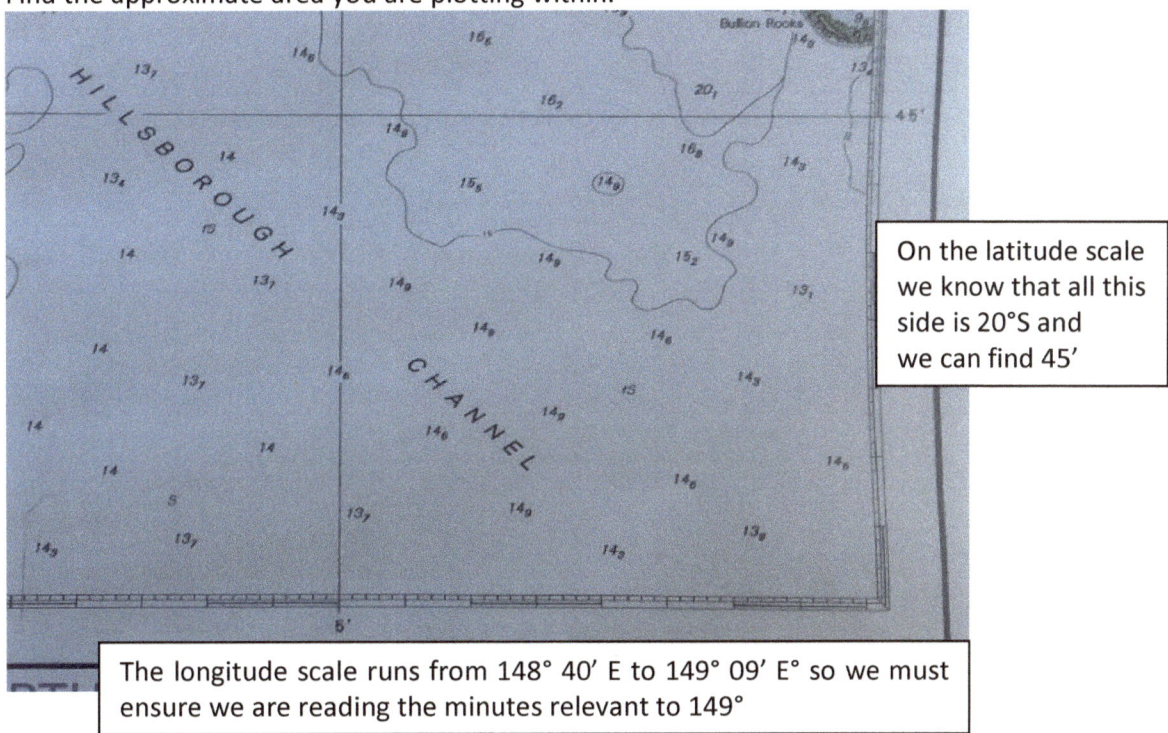

On the latitude scale we know that all this side is 20°S and we can find 45'

The longitude scale runs from 148° 40' E to 149° 09' E° so we must ensure we are reading the minutes relevant to 149°

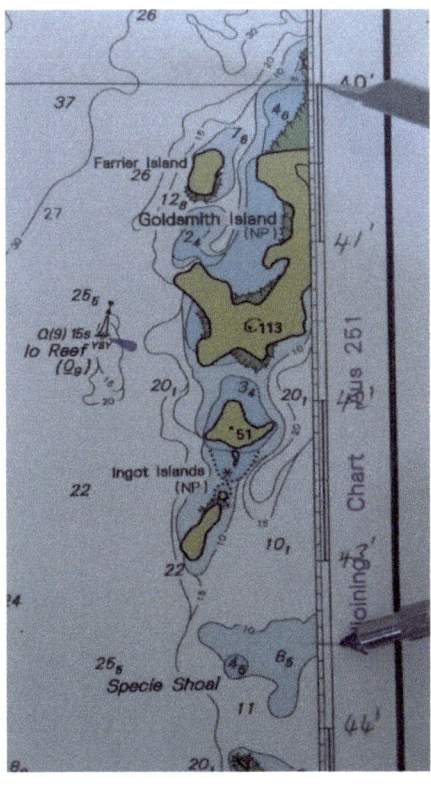

The minutes are written in increments of 5 on this chart

Pencil in the minutes between 40 and 45.

We measure from a latitude line (as a point of reference) and open the pencil compass to 43.5'

Maintain that compass width, while you take a look at the longitude scale.

©Jackie Parry

For the purposes of instruction, this diagram shows you the compass measuring the longitude scale.

Just use your eyes to visualise the distance shown, while maintaining the latitude measurement.

This is 149° 04.4'E

Note 1: The minutes have been pencilled in.

Note 2: The compass point is on the 5' longitude line as a reference point. (You can measure from the 149° longitude line if you prefer.)
We will measure this distance using the equipment in a moment, first just visualise the longitude measurement. We want to draw the Latitude measurement first.

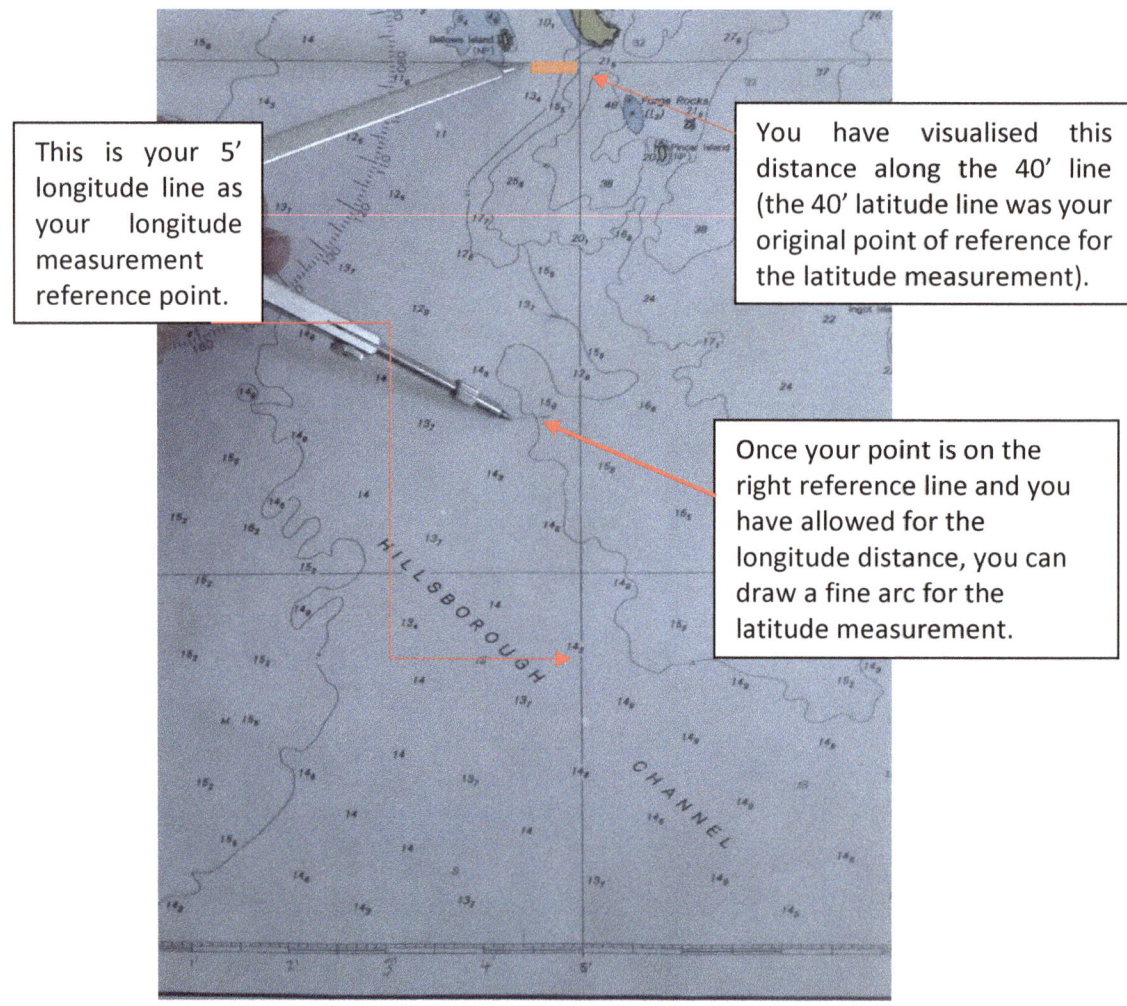

This is your 5' longitude line as your longitude measurement reference point.

You have visualised this distance along the 40' line (the 40' latitude line was your original point of reference for the latitude measurement).

Once your point is on the right reference line and you have allowed for the longitude distance, you can draw a fine arc for the latitude measurement.

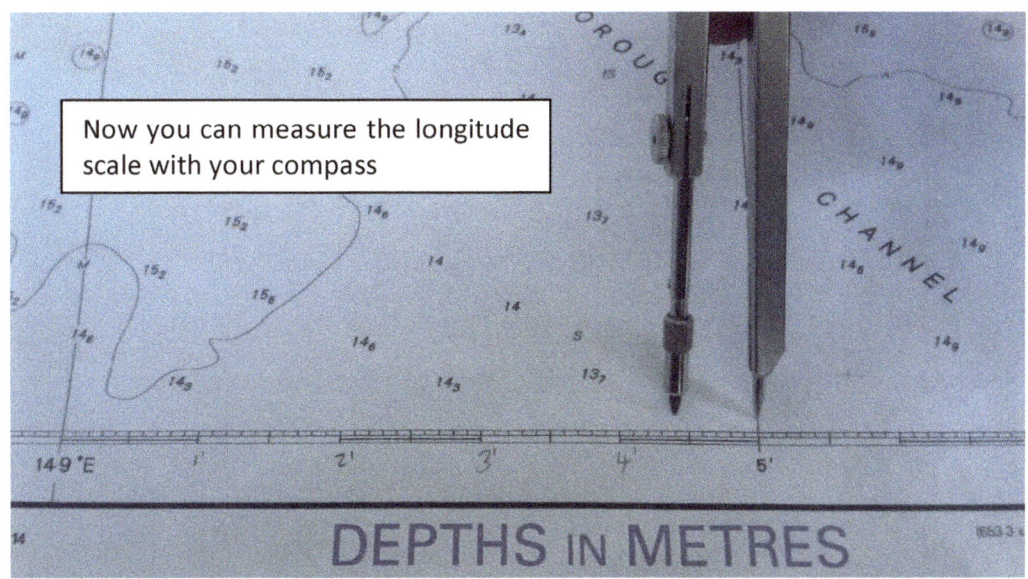

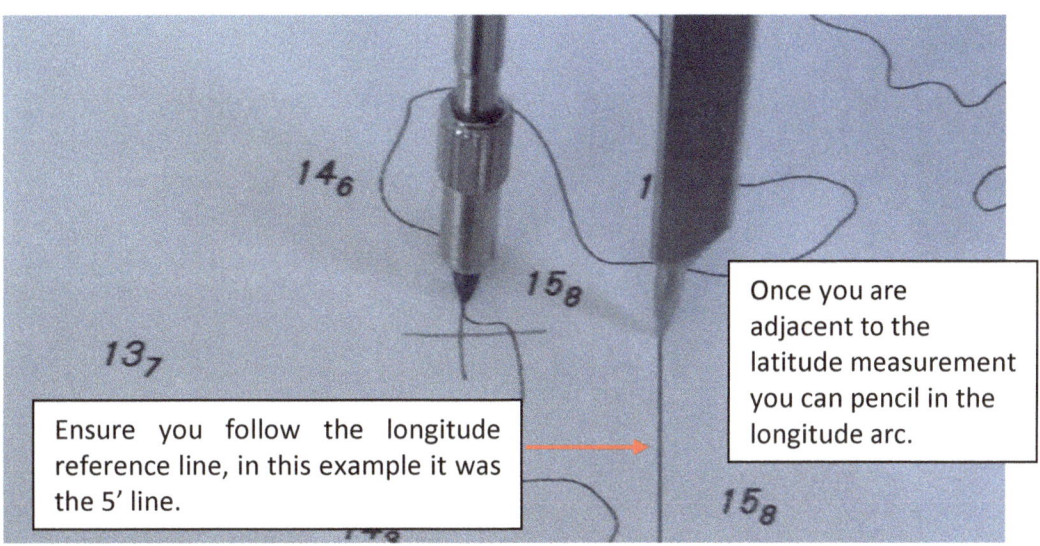

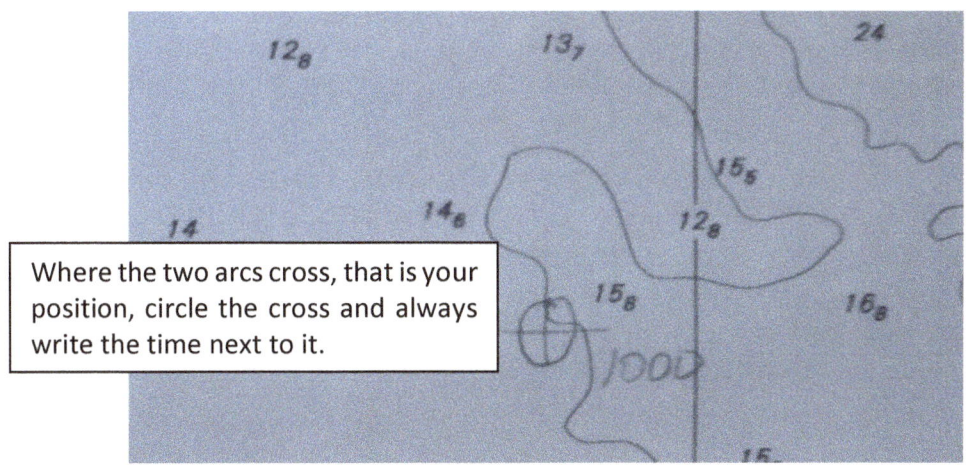

The following example is on a northern hemisphere chart. And shows how to use a parallel ruler in conjunction with a pencil compass to plot your position.

Your GPS reads 50° 29' N and 1° 41' W and you want to plot this on your chart.

Note 1: In the Northern Hemisphere, the minutes and degrees increase as you go up the chart, i.e. further north.

Note 2: In the area West of Greenwich, the minutes and degrees increase in value as you go towards the left on the chart, i.e. further west.

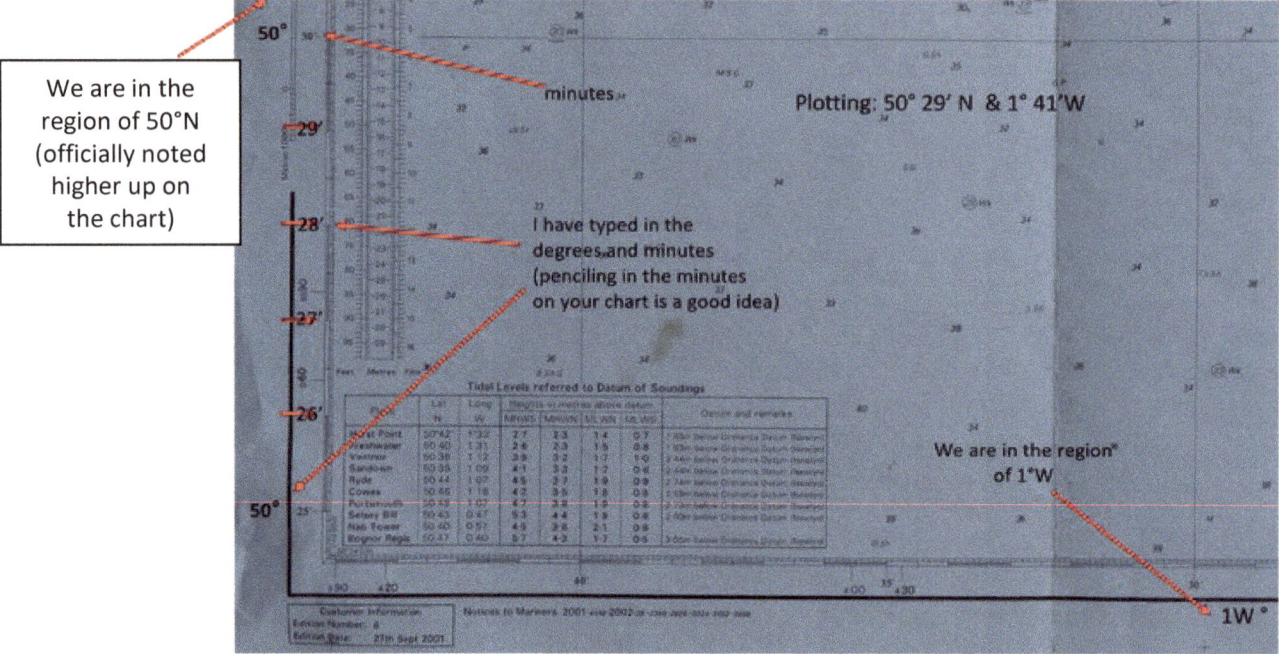

First, go to the approximate area on the chart and note in the minutes. The minutes are marked in five minute increments (on this chart). They are typed in here, but a light pencil notation is helpful to reduce errors. The latitude minutes are marked with a red line too, so you can see how they are divided up.

The distance between each minute can change with each different scale (i.e. on different charts), so take some time to become familiar with each chart. (Take extra care when moving to a new chart whilst sailing).

Typed in is: 50° N and 1°W. The degrees will be printed on the chart once, or maybe twice along the latitude and longitude line. On this image, the printed degrees did not show, hence the typed notation as a reminder.

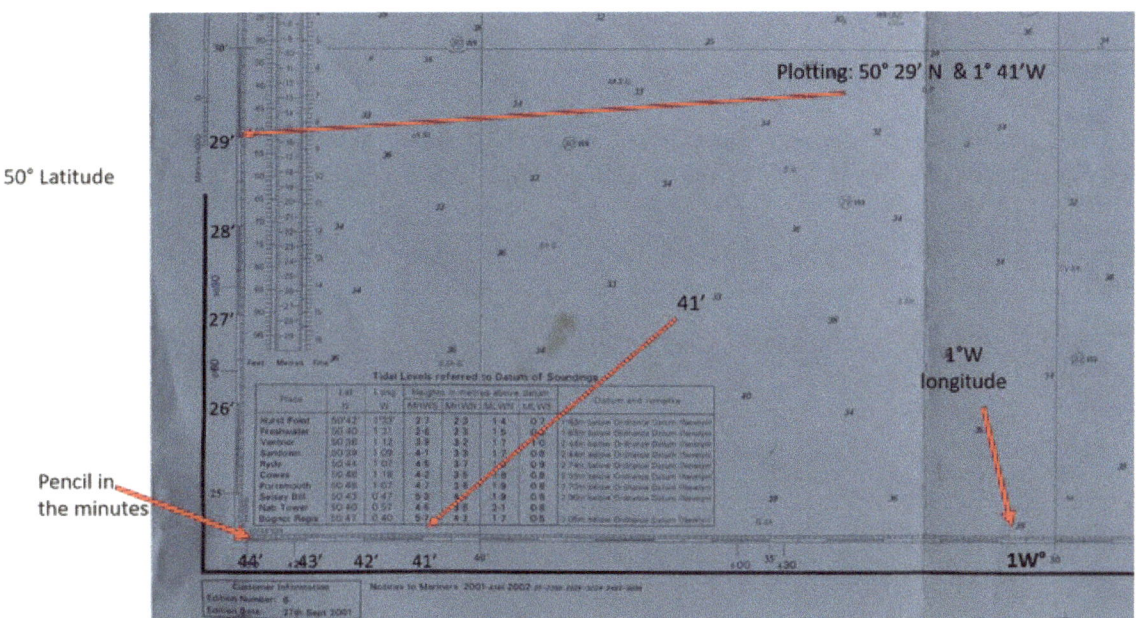

Looking at the longitude scale, we've once again noted the minutes, for the area we wish to plot. Now we have a very good idea where our fix will be.

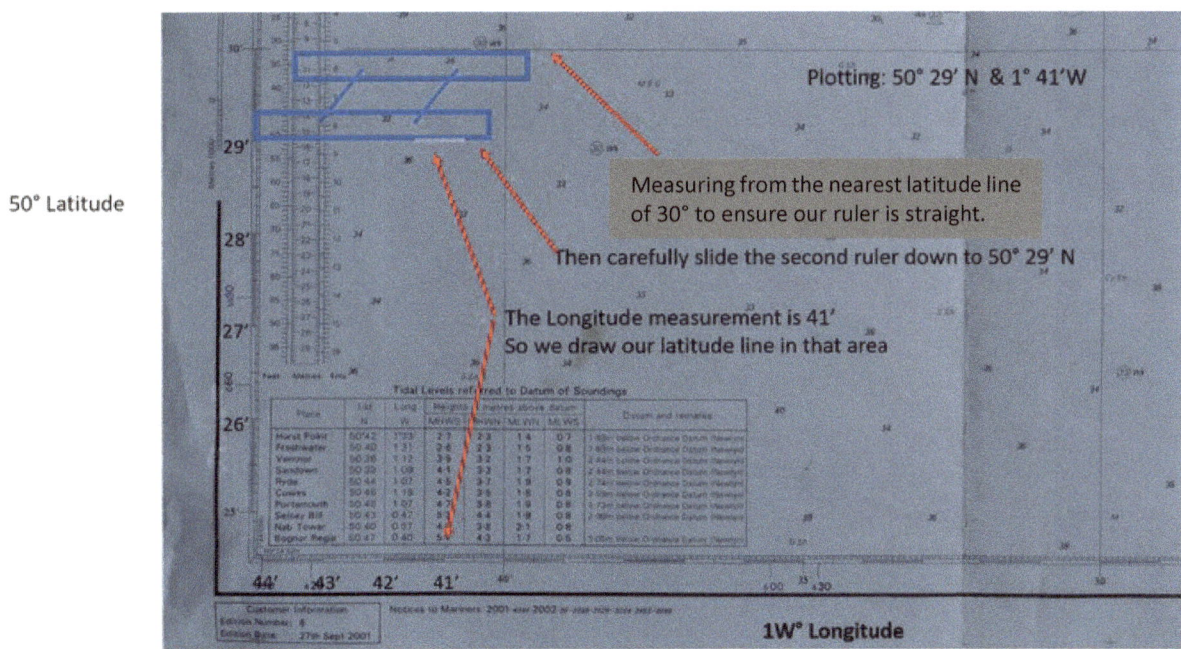

Using a pencil compass for both measurements is useful. Here we'll show you both ways to measure, with the ruler and the pencil compass, you can decide which is more comfortable for you, or use a combination of both.

Take your parallel rule and place one edge upon the nearest latitude line to where you want to measure the latitude co-ordinate. This is to ensure your line is parallel.

TIP: Study where your fix will be, approximately, and put the upper edge of the ruler on the right side of the latitude scale, i.e. so you are 'sliding' the other part of the ruler the minimum amount.

©Jackie Parry

Carefully open the ruler and slide it down to the correct measurement, the bottom of the ruler must lay against the correct measurement 29'.

TIP: At times the measurements are not conveniently near the chart's printed scale, this is why you should learn both how to use the ruler and the pencil compass to measure.

In the approximate vicinity of your longitude minutes, pencil in a small, light line where 29' (latitude measurement) is located.

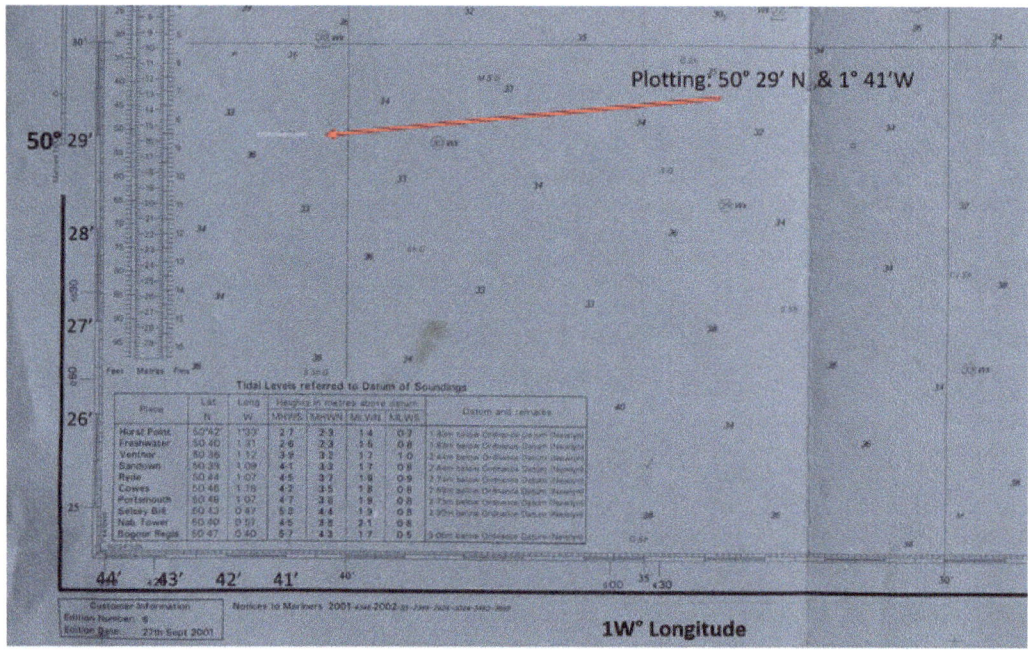

That's a lot of words for something so simple. Don't let the wordiness of it confuse you. Just take a step at a time and very quickly you will see how simple it actually is.

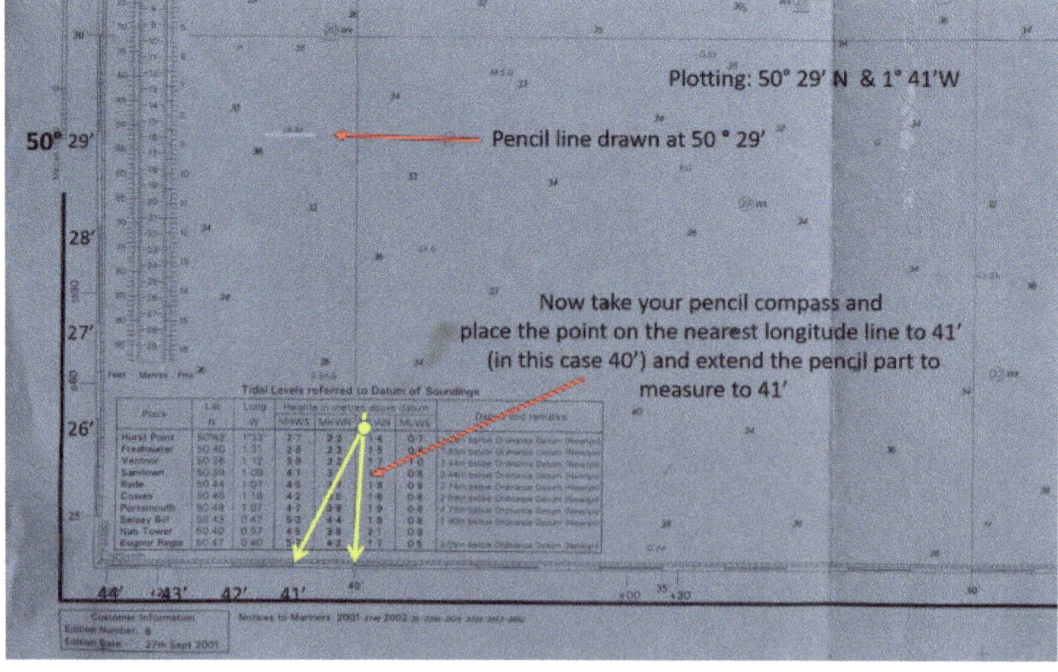

Now for the longitude measurement.

Take your pencil compass and place the point on the nearest longitude line that is printed on the chart (nearest to your measurement, in this case 40').

Open the compass to the correct measurement, ensuring the point stays on the correct longitude line.

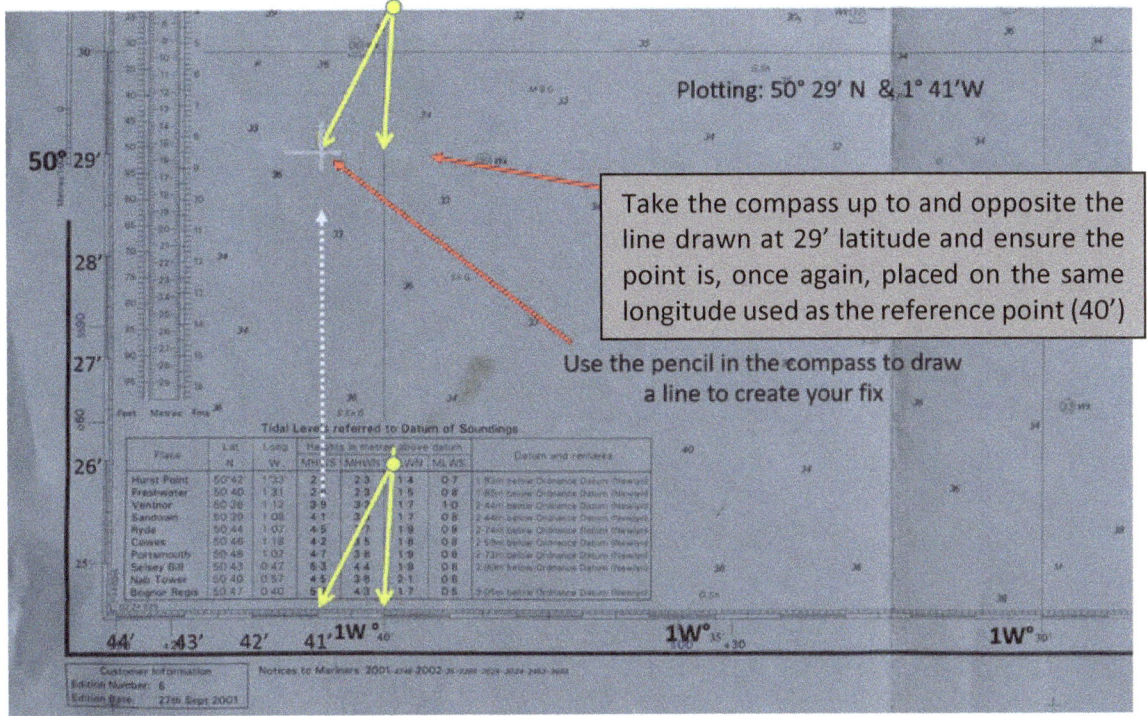

Take your pencil compass up towards your latitude marking, taking care not to alter the width of the opening. Your pencil compass needs to be fairly stiff.

Ensure you place the point on the SAME longitude line you originally measured from (in this case 40') and carefully draw a small arc to measure the longitude and to cross your latitude line that you have already drawn.

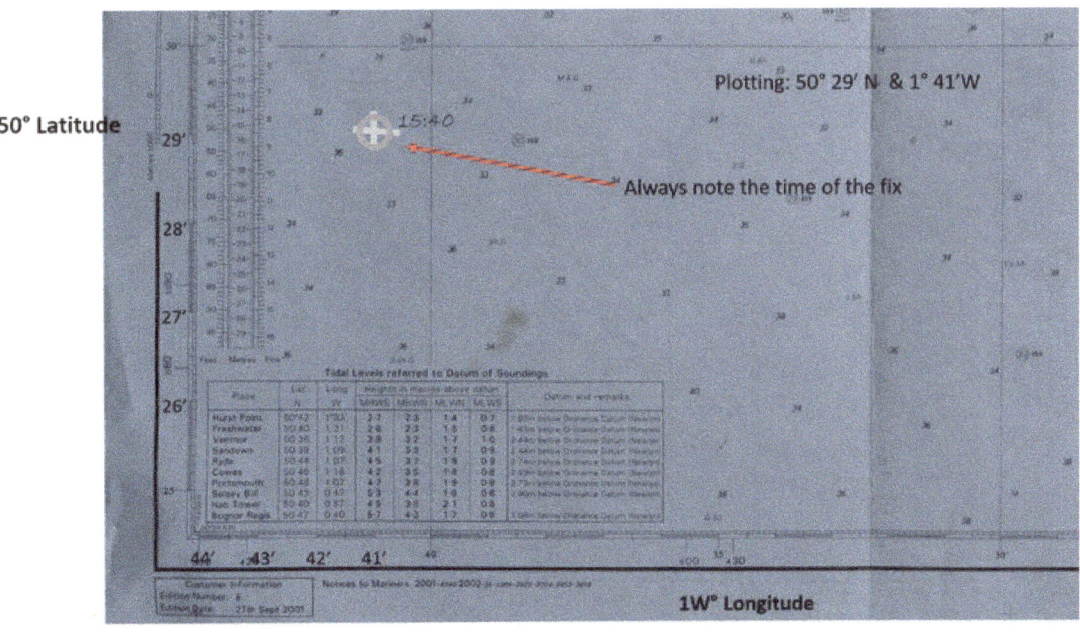

Again, that's a lot of words for something you will find very straightforward with a bit of practice. Always note the time of the fix (in case you need to calculate Deduced Reckoning (DR)).

©Jackie Parry   www.sistershiptraining.com   39

Take your time during each step. It is a simple process but it is also easy to make an error.
At this point it is a good idea to mark your planned course to check if you are heading into danger.

When route planning, it is beneficial to plot your waypoints and intended track between them onto a corrected paper chart. This shows your intended track and with careful study of the chart, dangers can be noted.

A paper chart of any scale will show all areas of danger, e.g. isolated rocks, etc., that may not show up on the scale chosen on your GPS plotter.

Exercise 5 – Position Practice page 9 in Questions and Answers Booklet
Answers 5 – Position Practice page 41 in Questions and Answers Booklet

POSITION FIXING BY BEARING AND DISTANCE

Distance
Distance is always measured on the latitude scale.

1 nautical mile (nm) = 1 minute of latitude

Measurement taken between Flashing light Fl(4)WRG, etc and Fort Albert

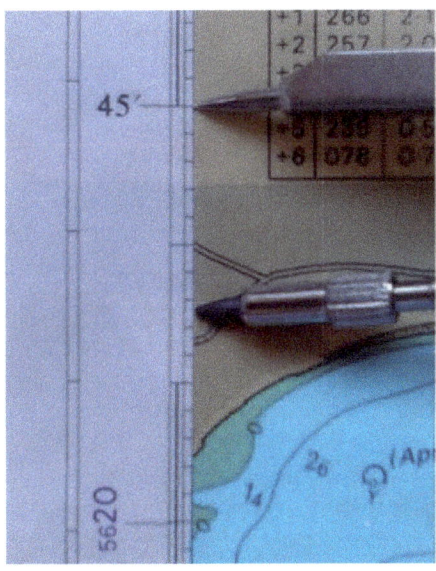

Measure on the latitude scale next to the area you are working (measuring) in.

Be cautious. As you measure adjacent to the area you work in, the measurement will not commence at 0.

The point is on 45' (minutes), that is your 0 (ie start) – but which line is one minute and therefore one nautical mile?

TIP: Note that in this example a northern hemisphere chart is utilised. The latitude scale increases as you move north on the chart. If a southern hemisphere chart was pictured, the latitude scale would increase as you move down the chart in a southerly direction.

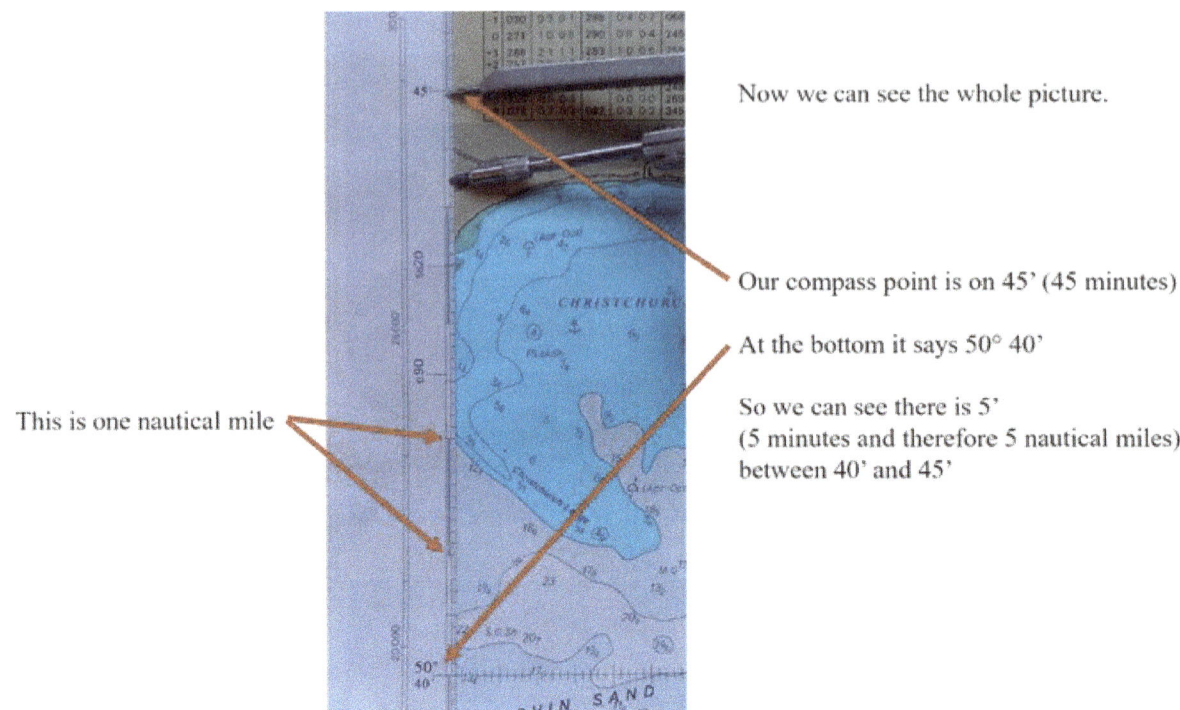

Now we can see the whole picture.

Our compass point is on 45' (45 minutes)

At the bottom it says 50° 40'

So we can see there is 5'
(5 minutes and therefore 5 nautical miles)
between 40' and 45'

This is one nautical mile

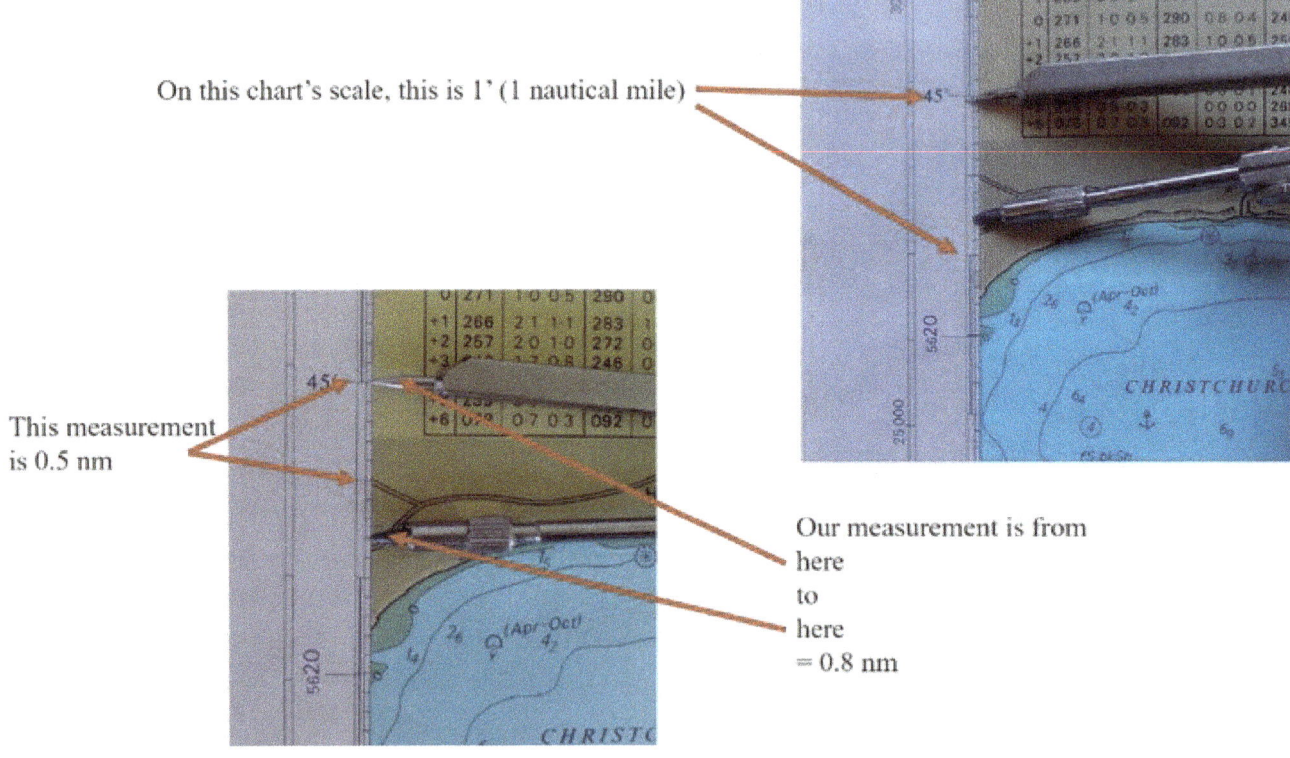

On this chart's scale, this is 1' (1 nautical mile)

This measurement is 0.5 nm

Our measurement is from
here
to
here
= 0.8 nm

Summary

We place our compass or dividers on two points. We want to know the distance between them.

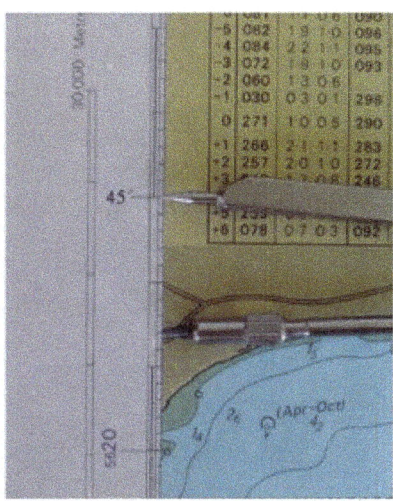

We moved our compass directly across to the **latitude** scale, carefully noting the scale, we can see that the distance measures 0.8nm

Measuring Over Large Distances

To measure larger distances, use dividers. Open your dividers up to 5nm.

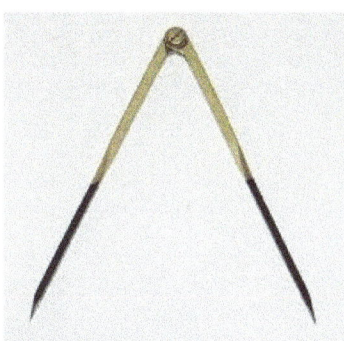

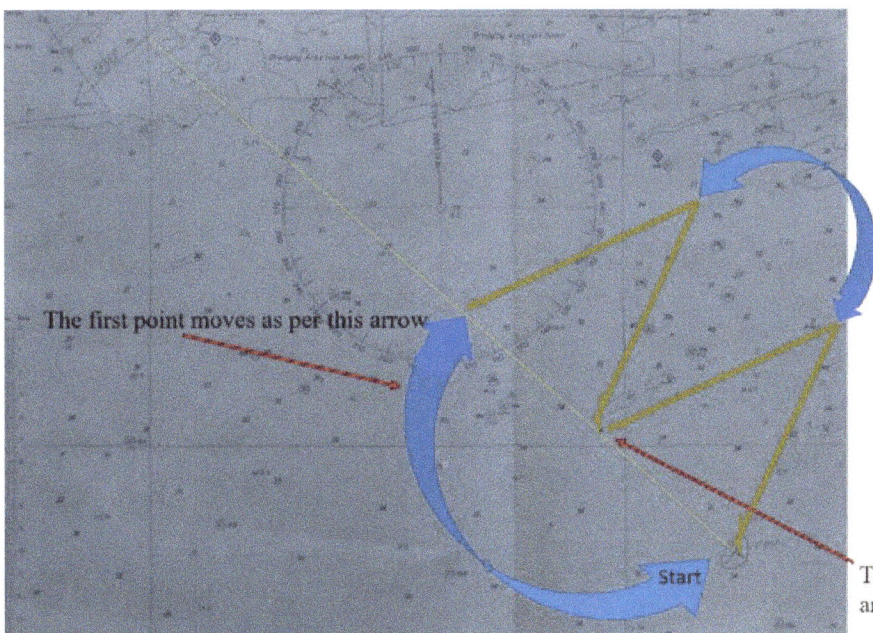

Hold the top of the dividers
And spin them 180 degrees

The first point moves as per this arrow

The second point stays in position and 'spins' on its point.

©Jackie Parry

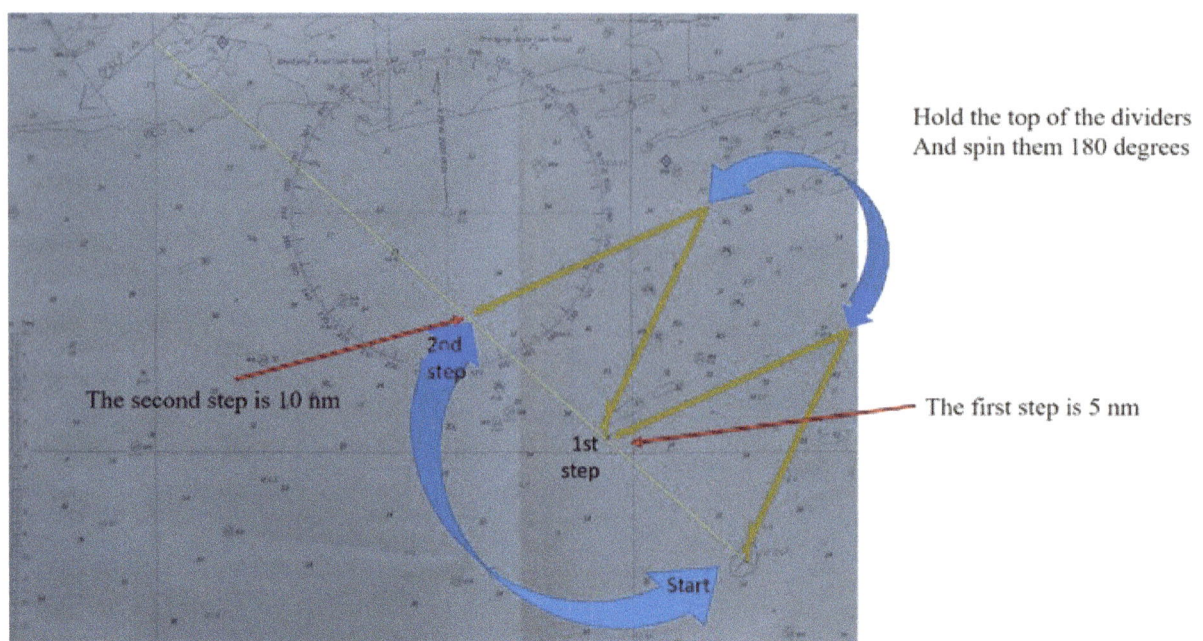

Hold the top of the dividers
And spin them 180 degrees

The first step is 5 nm

The second step is 10 nm

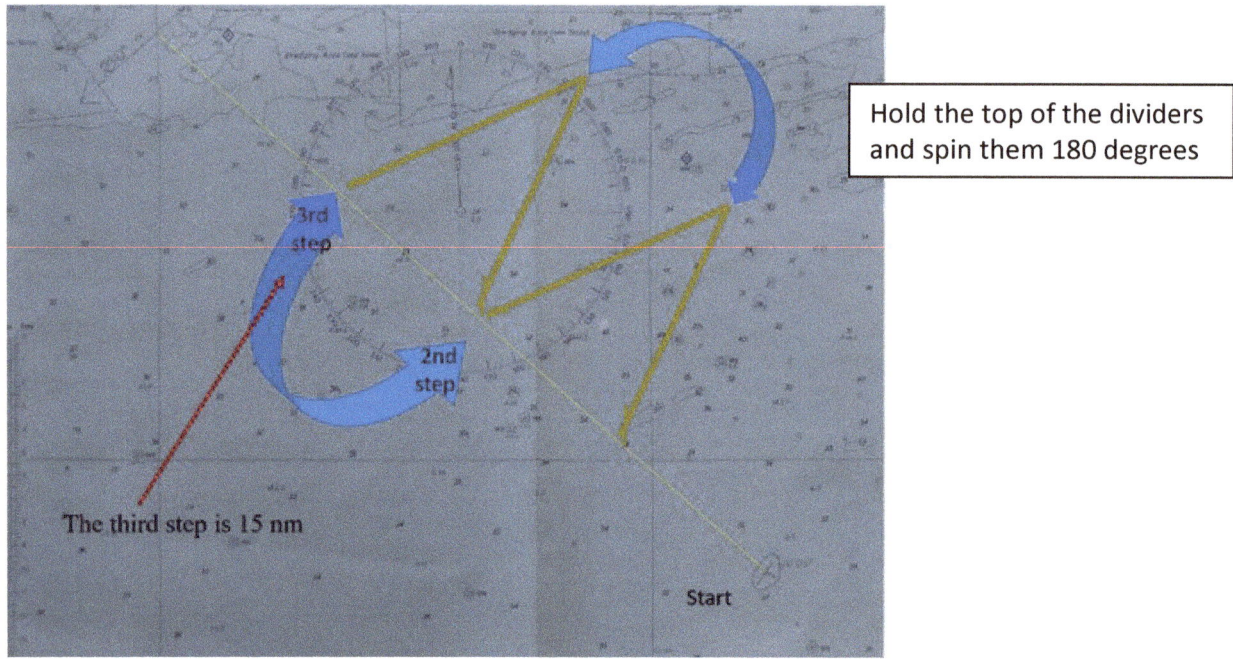

Hold the top of the dividers and spin them 180 degrees

The third step is 15 nm

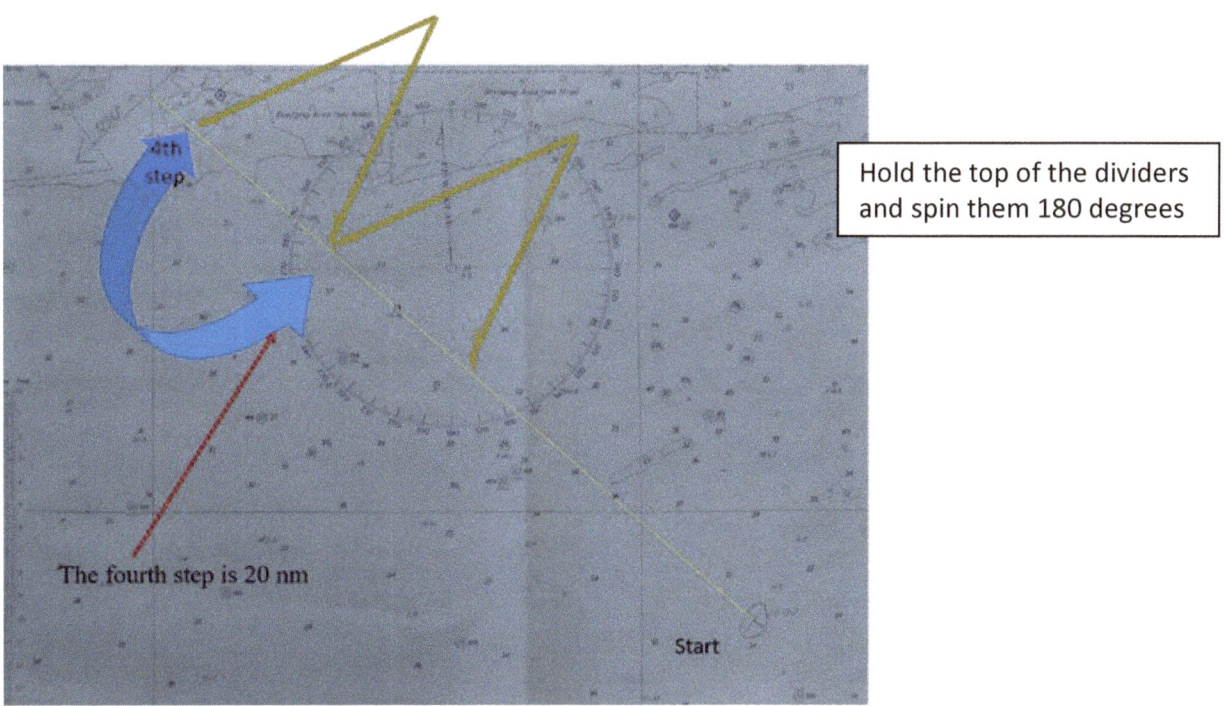

Hold the top of the dividers and spin them 180 degrees

The fourth step is 20 nm

Start

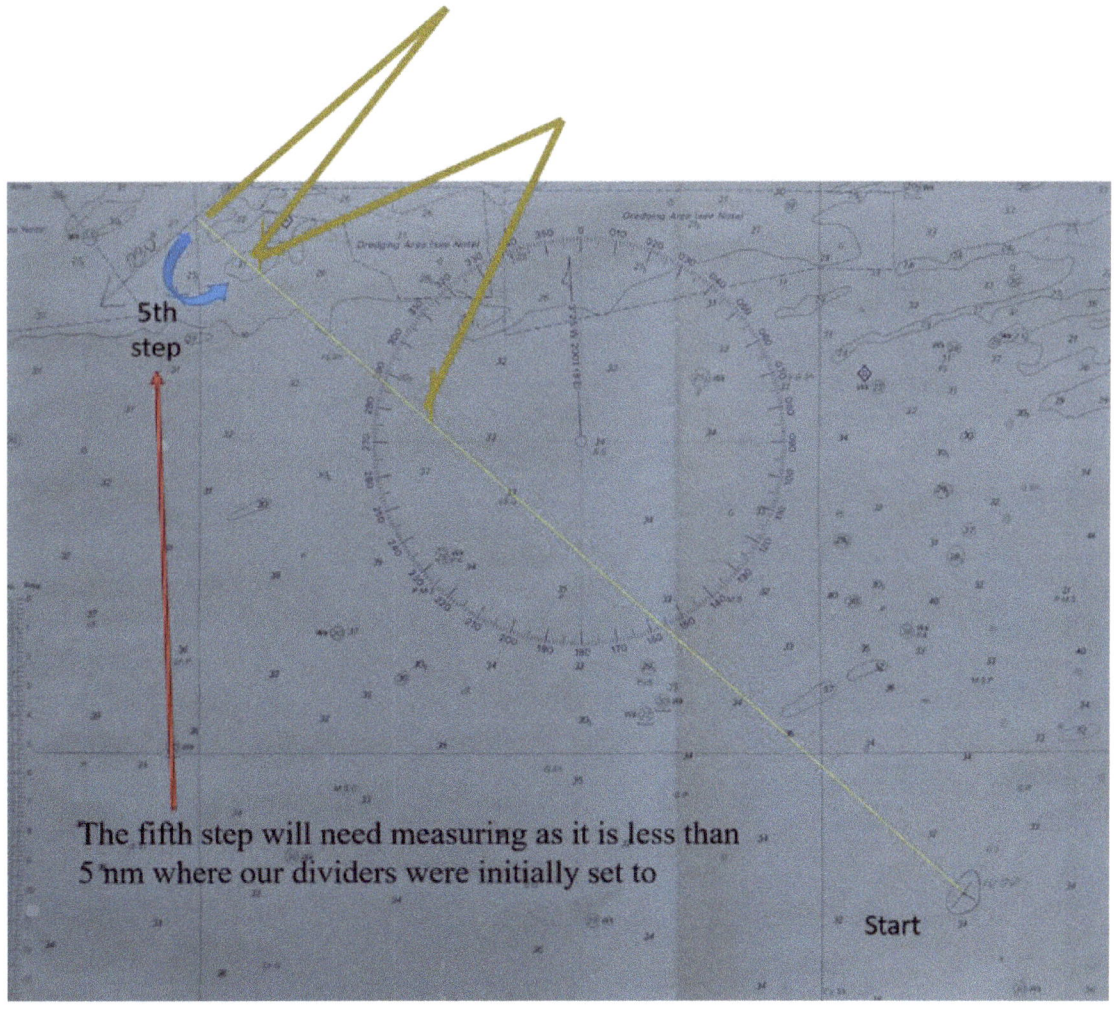

The fifth step will need measuring as it is less than 5 nm where our dividers were initially set to

Start

The dividers are set to a different measurement now (fifth step).

Take them across to the latitude scale and measure.

It measures 0.5 of a mile

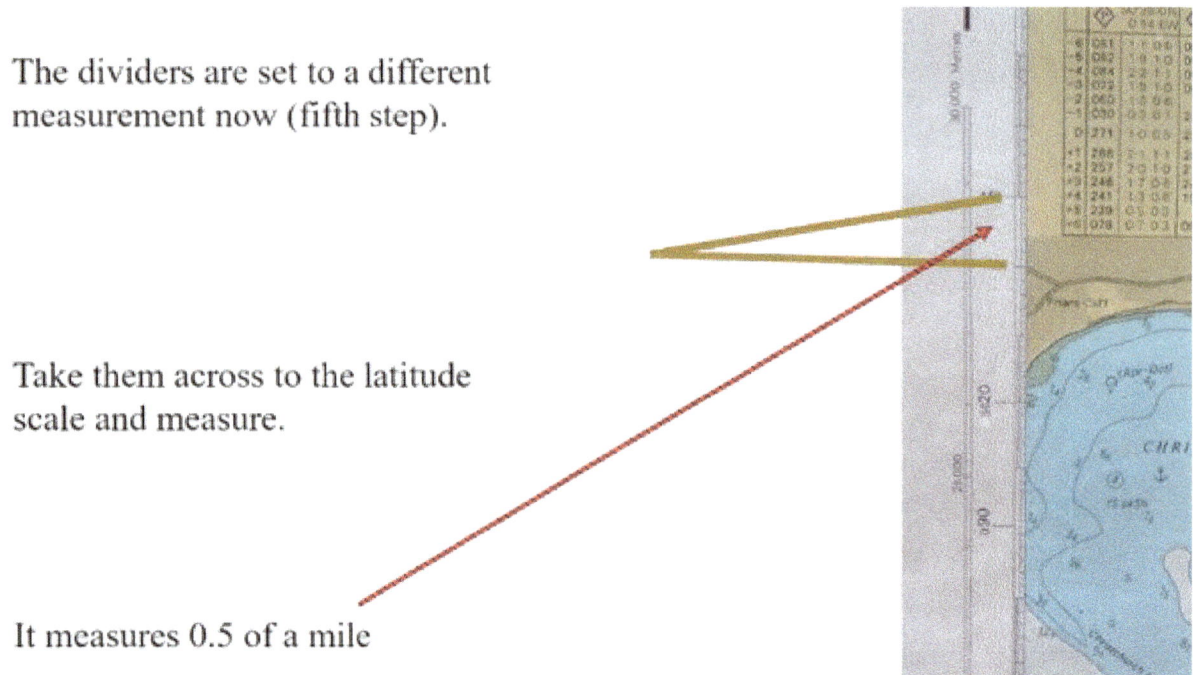

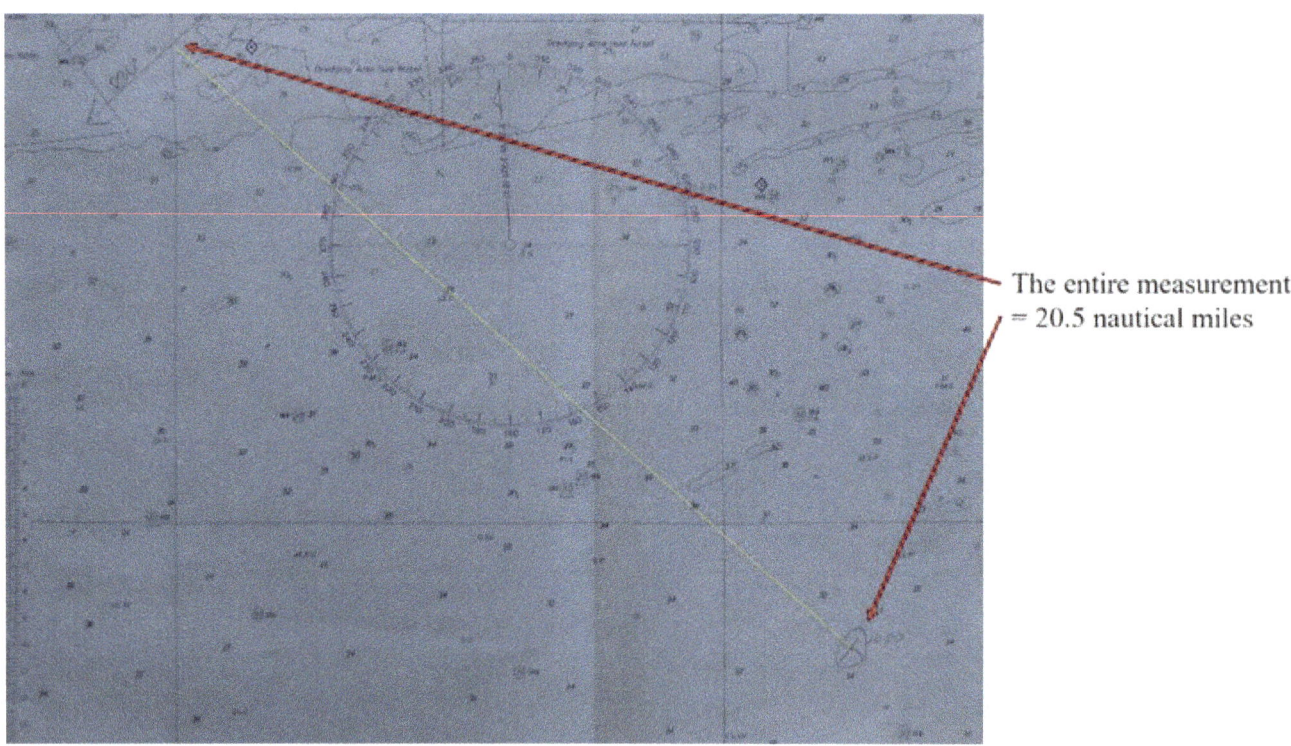

The entire measurement = 20.5 nautical miles

Exercise 6 – Distance page 9 in Questions and Answers Booklet
Answers 6 – Distance page 41 in Questions and Answers Booklet

BEARINGS
Direction
Direction is expressed in the angular difference in degrees from one position to another.

It's usually measured from north to the ship's head.

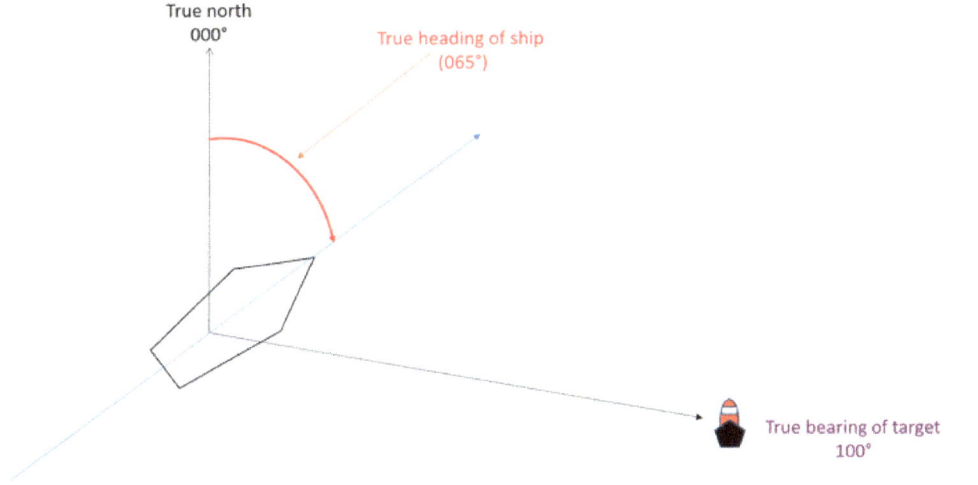

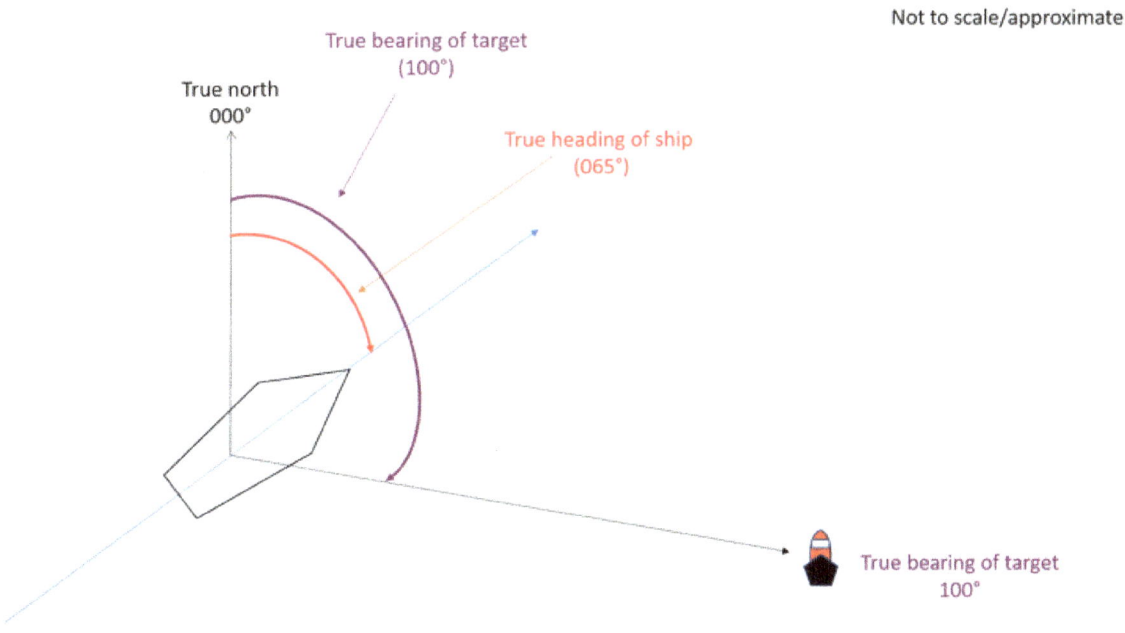

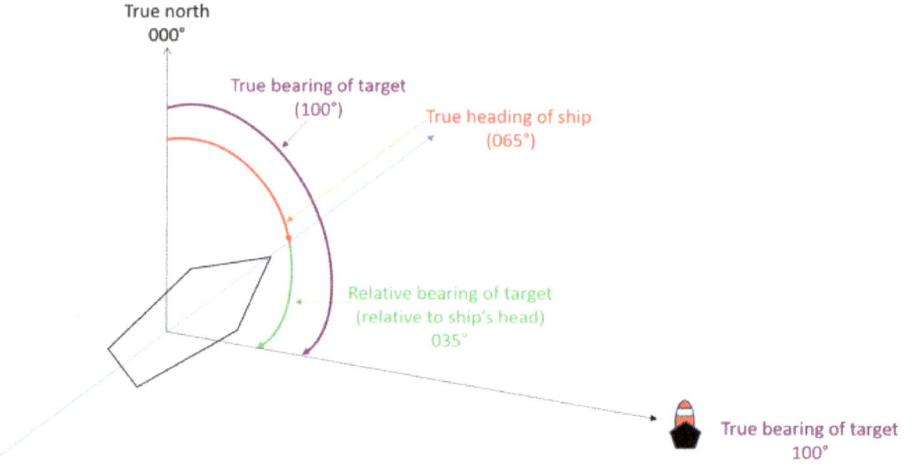

True Bearings

On a navigational chart the direction in which a place or object lies from the vessel is called the true bearing and is measured from north (000°) in a clockwise direction through 360°.

The diagram above shows a true north meridian with:
- The ship's head bearing at 065° TRUE
- The target's bearing is 100° TRUE
- The target's bearing is 035° RELATIVE to the ship's head (and also 035° Green)

TIP: In relaying your direction (or a target's direction) to crew or writing it in your log book you MUST make note (or say) that it is TRUE (as there are other bearings, such as compass, relative, radar, and red and green).

Compass Rose

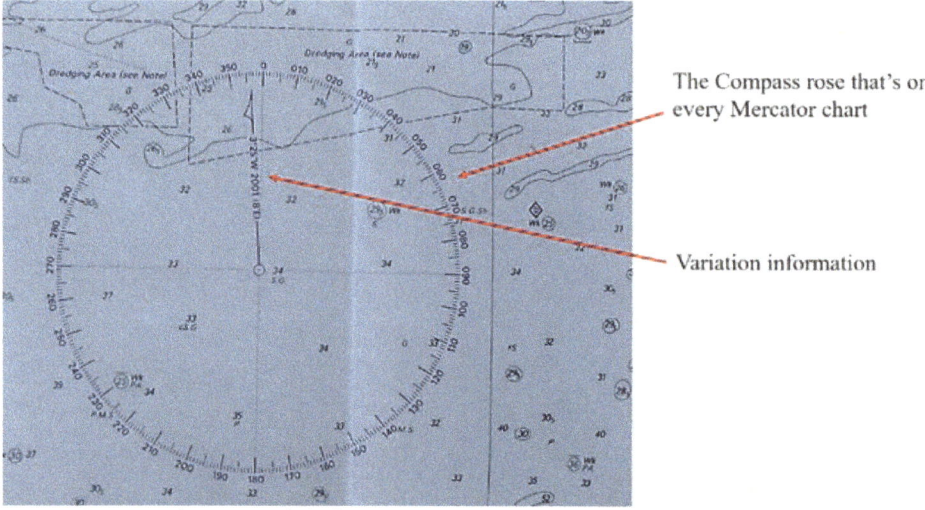

The Variation reads: 3° 25'W 2001 (8' E)

Usually, there is more than one compass rose on a Mercator chart, they are located at convenient places enabling the use of the rose for navigation work.

You can see the degrees (°) around the rose and the Variation. We'll go into more detail on Variation later on.

Finding your Course

The ruler is measuring 050° True (approximately a north east direction). Ensure the ruler passes through the centre of the rose

230° True is the reciprocal course

If you are heading in an approximate north-easterly direction you know that the bearing or course line is going to be around 045° (in this case 050° T).

Look at the image above again and note the reciprocal course of 230°T.

If you are heading in a north-east direction, you know the degrees must be somewhere between 000° and 090°. This is why we start at the beginning with degrees and directions. This is an excellent 'spot' check/back-up in your navigation work.

TIP: Reciprocal Courses and Bearings – If you have reciprocal dyslexia, an easy way to calculate the reciprocal course or bearing (180°) is to plus or minus 200, then adjust by twenty accordingly. For example, for the reciprocal of 050°, add 200° = 250°, then just minus 20° = 230°.

Direction and Bearings

Two commonly used rulers are the Bi-rola Chart Protractor (or the Portland Course Plotter) and the parallel rulers. We'll measure direction/bearings using both.

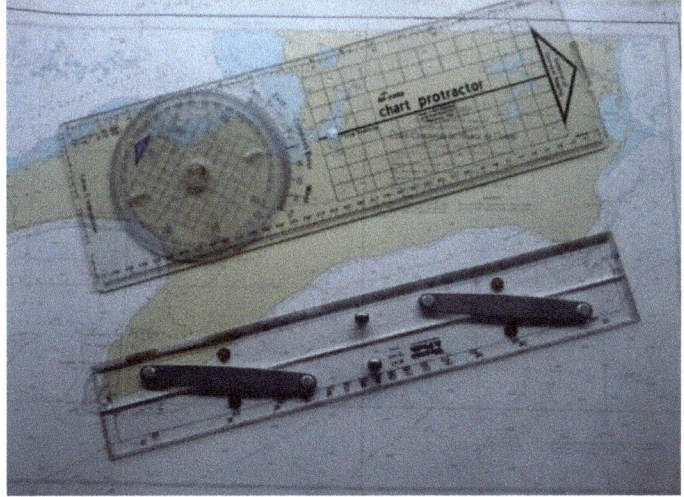

The Admiralty chart in use for this example is the Outer Approaches To The Solent. It's a chart we've used previously while sailing, so you may see some previous markings – they won't interfere with what we're doing.

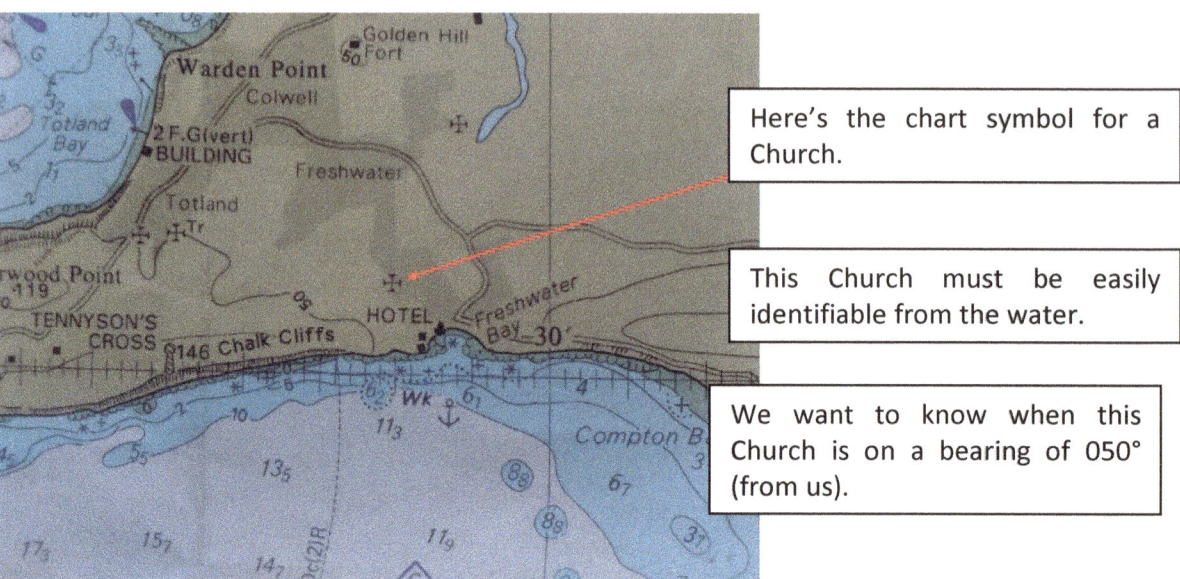

You've identified the church on the chart, you must ensure can identify the correct landmark by sight.

For this exercise we are going to assume you are heading in a north west direction and you want to know when the Church bears 050° True <u>from</u> our vessel.

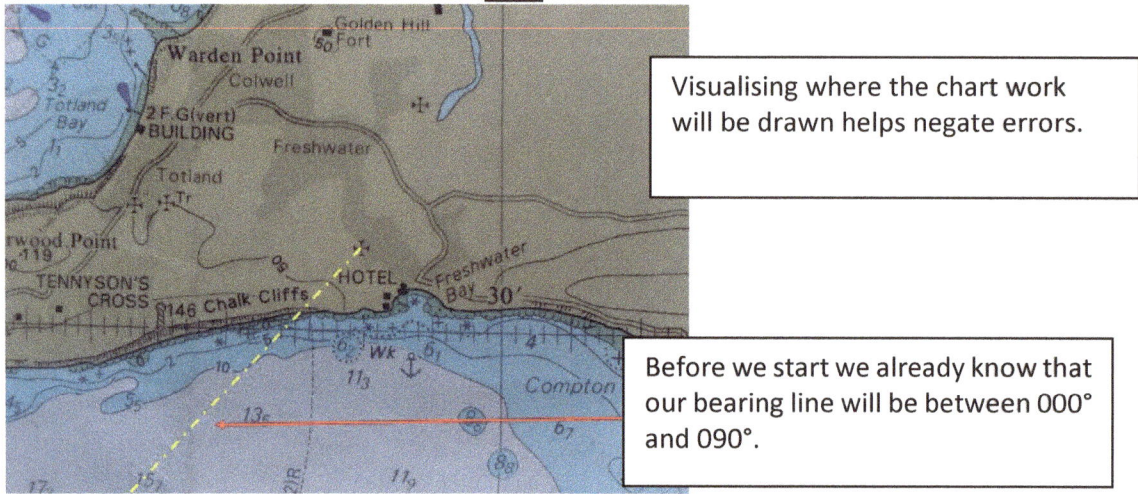

Visualising: Remember true north is always directly up on a Mercator chart.

The first part of this exercise will be completed with the parallel rulers.

©Jackie Parry www.sistershiptraining.com 50

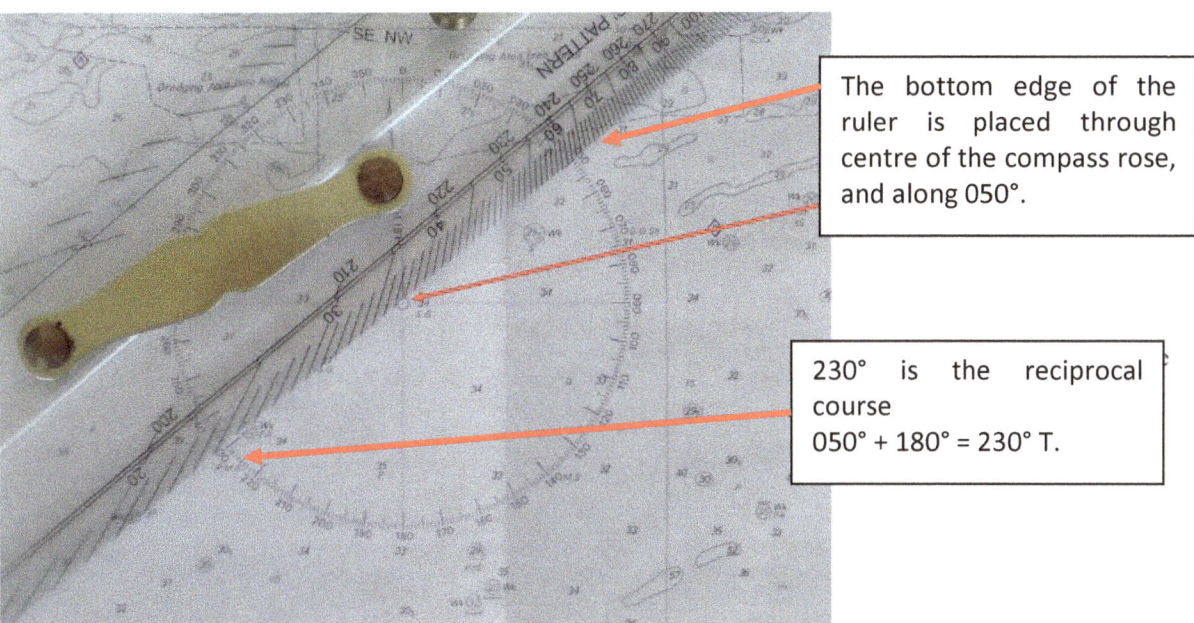

Reciprocal Course

230° is 180° in the opposite direction to 050°. Therefore, we can also say that <u>we</u> bear 230° <u>from</u> the Church.'

TIP: Always double check the direction you want, it's surprisingly easy to read the wrong bearing, especially in stressful conditions, and there are times on the water that are stressful as we all know.

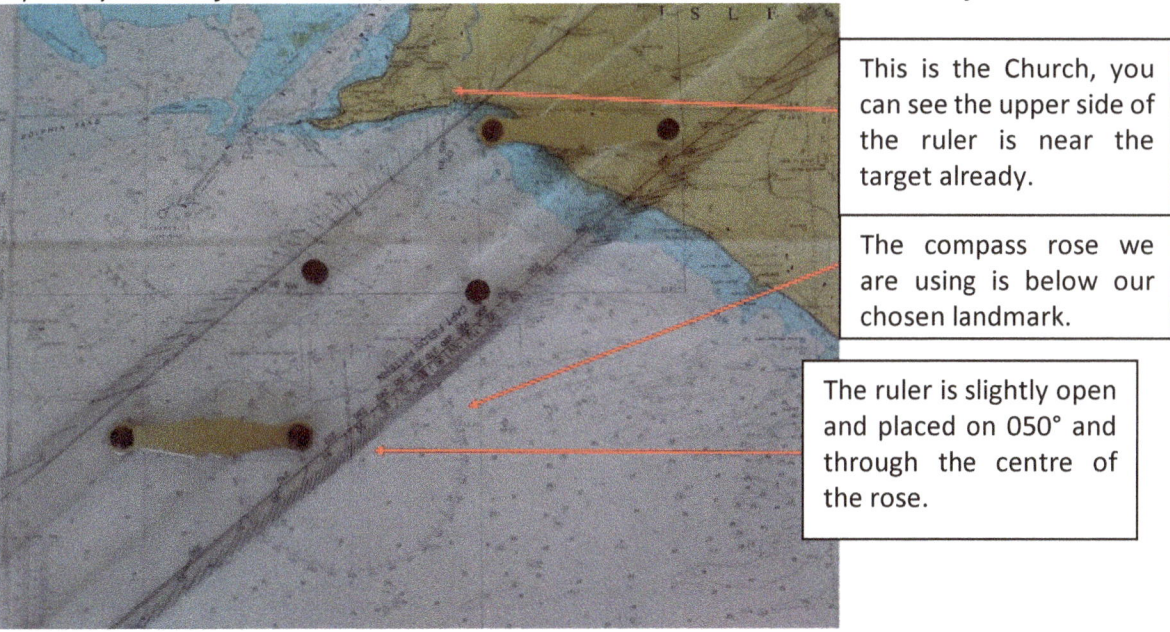

TIP: Note where the compass rose and landmark are in relation to each other, use this to your advantage. Prepare by opening the ruler slightly while placed in position on the rose – through the centre and on 050°. The bottom edge of the ruler is used here, so there are less 'walking' movements than if the upper edge of the ruler was used.

Hold firmly the part of the ruler that is on the rose.

Carefully slide the other part of the ruler towards the target, by opening the ruler more. You can continue to 'walk' the ruler as far as you need.

The Church (cross) is just above the hotel and our ruler cuts right through the middle.

With the ruler in place and held firmly, the bearing line can be drawn in.

In this example, the ruler was fairly close to the target. At times, it will be necessary to walk the ruler further taking great care to ensure it doesn't slip along the way (and if it does slip, you must start again).

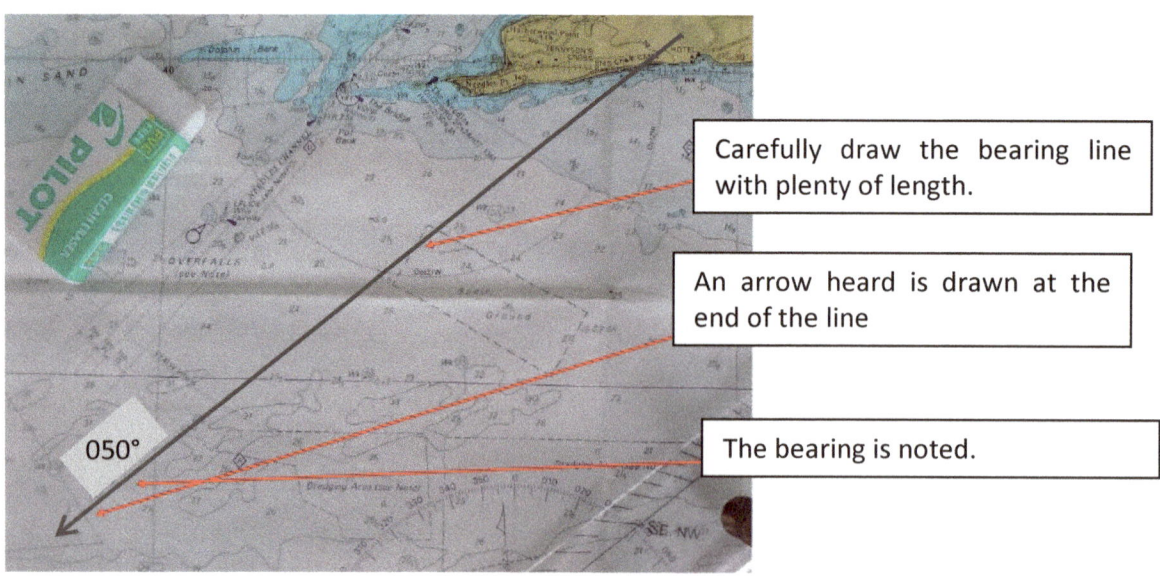

Carefully draw the bearing line with plenty of length.

An arrow heard is drawn at the end of the line

The bearing is noted.

©Jackie Parry

It is good practice and good seamanship on board to write and use the correct conventions (arrows, noting the bearing etc.). This means the next person on watch can look at the chart and instantly recognise the navigation work.

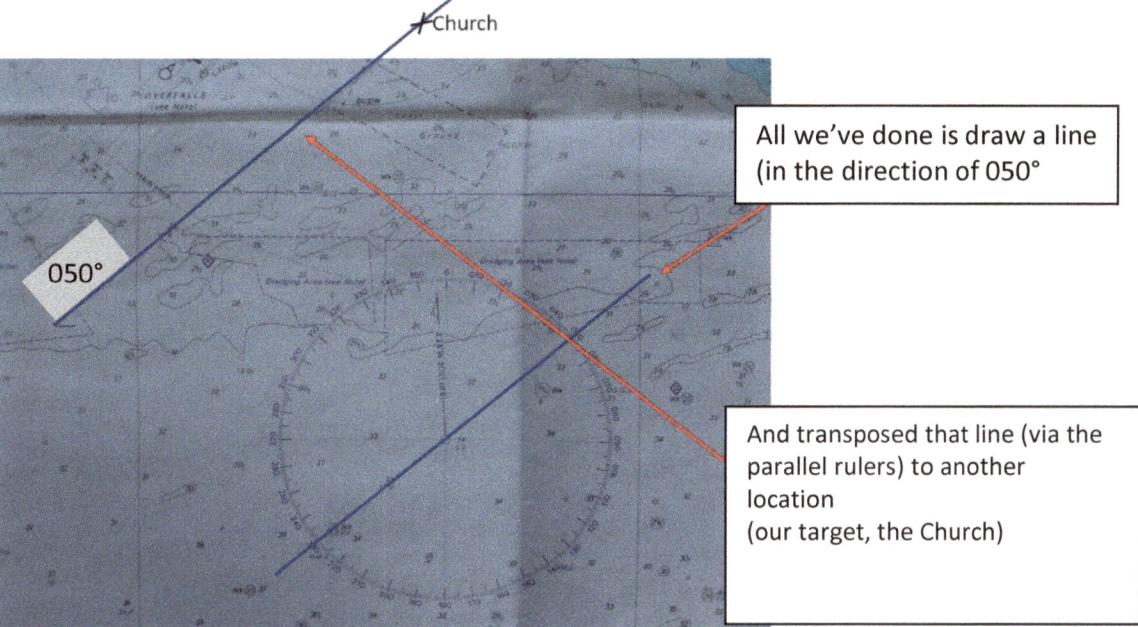

All we've done is draw a line (in the direction of 050°

And transposed that line (via the parallel rulers) to another location (our target, the Church)

Once practiced this, the entire procedure only takes a few moments – but it must never be rushed. Let's look at doing this with the Bi-rola/Portland Plotter now.

These types of chart protractors consist of two simple parts, the protractor 0° to 360° and the ruler with the large black arrow pointing in the direction of the bearing or course.

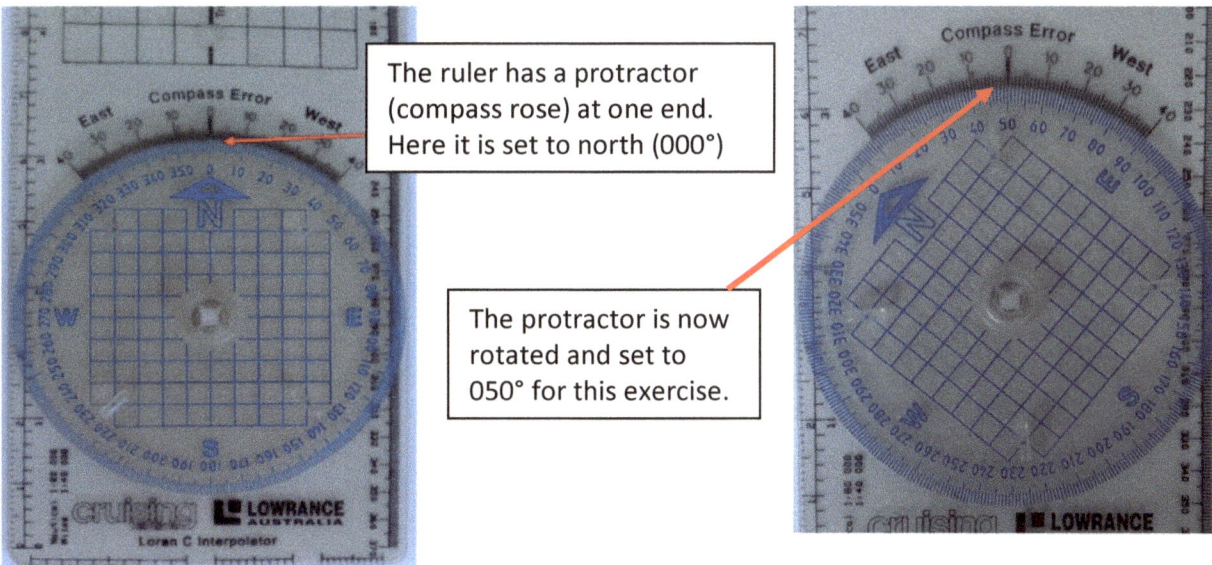

The ruler has a protractor (compass rose) at one end. Here it is set to north (000°)

The protractor is now rotated and set to 050° for this exercise.

©Jackie Parry   www.sistershiptraining.com   53

In summary: The protractor is set to 050° and the black arrow shows the True Reading of the Direction of Course or Bearing (in this case our bearing of 050°)

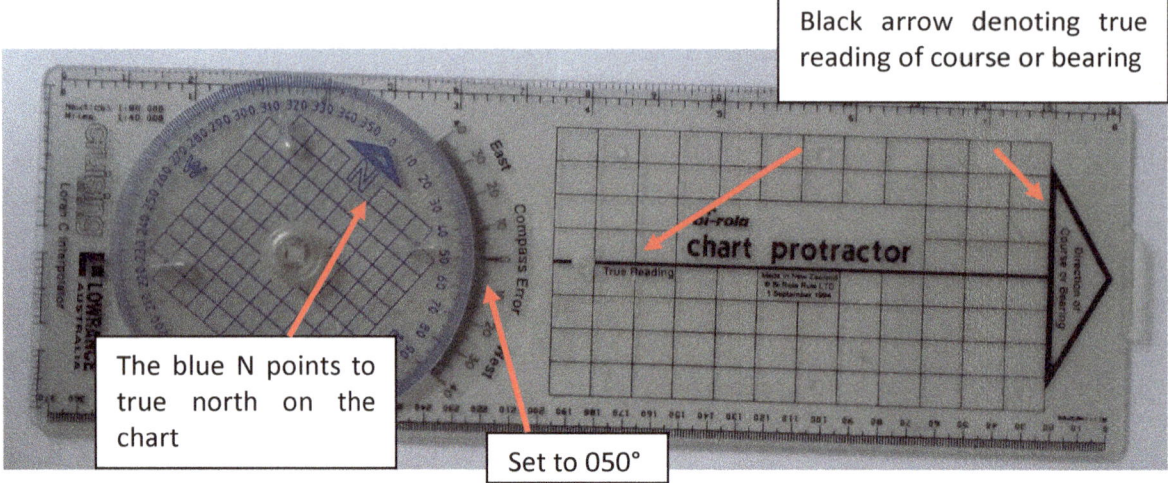

- Black arrow denoting true reading of course or bearing
- The blue N points to true north on the chart
- Set to 050°

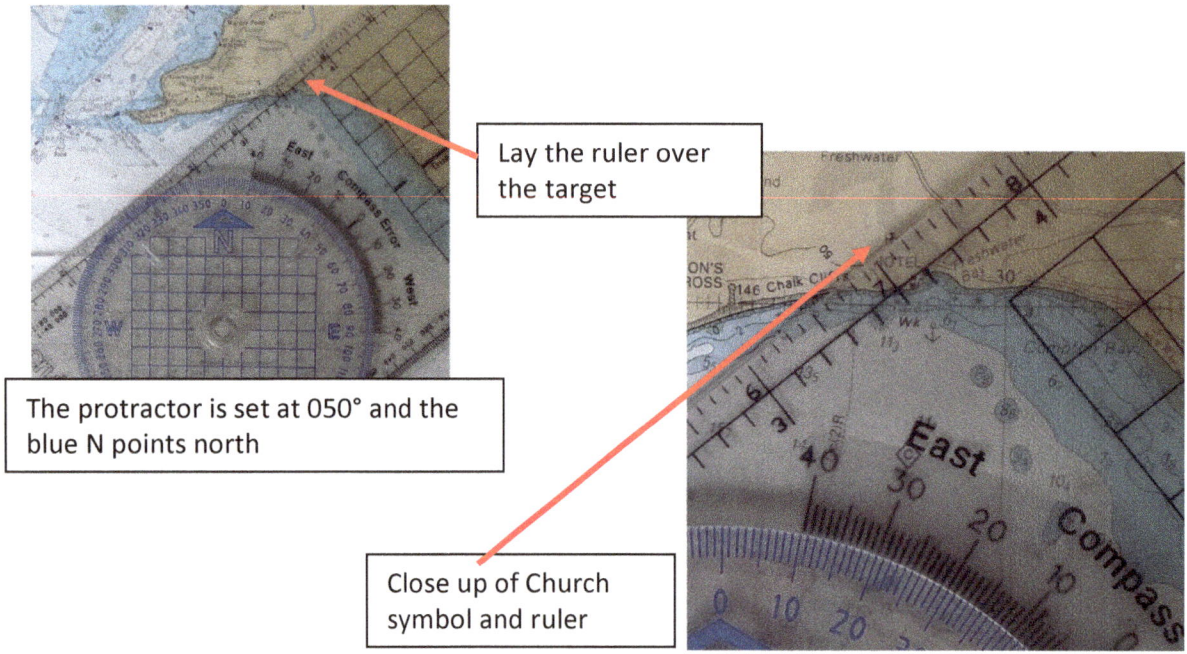

- Lay the ruler over the target
- The protractor is set at 050° and the blue N points north
- Close up of Church symbol and ruler

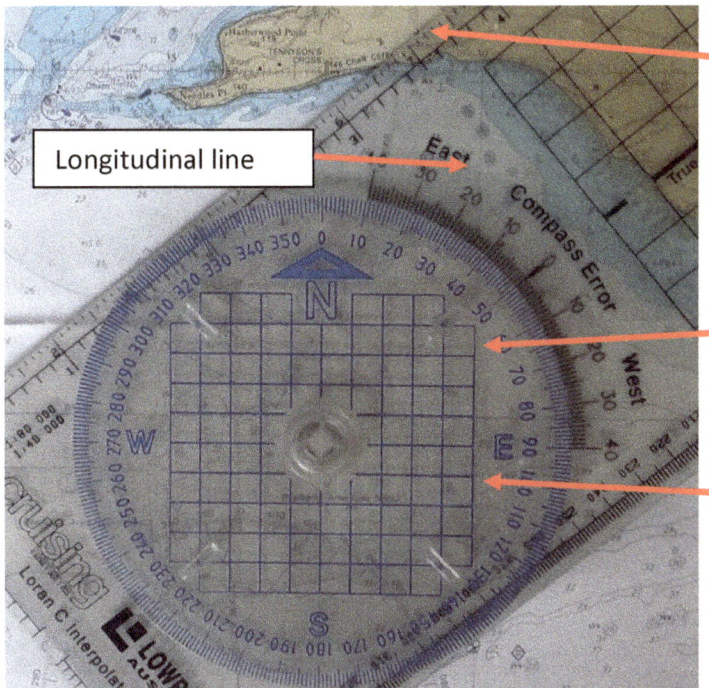

This is the target

Longitudinal line

Keep the edge of the ruler on the target and look at the blue grid on the protractor.

This grid must lay squarely on a straight line (lat. or long. line) on the chart to ensure the protractor is pointing directly to true north.

Here the grid is aligned with a longitudinal line.

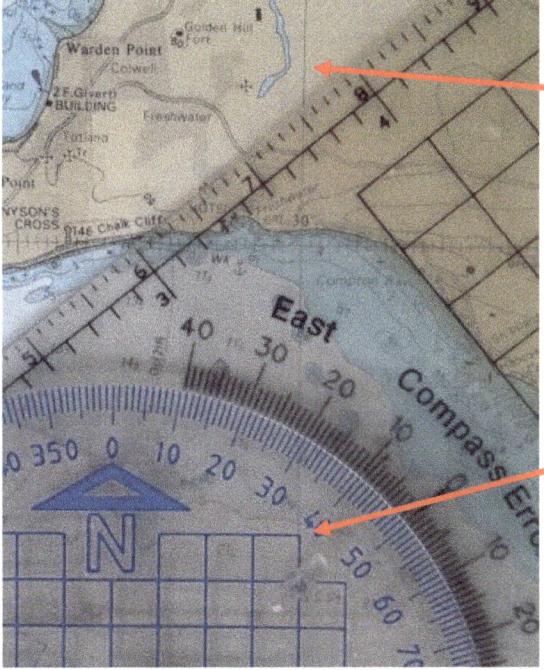

The longitude line runs right down the entire chart and through the blue grid

The blue grid is perfectly aligned with the longitude line

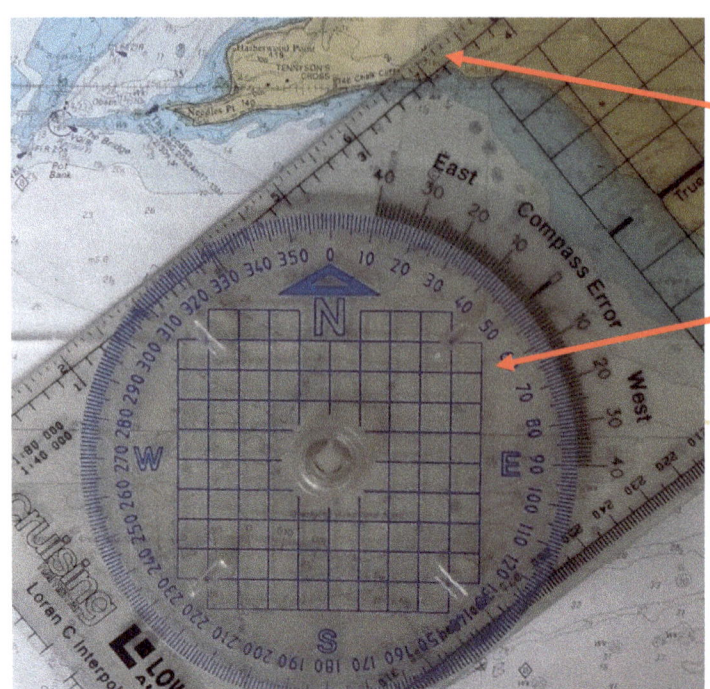

Once the ruler is:

1) Laying on the target (the Church in this case).

and

2) Squared up with the grid, the bearing line can be drawn.

Note: Once the protractor is set ensure the ruler and protractor are moved together to align to the grid, to ensure you maintain the protractor setting of 050°.

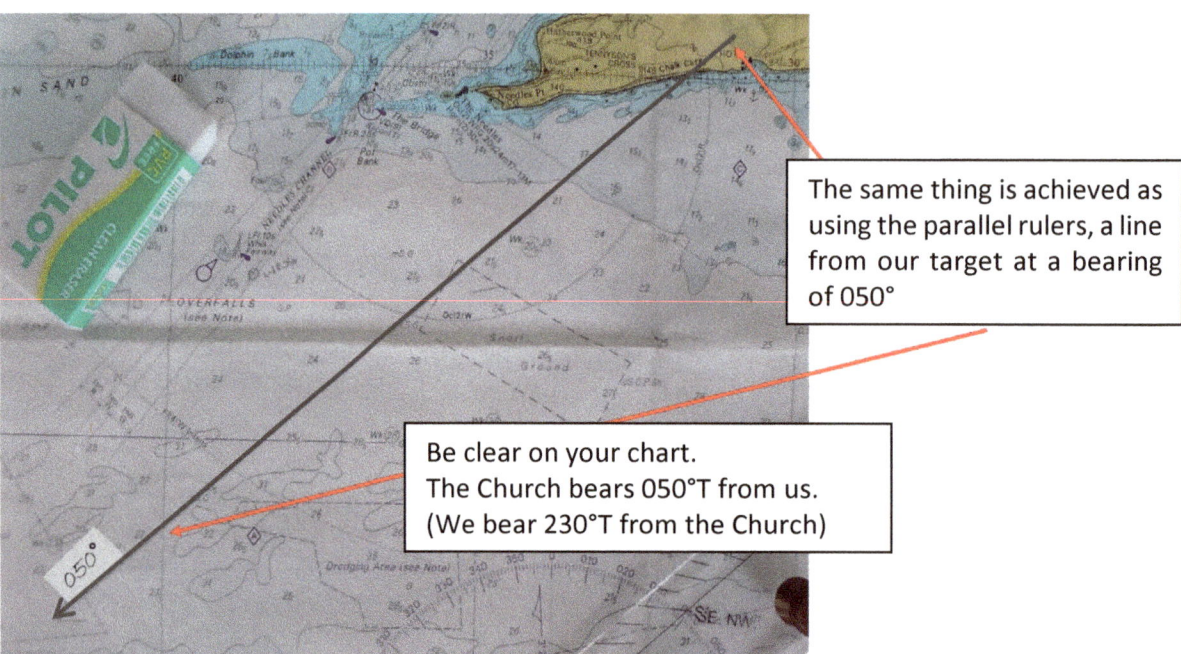

The same thing is achieved as using the parallel rulers, a line from our target at a bearing of 050°

Be clear on your chart.
The Church bears 050°T from us.
(We bear 230°T from the Church)

We'll use many bearings through this course for different navigation techniques. But the process for finding the bearing, whichever type it is, is the same.

Exercise 7 – Direction/Bearings page 9 in Questions and Answers Booklet
Answers 7– Direction/Bearings page 41 in Questions and Answers Booklet

SECTION SUMMARY

You have learned how to interpret the key information on a chart. You have also learned the basic principles of position, and direction on the Earth's surface and their relationship to a Mercator Chart. You've learned to plot a position, measure distances, and bearings.

SECTION TWO

THE COMPASS – TRUE TO COMPASS AND COMPASS TO TRUE

Compass
The compass functions as an indicator to Magnetic North. The magnetic bar, in the compass, aligns itself with the earth's magnetic field.

True North and Magnetic North
The difference between True North and Magnetic North is called Variation. (Variation is an error). The reason for this is that the Magnetic North Pole is not at the Geographic North Pole, around which the Earth rotates. The degree of Variation and its annual rate of change is indicated on nautical charts within the compass rose.

Cardinal points and steering
North, East, South and West are called Cardinal points. You should instinctively know which way to turn to achieve the compass degrees you wish to steer. Learning to steer by compass is important – what if your electrics or windvane fails? It is easier to steer by compass if the compass card is dampened correctly and positioned directly in front of the helmsperson.

Every boat should have a compass on board and everyone on board should know how to steer by compass. This sounds obvious and easy, but it can take time to learn this instinctively.

If you want to steer from 010° to 020° you would turn the boat in a clockwise direction, i.e. to starboard. Apply the opposite for fewer degrees, e.g. going from 020° to 010° you would turn to port.

Of course, knowing where north, east, south and west are in terms of where you are currently heading is natural for most of us, but for new crew this is something to be aware of – especially if the self-steering suddenly stops on a dark night in lumpy seas and in high density traffic.

Remember that if you turn to port, the numbers on the compass will get lower. If you turn to starboard, the numbers will increase. (When you reach 359° the next number is 000° which would still be 'increasing' the number.)

Selecting a marker to look at and head for, is the easiest way to steer by compass. This is okay if you are coastal sailing (i.e. steer your compass course then look/line up a marker/headland, then keep heading for that, ensuring you know how long you are in safe water). At sea, away from the coast, this is more difficult, but you can pick a star or even a cloud to temporarily aim for (if it isn't too windy!).

Points of a compass
Sometimes sailors indicate a direction to an object by using points of a compass, e.g. 'vessel two points off the starboard bow'. In navigation, a 'point' is 1/32 of a full circle. One point is 11.25 degrees. For example, four points to starboard = 045° to starboard.

True chart work
All chart work must be in True because north on Mercator charts is Geographic North not Magnetic North. When using your boat's compass you must convert Compass readings to True in order to lay off bearings or courses on your chart.

True to Compass (or Compass to True)

If you have found the course to steer on your chart, that will be in True. The helmsperson needs a Compass course to steer by, therefore you need to convert True to Compass.

Variation

In most parts of the world there is Variation. Variation changes with position, e.g. in the eastern Mediterranean Sea, Variation is minimal, but in the central North Atlantic, Variation can be much more. Moreover, some places will have a westerly Variation and some an easterly Variation.

In addition to the changes in Variation due to position, the Variation amount also changes over time (in the same position/area). This occurs because the position of the Magnetic North Pole slowly moves in a small circle. The movement of the Magnetic North Pole is known as Secular Variation or Secular Change and is indicated in the compass rose.

The Secular Change is indicated by the figure in brackets, next to the current Variation on the compass rose on your chart.

Example - Variation:

8°20'E 2014 (1'W) (from Chart AUS252)

This means that in 2014 the Variation was 8°20'E. Every year, thereafter, it moves 1' West.

From 2014 until 2020 = six years.

Therefore, apply 6' West to 8°20' (i.e. one minute for each year).

You start with 8°20'E, apply 6'W = 8° 14' E (it's easier to see in diagrammatical form):

> If we apply 6' West, then you can see that moving in a westerly direction 8° 20' East becomes less (e.g. subtract the total yearly change).

If the Secular change was East, you can see that 8° 20' East would become more (e.g. add on the yearly increase).

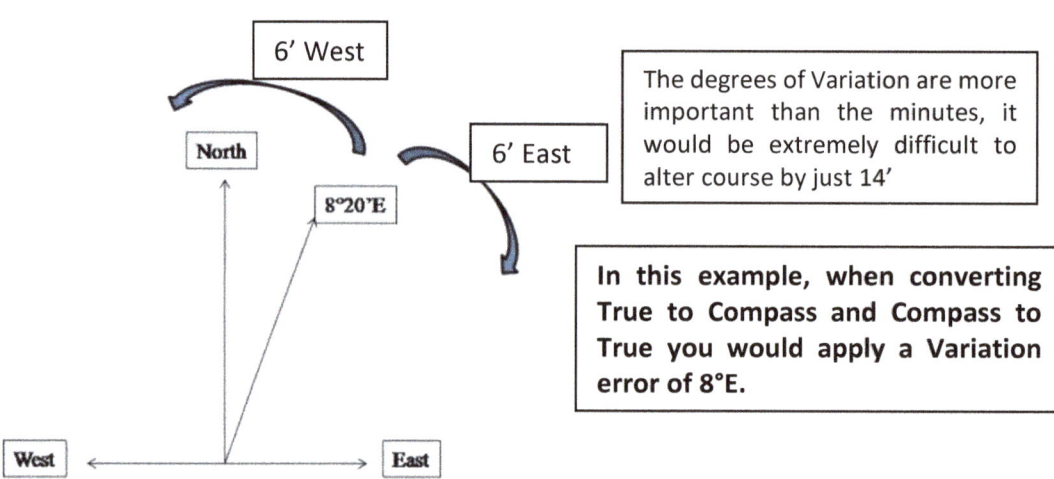

The degrees of Variation are more important than the minutes, it would be extremely difficult to alter course by just 14'

In this example, when converting True to Compass and Compass to True you would apply a Variation error of 8°E.

More Variation Examples
1)

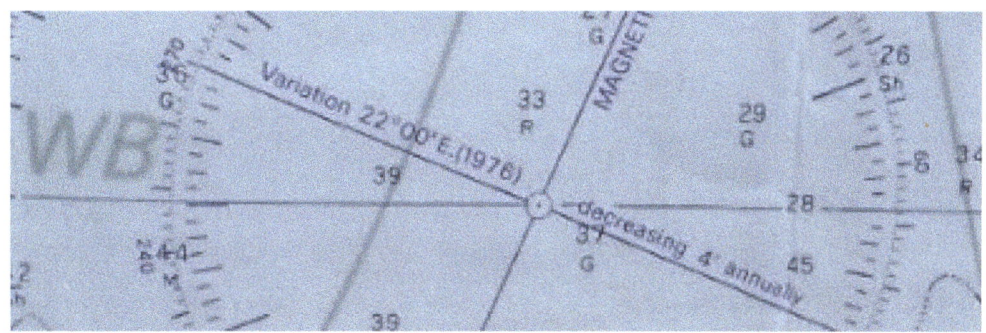

Answer: Variation for 2020 = 19° E

Calculation:
44 years (difference between 1976 and 2020) x 4' = 176'

How many whole degrees make up 176'? = 3° = 180' (this is within 4 minutes (') of 176' and definitely close enough to steer by).

Therefore, we have 3° to subtract (West = subtract: the chart compass rose tells us the variation is decreasing).

22°E - 3°W = 19° E

2)

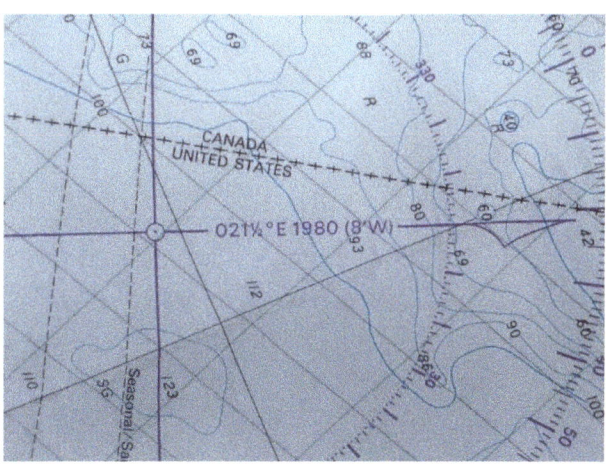

Answer: 16°E
40 years (difference between 1980 and 2020) x 8'W = 320' minutes

320' / 60 (1 degree) = 5° 20'

Take care with the remaining minutes.
You've calculated that there are 5° in 320'

5 x 60 = 300, so you have just 20 minutes left (320 – 300).

Adjusting your Variation to 2020, as follows:

21° 30'E - 5°20'W = 16° 10'E

Round down to 16°E

TIP: Draw it out. A visual aid helps confirm you are on the right track.

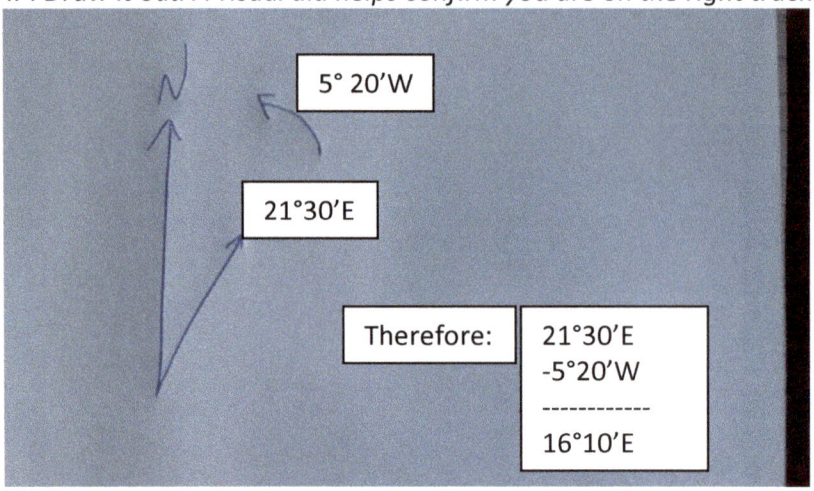

A rather crude sketch, but it helps to see what is actually occurring.

3)

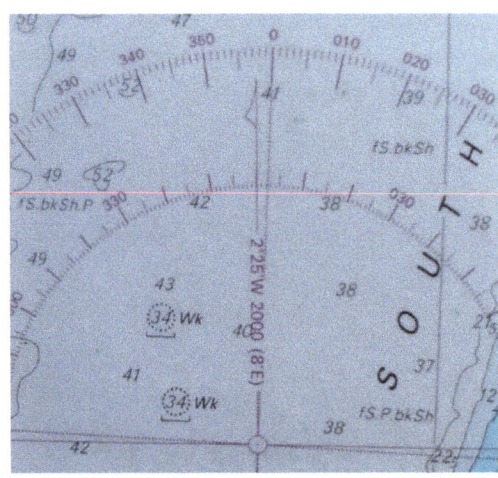

Answer: 1°E
2°25'W 2000 (8')

Calculate answer:
20 years x 8 = 160'

There are two whole degrees in 160 minutes, plus 40'
2 x 60 = 120

We had 160 minutes, we subtract 120 minutes (as that is 2 degrees) and we are left with 40 minutes, that is close to another whole degree. Due to the vessel yawing, rounding up in this situation is fine: 3°E

We are adding on the East figure, therefore, looking back at our chart.
2°25'W plus 3°E = 0°35'E (again disregard the minutes), so our answer is 1°E

If you are finding this part tricky, you can turn the degrees into minutes to use simple mathematics. Starting with a negative (West) is harder.

Simplify where you can: There are 60 minutes in a degree, therefore:
2°25 is the same as 145 minutes
3° is the same as 180 minutes

180 – 145 = 35'E.

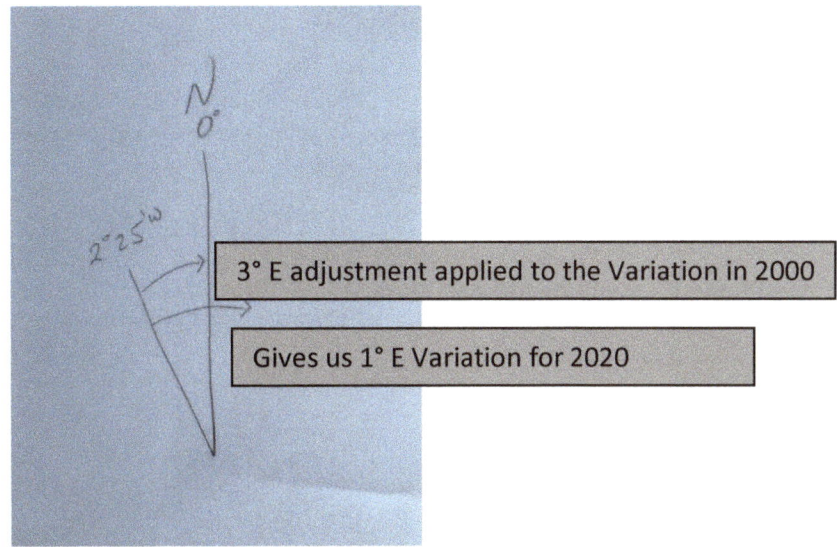

- 3° E adjustment applied to the Variation in 2000
- Gives us 1° E Variation for 2020

Converting True to Compass and Compass to True

If you use a hand-bearing compass, there will be no known Deviation (Deviation is the second error). Deviation is caused by magnetic material onboard altering the compass point by so many degrees and only applies to your ship's compass.

To convert Compass to True or True to Compass there are two useful memory aids to utilise.
First, write down the key points:

CAN	C	**C**ompass (your boat's steering compass)
DEAD	D	**D**eviation (from your boat's Deviation card, created by Compass Adjuster)
MEN	M	**M**agnetic (Ship's Compass with Deviation applied or hand held Compass)
VOTE	V	**V**ariation (found on your chart, always either east or west of true north)
TWICE	T	**T**rue (all chart work must be in True)

(Or, Tele Vision Makes Dull Company, which are the above letters in reverse.)

Example – Compass to True

You have taken a bearing with your ship's compass of 100°C and on that heading there is a Deviation of 2° East (taken from your ship's compass Deviation card). Variation is 5° West (from the compass rose on the chart in use, nearest to the area you are in).
First, write down what you know:

C	100°	
D	2°	East
M		
V	5°	West
T		

There are two ways of calculating the answers:
1) Use the rhyme: Error East Compass Least; Error West Compass Best
Start with 100°C, now apply 2° East, (error East Compass Least) which means C must be less than M) therefore M = 102°.

M = 102°, now apply 5° West (Error West, Compass Best), M (Magnetic Compass) must be more than True (T), therefore = 097° True.

C	100°	
D	2°	East
M	102°	
V	5°	West
T	097°	

Note: Magnetic is a compass reading with the Deviation applied

You can now plot the bearing 097°T on your chart.
2) Write out the process using CADET. The word CADET tells you that from Compass to True you must ADD EAST (AD E).

C → AD E → T

Using this word and expanding the meaning provides us with a picture that is easy to follow. Simply apply the opposite for True to Compass.

©Jackie Parry

www.sistershiptraining.com

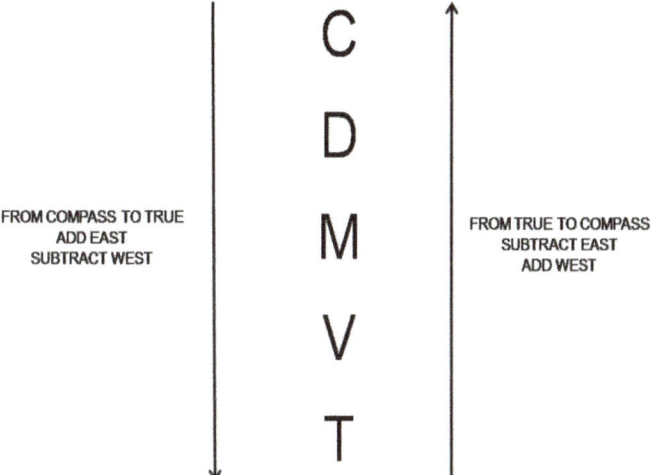

Above we have:
- Written out CDMVT with opposing arrows each side.
- We know by using CADET, when going from Compass to True we ADD EAST (AD E). So draw a line pointing from C to T and write, next to this line 'Add East'. If you add east you must subtract west – write this on the same side.
- On the other side of CDMVT, draw a line with an arrow going in the opposite direction from the first arrow on the other side.
- The instructions for East and West are the exact opposite. Therefore, write subtract East, add West.

Simply follow the directions
As per our example, we have 100° Compass to convert to True. Using the above, it states that from Compass to True (C → T) you have to add East and subtract West.

Therefore 100°C + 2° East = 102°M, then 102°M – 5° West = 097° True

You can now plot the CONVERTED bearing line of 100° Compass as 097° True on your chart.

DEVIATION

As a reminder, Deviation is the deflection of the compass needle from its proper orientation. It is usually caused by magnetic materials on the boat (or indeed the boat itself). Deviation can be East or West, or zero, depending on the magnetic conditions on the vessel. <u>The value of Deviation changes with the boat's heading.</u>

Deviation is usually calculated by a professional Compass Adjuster; however you can check Deviation errors yourself by lining up your vessel on a set of leads and noting your compass heading.

Calculating Deviation
Choose a set of leads and place yourself right on the leads with your bow facing them. The chart, will provide the True bearing of those leads. The boat should be stationary for this exercise. You can determine the Deviation on different headings (of the vessel) by rotating the boat in a fixed point and taking true bearings from different landmarks (as you rotate) with your Bi-rola or Portland Protractor. Note your compass reading for each true heading and then by using the Variation you can calculate the deviation for different headings.

In our example, we will assume the bow is facing the leads:

Note your ship's compass heading.

Apply Variation for your area (noted on the compass rose on your chart).

The difference between the Magnetic bearing (True with Variation applied) and your Compass reading (C) is your Deviation for that heading.

The Deviation is usually slightly different for each course the vessel is on, and the Deviation error is usually noted in multiples of 10° on a Deviation card.

Example Deviation Card

Ship's Head By Compass	Deviation	Ship's Head By Compass	Deviation
000°	3½°E	180°	2½°W
010°	4°E	190°	4°W
020°	4½°E	200°	5°W
030°	5°E	210°	5½°W
040°	5°E	220°	6½°W
050°	5°E	230°	6½°W
060°	5½°E	240°	7°W
070°	5½°E	250°	6½°W
080°	5°E	260°	6½°W
090°	5°E	270°	5½°W
100°	4½°E	280°	4½°W
110°	4°E	290°	3½°W
120°	3½°E	300°	2½°W
130°	3°E	310°	1½°W
140°	2°E	320°	½°W
150°	1°E	330°	½°E
160°	½°W	340°	1½°E
170°	1½°W	350°	2½°E
180°	2½°W	000°	3½°E

Don't forget:
- Your charts will show the TRUE bearing.
- Use the Variation to work out the Magnetic bearing (M).
- Find your COMPASS heading.

Note the difference between Magnetic and Compass, that will be your Deviation – FOR THAT HEADING ONLY.

Example: Calculating Deviation
Our example utilises the transit bearing of the two northern island tips on AUS252 (location 20° 5' S)

- Choose a transit bearing (set of leads is best)
- Bow facing leads: lay off True bearing (e.g. 100° True)
- Boat is stationary
- Bow facing transit bearing
- Note your compass course. (e.g. 095° C)

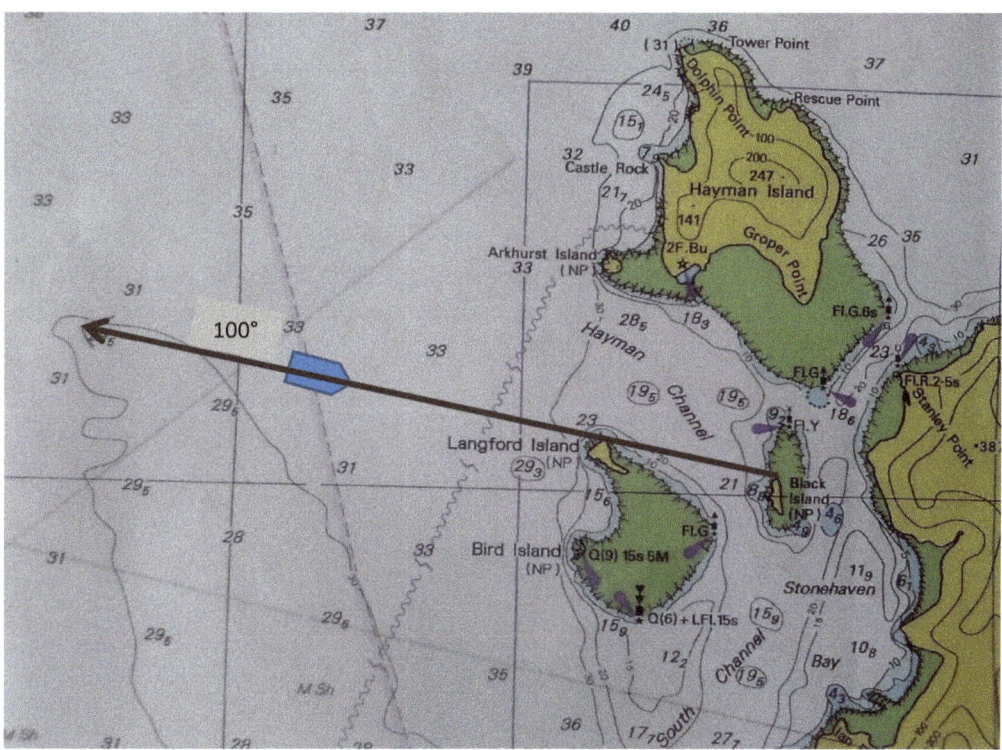

Write out what you know:

C	095°	
D	°	?
M	°	
V	8°	East
T	100°	

C	095°
D	°3 West
M	092°
V	8° East
T	100°

©Jackie Parry

1. Fill out what you know
2. Calculate M (using the memory aids)
3. The difference between Magnetic and Compass = Deviation

How do we know if the Deviation is East or West?   **-Use your memory aids**

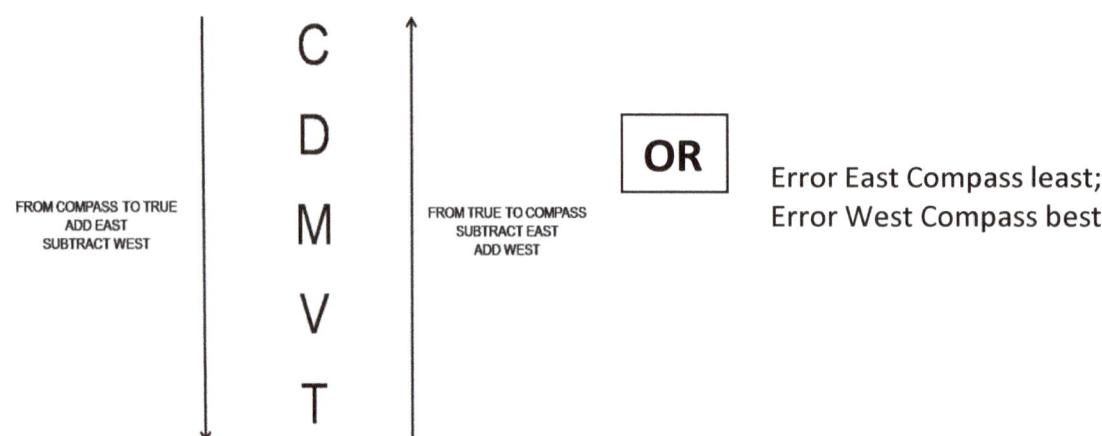

Error East Compass least;
Error West Compass best

If you use your GPS to check your Deviation, ensure your GPS is set to TRUE. This only works if you do not have a tidal stream or leeway to account for. (GPS gives course over the ground, not through the water.)

C	103°	
D	°	
M	098°	
V	2°	East
T	100°	

Above, we have:

The True bearing, i.e. the line you are sitting on (on your boat).

Your Compass reading (103°) (while you are pointing at the leads).

The Variation (from your chart) can be added in and now you have calculated Magnetic (error East, Compass least which is 2° in this example).

Now, you just need to calculate the Deviation (remember it is for that course only).

The difference between 103° and 098° is 5°. So, the Deviation is 5°, but you must make sure you note whether it is East or West Deviation. As the Compass number is the higher than True, the Deviation must be West (error West, Compass best).

C	103°	
D	5°	West
M	098°	
V	2°	East
T	100°	

On a Compass bearing of 103° C you have a Deviation of 5°W to apply. The Variation of 2°E helps you to determine your True bearing of 100°T or vice-versa if going from True to Compass. The Compass Adjuster (or via DIY) determines the corrections for Deviation at 10° intervals from 000 to 360° on the compass, and he or she then records this information on the vessel's Deviation card.

TOTAL ERROR

If you will be taking several bearings while steering the same course it makes sense to arrive at a single correction to apply to all those bearings. This is called the Total Error.

The Variation remains the same in the same area and that deviation only changes when we change course. With this is in mind we can find the total compass error for the course being steered and apply that to all bearings taken whilst on that course.

Example – total error
While steering 076°C the deviation (from the deviation card for 076°) = 2°W and the variation from the chart is 13°E.

The total compass error (combined variation and deviation) is therefore 11°E.

If the suffix is the same for both errors (e.g. Variation is East and Deviation is East) then add them together using the same suffix on the result

e.g. Variation = 10°E and Deviation 2°E, then the total error will be 12°E

If the suffix is different (e.g. Variation is East and Deviation is West) then subtract the smaller number from the larger number and use the suffix from the larger number on the result.

e.g. Variation = 10°E and Deviation = 2°W, then the total error = 8°E

BEARINGS
Hand-Bearing Compass
This piece of equipment is invaluable when in a busy waterway.

You can take bearings of other vessels (relative to you) and jot them down. A few minutes later you do the same and compare with the first bearing. This will show you whether you are on a converging course.

Remember, if the distance is diminishing between you and the target and the bearing is steady (or near to steady) you are both heading for the same bit of water and will collide.

Note: When taking a relative bearing of a target, Variation and Deviation do not matter as you are only worrying about whether the bearing changes over time and not plotting it on your chart.

When you are converting bearings to True (e.g. for plotting using a three-bearing fix) remember that you do not apply Deviation to a Hand-bearing Compass – there is likely to be some Deviation but it will be dependent on where you are standing on your vessel, but you will apply Variation).

Exercise 8–Compass to True and True to Compass page 10 in Questions and Answers Booklet
Answers 8–Compass to True and True to Compass page 42 in Questions and Answers Booklet

THREE BEARING FIX

Three bearing fix: This is a great way to double check your position. You should use three bearings, although you can use two. (Two bearings will not show an error though, if one has been made).

Choose distinct objects to ensure that you do not incorrectly identify the landmark. Lighthouses and towers are good to use in this exercise.

When taking bearings of edges of land, vertical embankments and steep cliffs are preferable over gently sloping shores. The rise and fall of the tide can change the shape of the coastline.

Do not take a fix from objects that can drift. Buoys should not be used.

TIP: Remember to convert all your bearings to True before laying them off on your chart.

On your chart select three conspicuous landmarks to use. Take bearings (of the landmarks) with your handheld compass in the following order. This reduces errors when underway.

First bearing: closest to your stern.
Second bearing: closest to your bow.
Third bearing: abeam (090° from your bow).

You must be 100% sure that you visually identify the correct landmarks and, ideally, the landmarks should be around sixty degrees apart.

TIP: You will need to apply Compass error (Variation), but no Deviation if using a handheld compass (Deviation is only applied if you are using the ship's compass with known Deviation).

Example – Three Bearing Fix:
You've identified three conspicuous landmarks and taking a bearing with a handheld compass.
TIP: Always note the time the bearing is taken.

- Edge of building 082°C 0959hrs
- Church 051°C 1000hrs
- Needles Point 024°C 1000hrs

We cannot lay these bearing lines on our chart until they are converted to True. Look at the Variation:
Variation for this chart is 3°25'W 2001 (8'E)

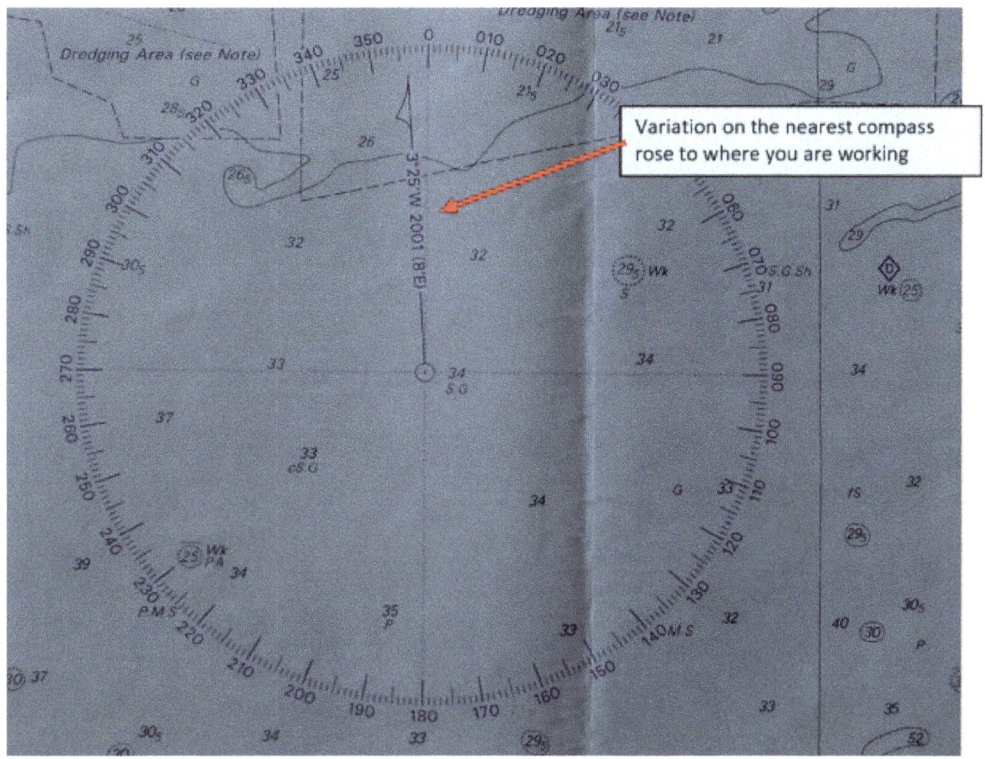

From 2001 to 2020 there are 19 years. For each year the Variation has changed by 8'E, therefore:

8 x 19 = 152'

We know that a degree is 60 minutes and two degrees is 120 minutes, with 32' left.

We therefore have a change in Variation of 2° 32'E (between 2001 and 2020).

The Variation in 2001 was 3°25'W (in the rose) and you can see in the picture above that it is West (left of 360°) and therefore considered a minus.

If the amount of change in the Variation (2001 to 2020) is East, then we add the calculated 2°32'E.

-3° 25'W + 2°32' E = 0° 53'W

In Variation calculations think of West as a minus, illustrated in the following diagram. We can round up to 1°W.

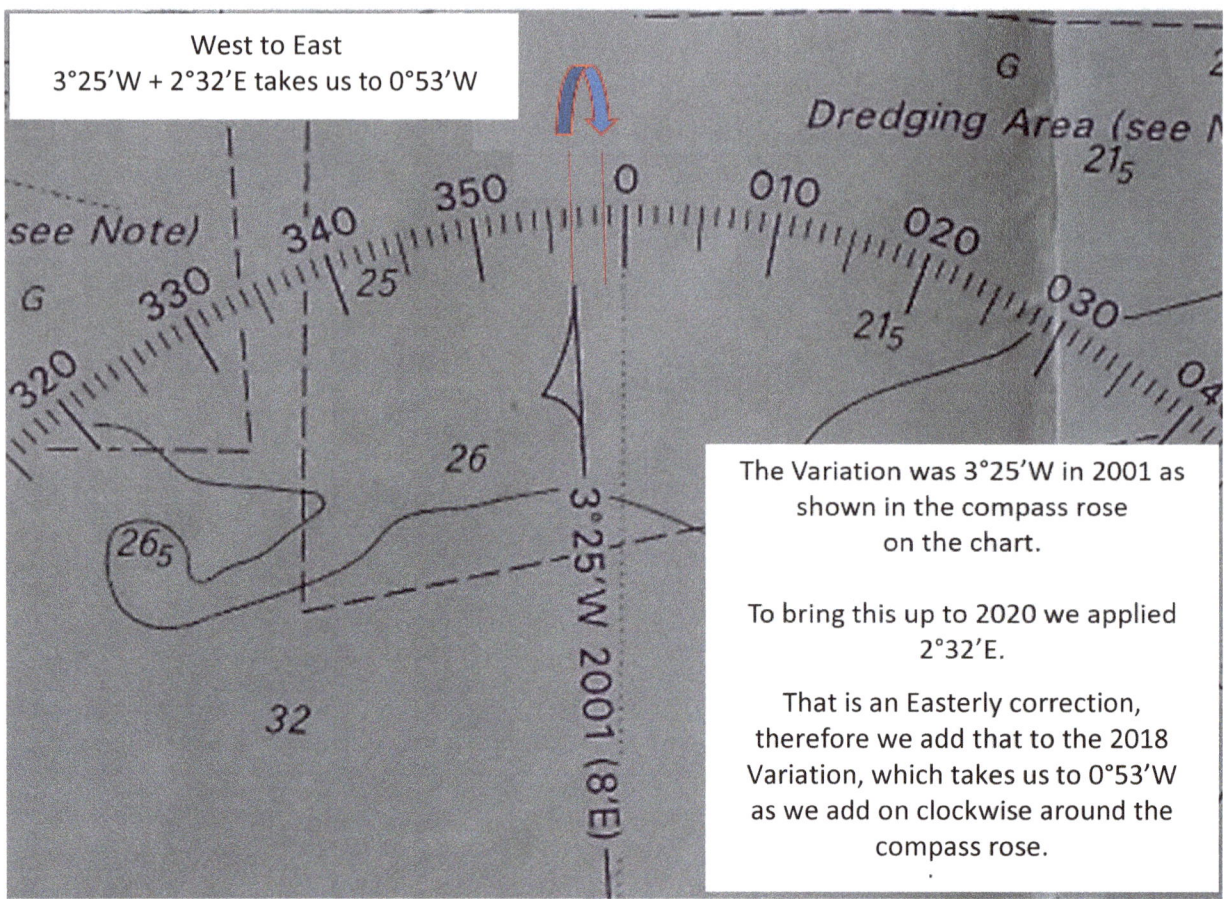

It is impossible to steer by minutes, so we'll use 1°W as our Variation.
Now we can convert our Compass bearings to True for our chart work.

Deviation: Is the compass error induced by magnetic influences onboard.
Remember, there is NO deviation applied to a handheld compass. The Deviation card on board is for the ship's Compass only. Moving a handheld compass around the vessel will mean the compass has different readings for Deviation. It's good practice to try to be as far as possible from magnetic items on board (without falling overboard!).

Write out the conversion for three magnetic bearings 82°, 51°, 24°, taken by the handheld compass:

C (this is the ship's compass which we didn't use)
D (there is no known deviation as we used a handheld compass)
M	82°	51°	24° (handheld compass bearings)
V	1°W	1°W	1°W (error West compass or magnetic Best)
T	81°	50°	23°

These True bearings can be drawn on the chart.

©Jackie Parry   www.sistershiptraining.com

Remember: If you use your ship's compass to take bearings and you have a deviation card, use the deviation of the ship's heading (when taking the bearing) not the bearing itself.

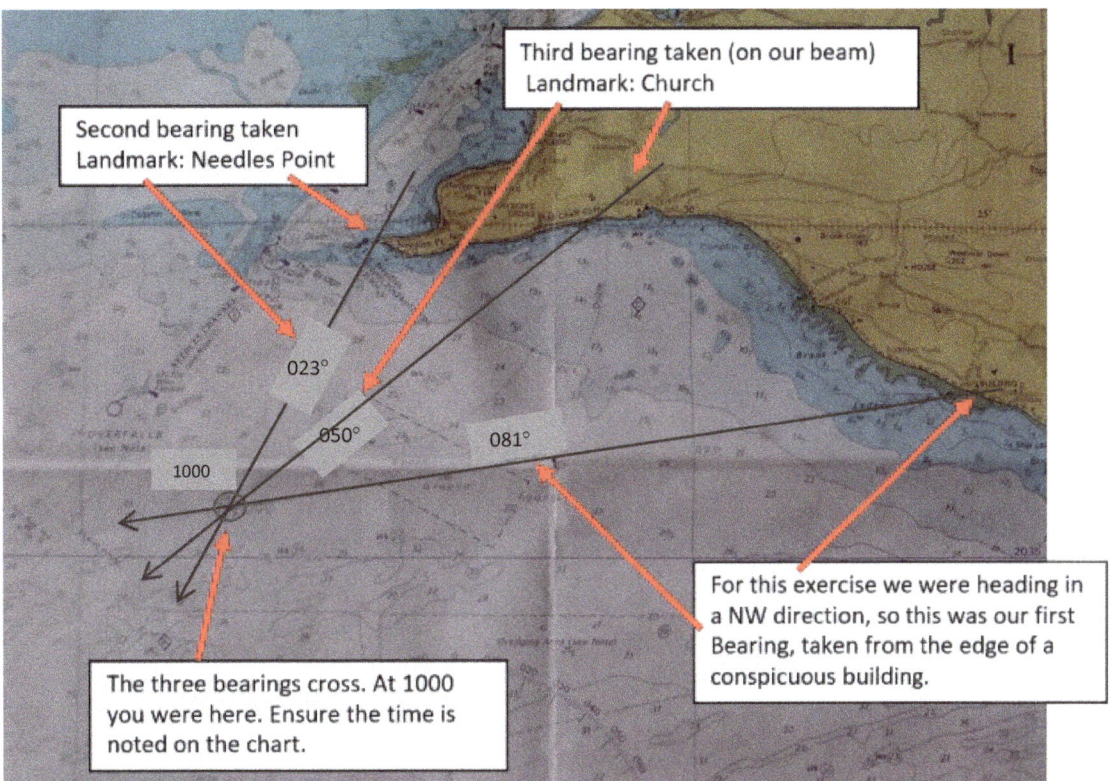

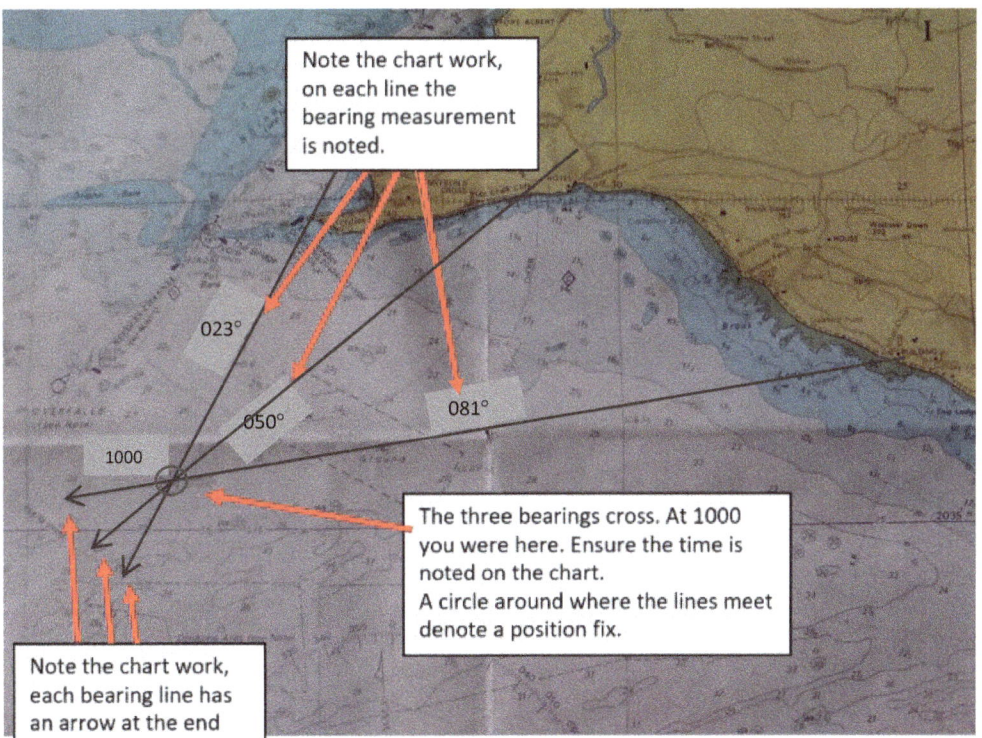

Once you have converted the Compass bearing to a True bearing, plot the bearings on your chart. Where the three bearing lines cross, this is your fix position. The time of the bearings taken is noted on the chart next to your fix position. This is very important, especially when using DR.

50° 36.95'N 1° 37.55'W

©Jackie Parry   www.sistershiptraining.com

Once you have your position marked, measure the latitude and longitude scale, check it and note that time and position in your log book. In the comments section, explain the fix was obtained via bearings with a handheld compass.

Remember: Do not use navigation buoys for bearings, as they may have moved from the charted position.

Two bearings can be used, but they will not show any errors that may have occurred, as three bearings will.

With three bearings, you may end up with a cocked hat where the three bearing lines meet (usually looks like a witch's hat, see picture below). If it is not too big, mark your position in the cocked hat at the closest point to danger and have another go (in the example below, that position would be nearest to land). Cocked hats occur with errors (plotting, wrong identification of object, compass error incorrectly applied or unknown compass error), or this could occur with the imprecise reading of the compass or an unsteady hand when at sea.

Cocked Hat

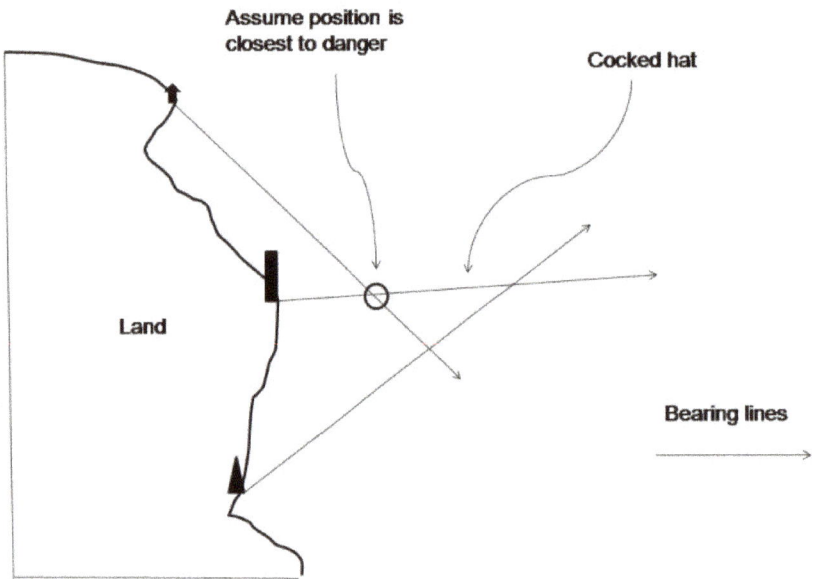

Let's run through it ourselves

This will be the end result:

Mount Arthur (250) on Shaw Island: 013°T
Thomas Island Peak (179): 063°T
CopperSmith Rock Light: 105°T

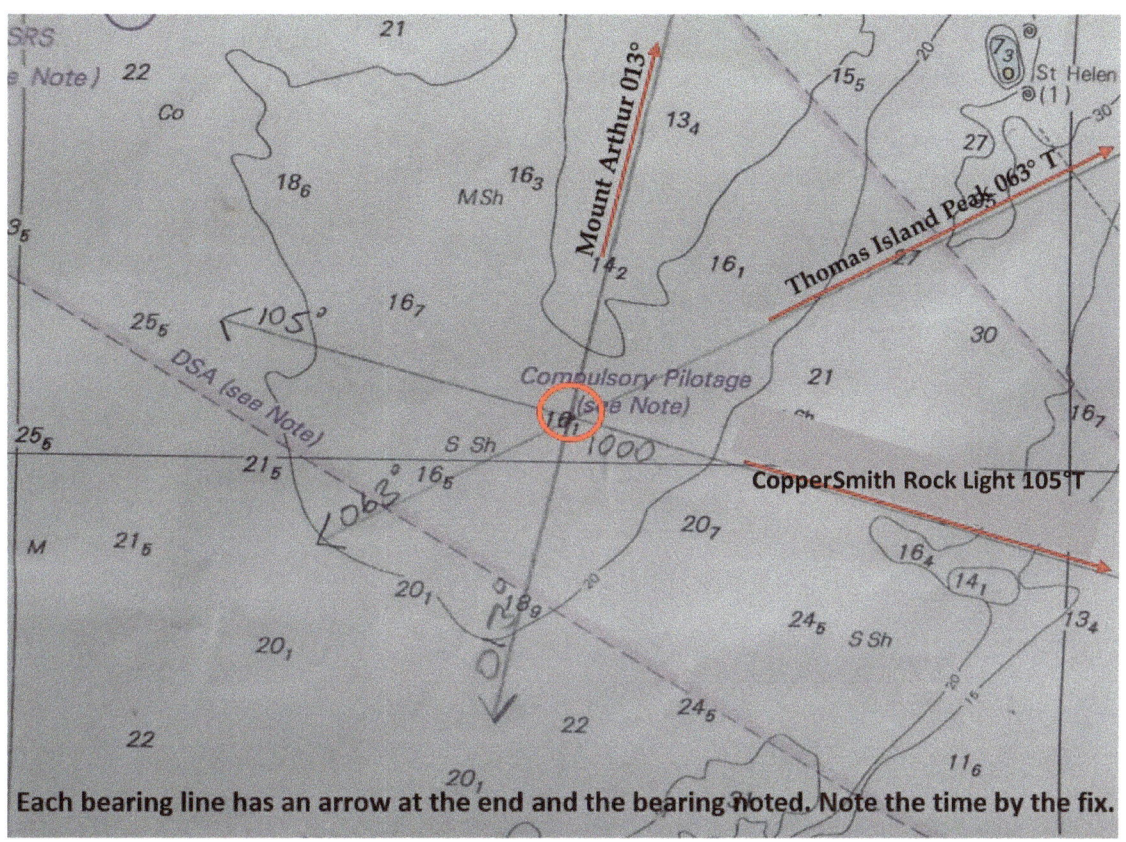

Each bearing line has an arrow at the end and the bearing noted. Note the time by the fix.

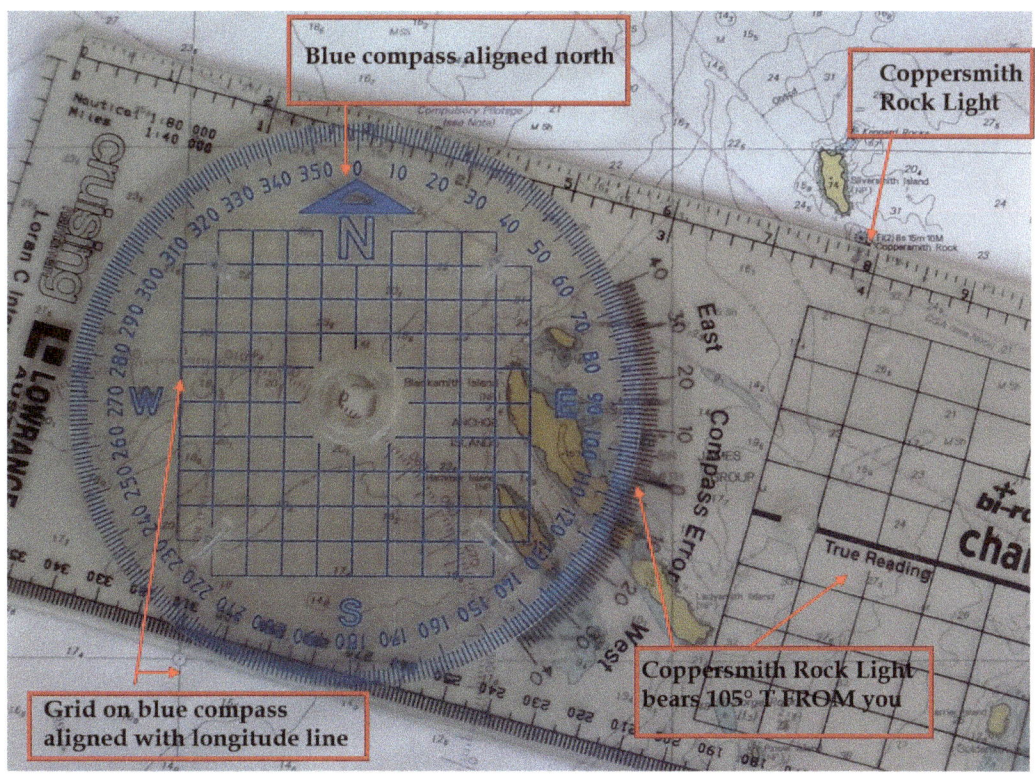

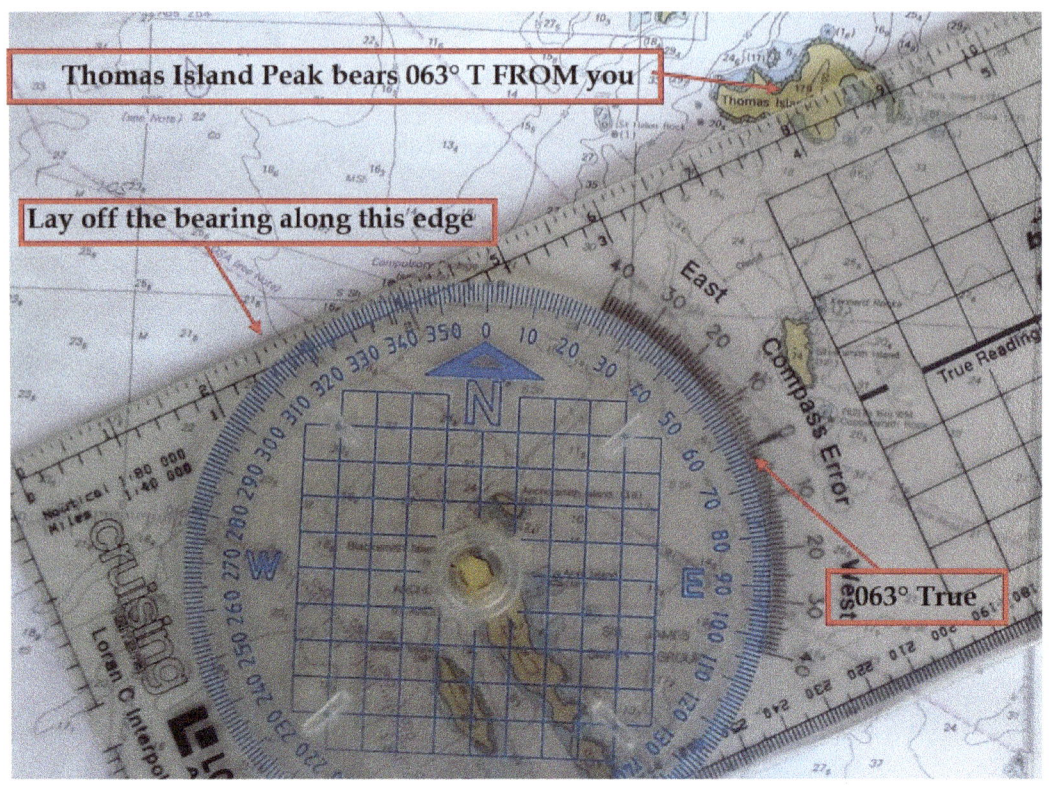

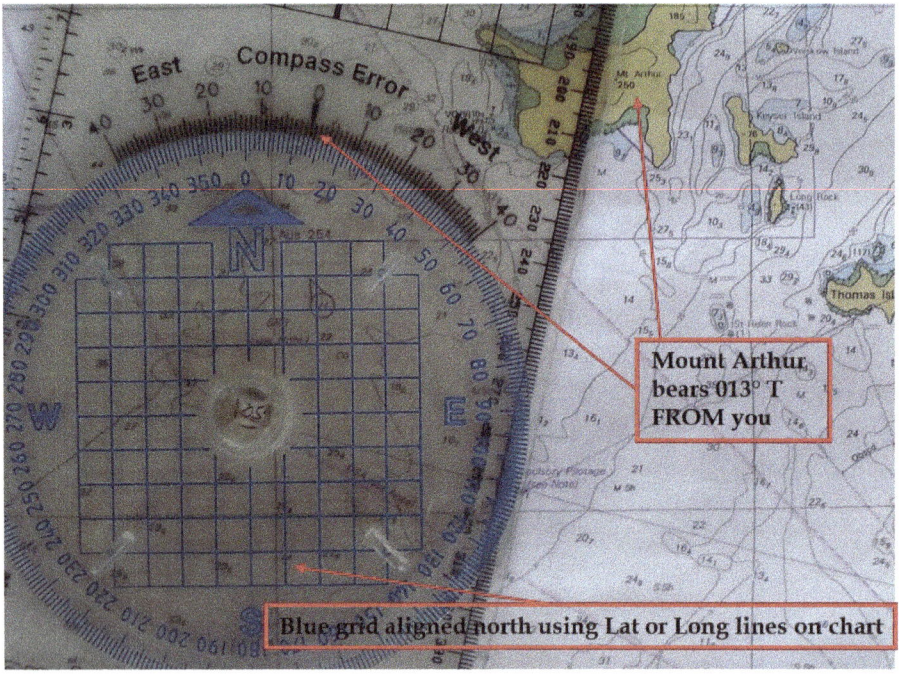

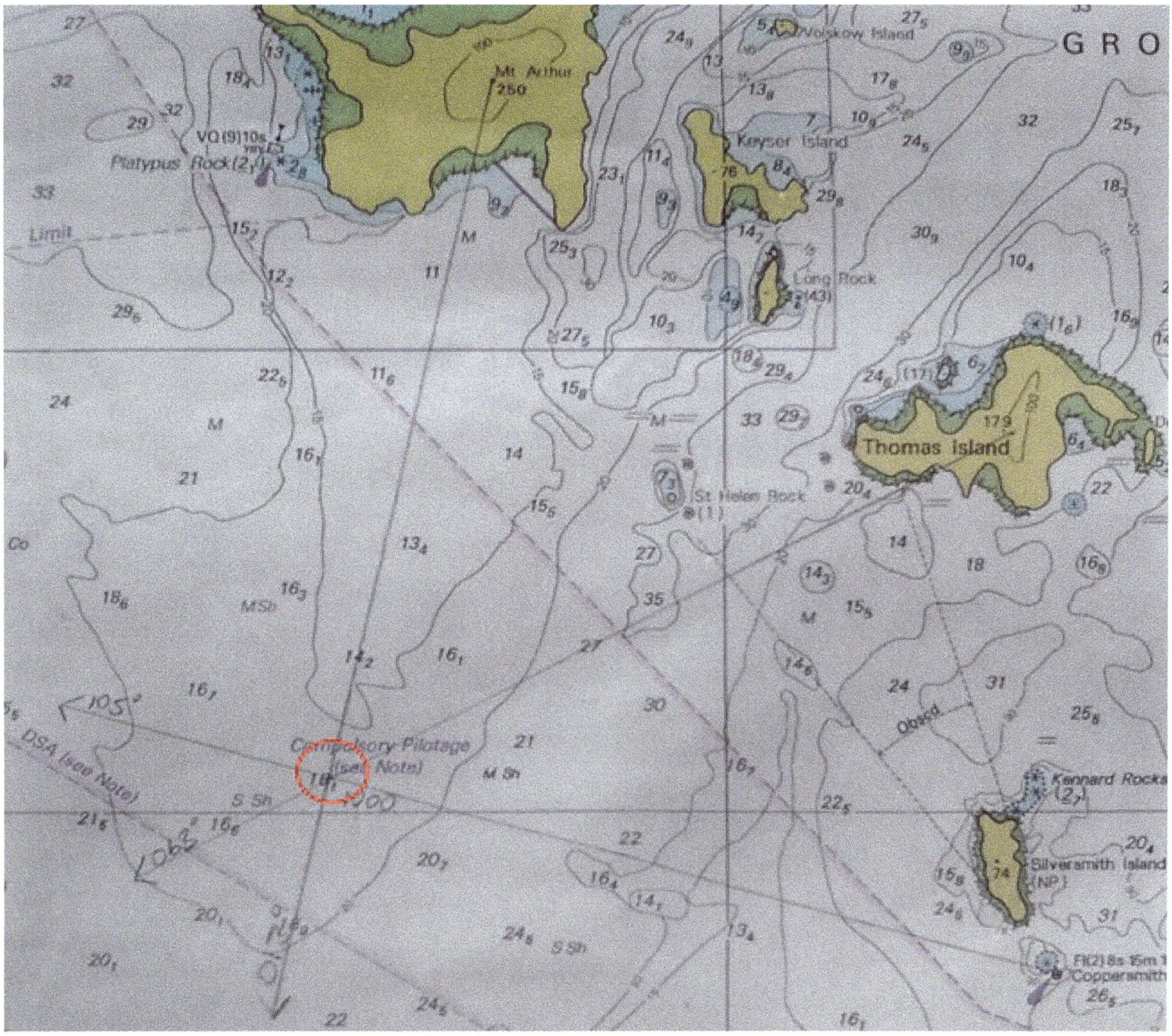

[Nautical chart image]

This is your completed 3-bearing fix plot: 20° 34.8'S 149° 02.6'E

Exercise 9: Three Bearing Fix page 14 in Questions and Answers Booklet
Answers 9: Three Bearing Fix page 44 in Questions and Answers Booklet

POSITION BY BEARING AND DISTANCE

Using the compass rose (direction) and the latitude scale (distance) we can plot our position.

You can also use radar bearings. These are not as accurate as radar ranges as the boat is often yawing, but it is good practice to use several methods to confirm your position (other than just using the GPS).

Example: At 1000 hrs you take two radar ranges between known islands. And you've also shot a bearing from the tip of Blacksmith Island of 098°T (already converted to True), so you can double check where you are.

For the sake of this course we know we are between these islands
5 nm west from tip of Blacksmith Island
4.8 nm east from the east side of East Repulse Island

Practice measuring distance.

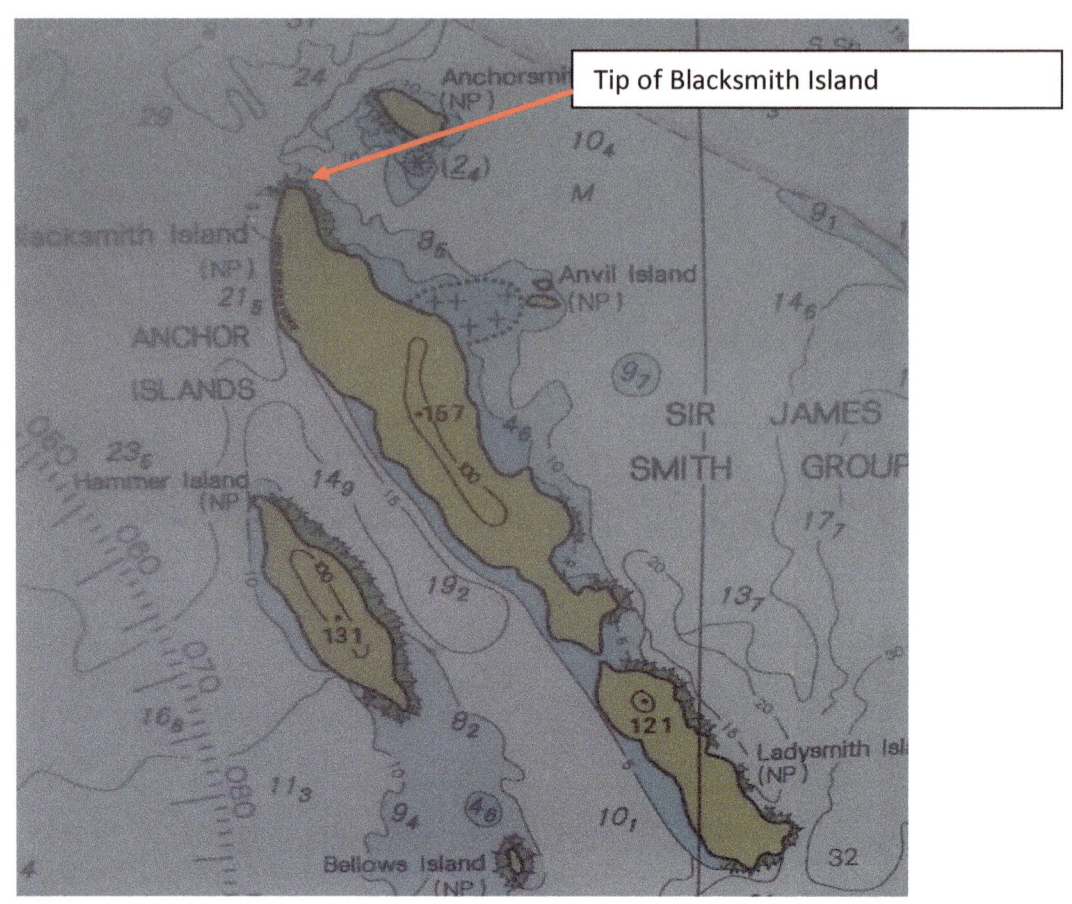

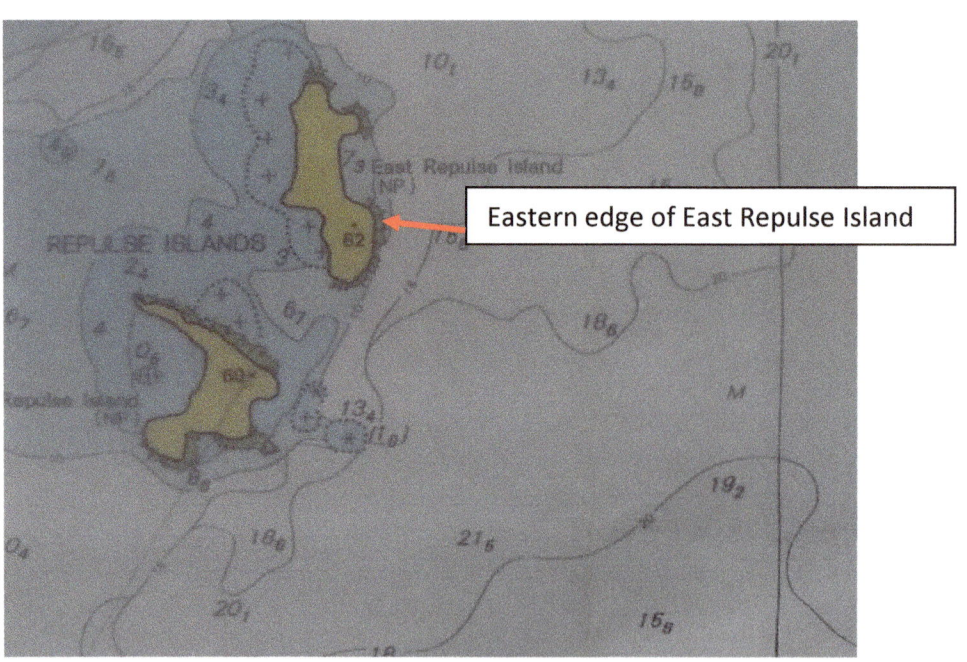

Practice drawing in a bearing.

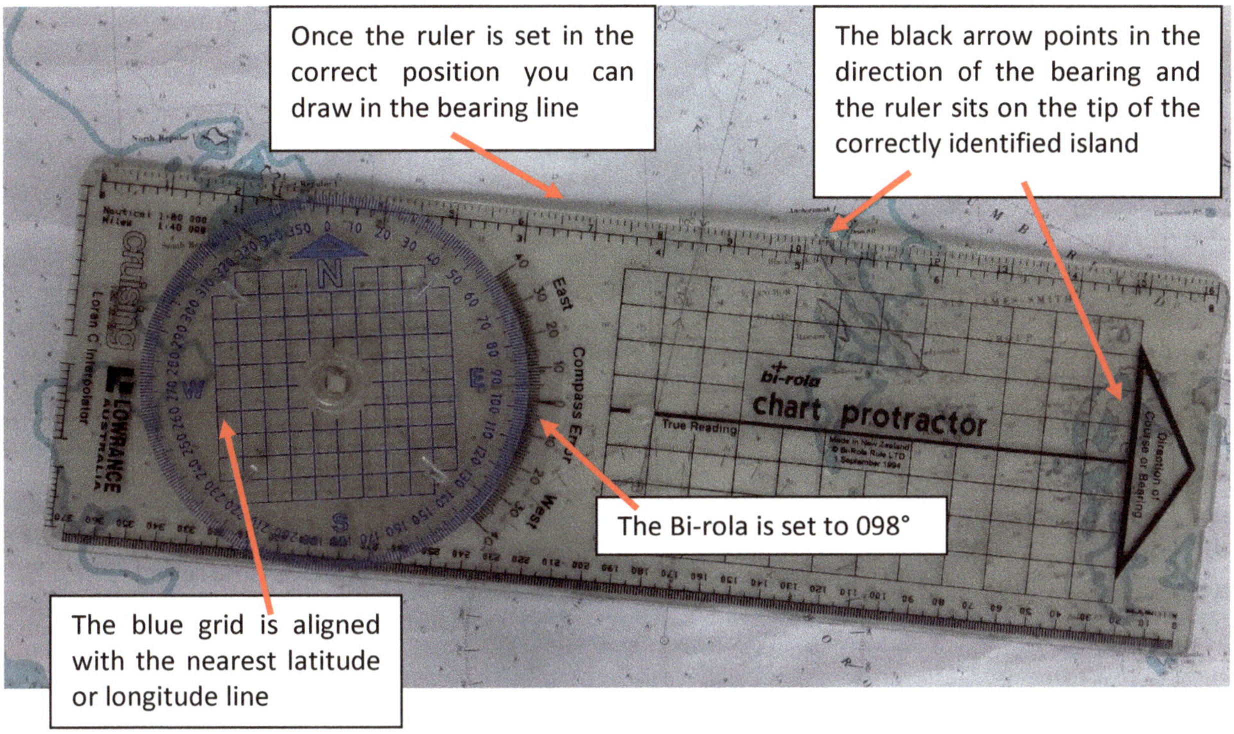

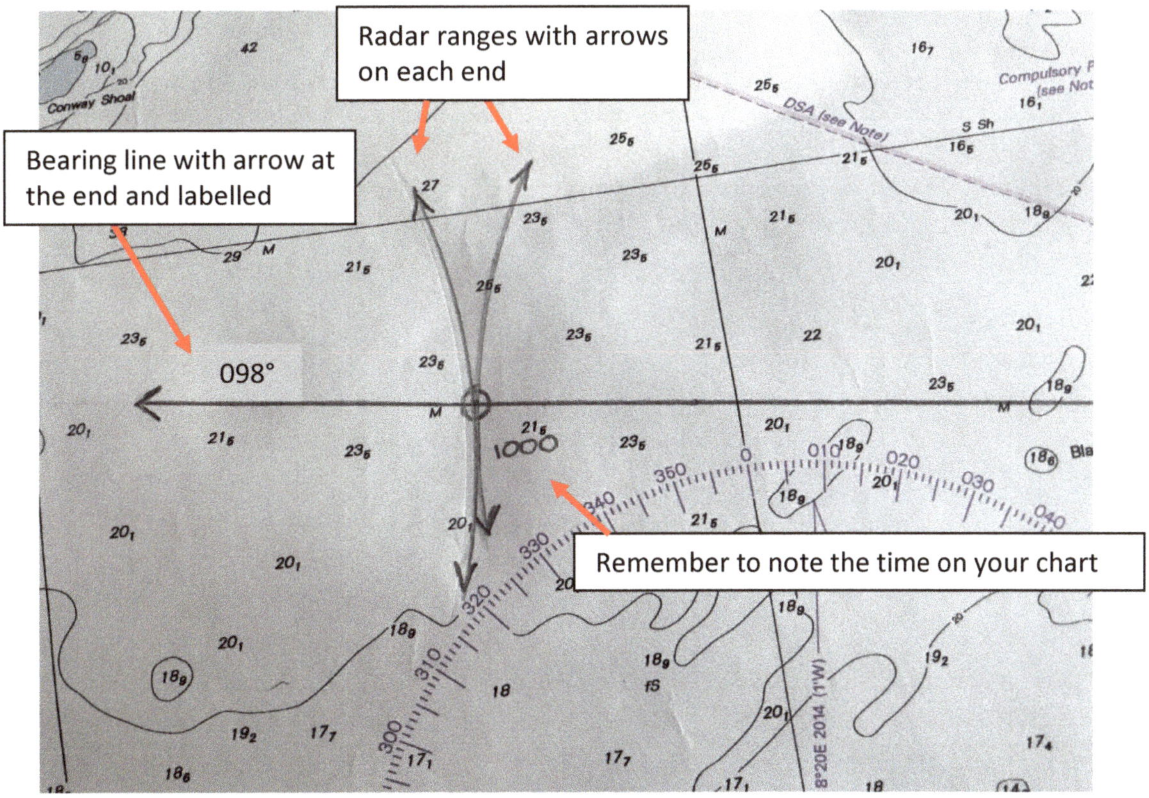

20° 36.4'S 148° 58.1'E

Exercise 10– Radar Range Fix page 14 in Questions and Answers Booklet
Answers 10– Radar Range Fix page 44 in Questions and Answers Booklet

Additional Notes on Radar Use

The horizontal beam from radar produces a certain width (called the horizontal beam-width) and this will change the bearing by a few degrees. The wider the scanner, the narrower the beam-width and therefore the more accurate it is.

In Heads Up mode, simply use the EBL (Electronic Bearing Line) on your radar to obtain the Relative bearings on screen. Remember, only TRUE bearings can be drawn on your chart.

To convert the Relative bearing to a True bearing add your TRUE course to the Relative bearing. This is then the True bearing of the object or target and can be laid off on your chart.

True bearing (of object or target) = own ship heading (True), plus Relative bearing (of object or target).

Relative Bearings

Relative Bearings are Relative to the ship's head. They are different from Red and Green bearings. Relative bearings range clockwise from 000° to 360°; Red and Green bearings range from 000° to 180° on either port (Red) or starboard (Green) side. Relative bearings are easier to convert to True.

Relative bearings: Looking straight over the bow = 000°, over the stern = 180°, port beam is 270°, starboard is 090°.

Red/Green Bearings: If a vessel is abeam on your starboard side, she is also '090° Relative' or '090° Green'. If a vessel is abeam your port side, she is '270° Relative' or '090° Red'.

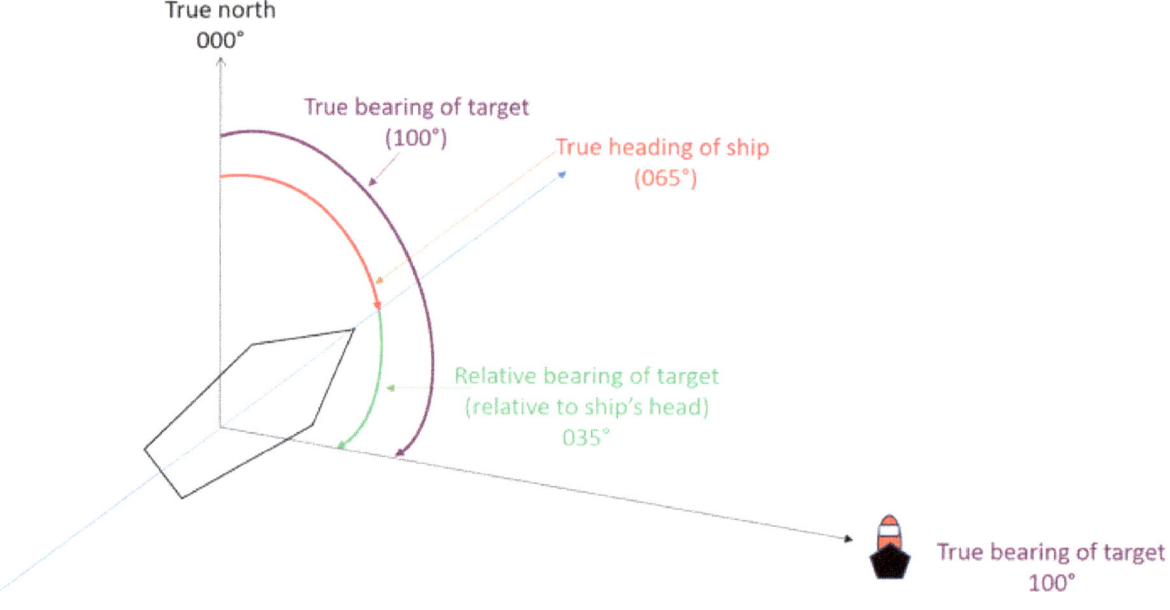

Position fixing bearings

Read these notes (below) while looking at the diagram above.

The red line and text shows the vessel's course is 065° True.
Onboard, we would say, "heading 065° True".

©Jackie Parry

The purple line and text shows the True bearing of the target (100° True).
Onboard, we would say, "target bearing 100° True".
The green line and text show the relative green bearing (035°).
Onboard, we would say, "target bearing green 035°."

TIP: Remember to convert all your bearings to True before laying them off on your chart.

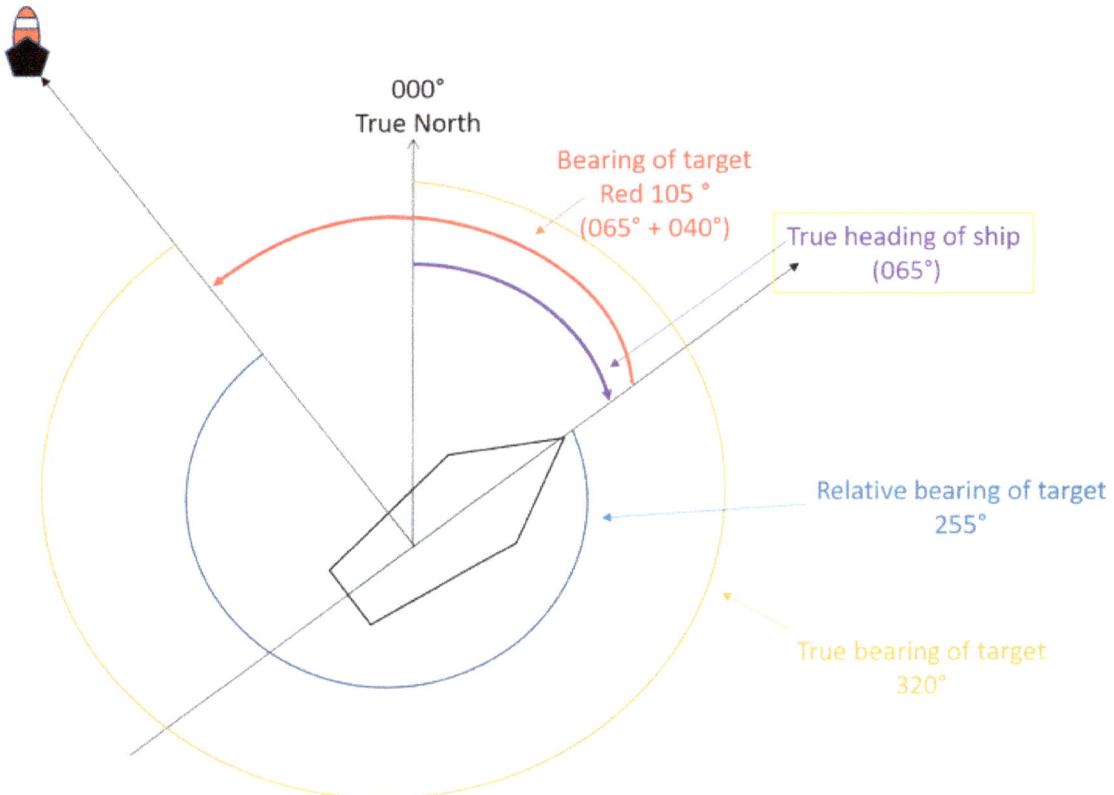

Bearings Illustrated
Read these notes (below) while looking at the diagram above.

The purple line and text shows the vessel's course is 065° True.
Onboard, we would say, "heading 065° True."
The red line and text shows the relative red bearing of the target (Red 105°).
Onboard, we would say, "target bearing red 105°."

Upon hearing "red", instantly the person hearing this message will look to port. I'd start looking at approximately 090° and work my way around until I could see the target.

In reality, the target will be viewed abeam of the vessel's port side. Most navigators/crew will be able to have a good guess at the angle without physically doing the calculations in the first instance.

We know that if a target is slightly abaft the beam it is going to be just over 90°.

The blue line and text shows the relative bearing of the target read from the radar in Course Up (CU) Mode as 255° (to the ship's head).

On board, we would say, "target 255° relative." (To be recorded, with the time, for chart work.)

©Jackie Parry

The orange line and text shows the True bearing of the target.

On board, we would say, "target bearing 320° True." (Which is our True course (065°) plus the Radar Relative Bearing (255°) = 320°T. In reality we would use Red/Green bearings in conversation between crew or other ships. And Relative Bearings for noting in the log, and true bearings on the chart.

Convert Red and Green bearings to True (for chart work): If you have taken a Green bearing, add this to your ship's True heading. If you have taken a Red bearing, subtract this from your ship's True heading.

True bearing = Ship's heading (T) + Green bearing
True bearing = Ship's heading (T) – Red bearing

Note: If you end up with a negative number, just add 360, as we work within 360°.

E.g.
Our ship is on a course of 054° True and the first mate has spotted a vessel "target red 085°".
Covert to True to lay it off on your chart.

True bearing	=	Ship's Heading (T) – Red bearing
	=	054° (T) – 085° (Red bearing) = -031°
	=	-31 + 360
True bearing	=	329°(T)

(If you can see that you will end up with a negative number, you can add on the 360 first if you wish.)
e.g. 054° – 085° + 360° = 329°

Additional Notes for Radar Settings
Notes on radar: Relative motion Course-Up (stabilised) or North-Up (stabilised)

With the addition of heading information from the vessel's electronic compass and/or GPS, the stabilised capable radar can provide True bearings. These True bearings can indicate the vessel's True course and the target's True bearing, and the effect of yawing is minimised on the screen.

Course-Up: display provides the more realistic view as the top of the screen is the direction of the ship's heading and so targets viewed on the righthand side of the screen are seen on the starboard side of the wheelhouse.

North-Up: display relates directly to the view of a chart that is read north up. It will have a different orientation to the view looking out of the wheelhouse.

Example for Relative Bearing Calculations

A vessel is steering 073°C. Deviation is 4°W. Variation is 9°E. The relative bearing of Edward Island Light is 274°. What is the true bearing of Edward Island Light?

True Bearing	
Relative Bearing	274°Rel
True Course	
Variation	9°E
Magnetic	
Deviation	4°W
Compass	073°C

> Write out what you know first.

True Bearing	
Relative Bearing	274°Rel
True Course	078°T
Variation	9°E
Magnetic	069°M
Deviation	4°W
Compass	073°C

> Then fill in the blanks, using the memory aid:
> Error West Compass Best
> Error East Compass Least
>
> or
>
> CADET

True Bearing	352°T
Relative Bearing	274°Rel
True Course	078°T
Variation	9°E
Magnetic	069°M
Deviation	4°W
Compass	073°C

> Now the True bearing can be found by adding the vessel's True Bearing to the Light's Relative Bearing:
>
> 78 + 274 = 352°T

Exercise 11 – Bearings page 14 in Questions and Answers Booklet
Answers 11 – Bearings page 44 in Questions and Answers Booklet

SECTION SUMMARY

You have now arrived at the situation where you can convert compass courses and bearings to layoff on the chart and vice versa. You have the knowledge to position yourself, using various methods, on the chart and layoff courses and measure your distance. You have also learnt how to check your compass error and work out the deviation for the ship's head you are steering.

SECTION 3

DEDUCED RECKONING (DR) AND ESTIMATED POSITION (EP)

Position - DR

In navigation, Ded Reckoning (DR) is the process of calculating your position by using a previously determined fix. You advance your first fix based upon known or estimated speeds over lapsed time, and course.

You must maintain the same speed, time, and course for the duration (note length of time) or calculate an average. Of course, set and drift (effects of current) need to be accounted for, at times, to provide an Estimated Position.

To rely on a DR position, you must ensure your first fix is correct. As the new calculation is based on this position, if it is wrong the errors will accumulate.

Example – Deduced Reckoning

You have obtained a good fix and for an hour thereafter you have been sailing at 5 knots. During this time, you have travelled five miles through the water.

When travelling at 5 knots over an hour, your distance is 5 nm

If your course has remained the same during this hour, simply extend your course line and mark off five nautical miles (measure miles off the latitude scale nearest to your location). This is assuming no set and drift.

The following example is a vessel travelling at 6 knots for one and a half hours (you will need to remember the speed, distance, time, formula for more complex calculations).

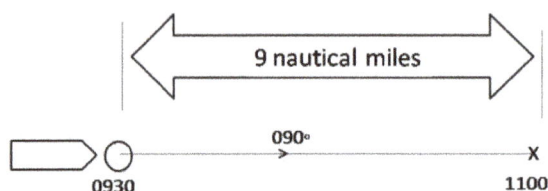

Course 090°, speed 6 knots.

After 1.5 hours distance = 9 nautical miles

The circle is the convention for a position fix by ranges and/or bearings. The cross is the convention for a DR position fix.

In one hour at 6 knots you would travelled 6 miles, in another half an hour you would travel another 3 miles, therefore over an hour-and-a-half you would have travelled a total of 9 nautical miles.

The DR position is marked with an X and the time noted. Remember, this example does not allow for set and drift. Estimated Position (EP) is DR with estimated set and drift applied.

POSITION – ESTIMATED POSITION (EP)

This is a two-stage process:

Plot your DR position on your chart.

From your DR position, lay off the estimated set and drift of the current (direction in degrees and distance in nautical miles). Remember to construct the plot over an hour if possible, to maintain simplicity (e.g. travelling at 4 knots over an hour means you travel for 4 nautical miles).

TIP: If your chart is large scale you may need to work your calculations over thirty minutes, just remember to half everything. When travelling at 4 knots, in half-an-hour you will have travelled 2 nautical miles. It is the same for the drift, if the drift rate is 2 knots, for half-an-hour the drift rate will be one knot (because the drift rate is given (on charts) over the hour.

In navigation, **'set' is the bearing of the current (in degrees) and 'drift' is the speed (in knots).**
Example

If the current is running to the north at 2 knots and you have worked your DR course over one-and-a-half hours, then plot the EP from your DR position. This will be 2 (knots of current) x 1.5 (hrs), giving you a distance of three miles. From your DR position, draw a line heading north (direction of current) and the distance of three nautical miles will be your EP. See diagram below.

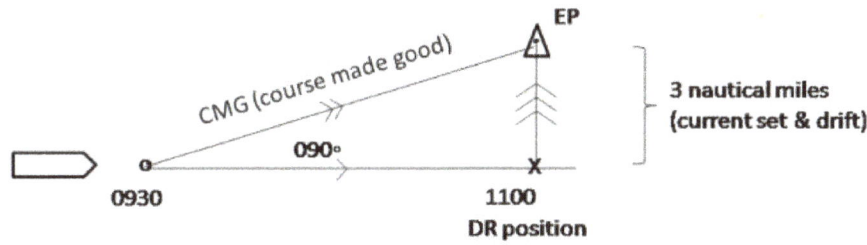

Northerly current is 2 knots, therefore over 1.5 hours the distance = 3 nautical miles.

Plot this on your chart to obtain your EP (Estimated Position). Note: the standard convention for EP is a triangle.

The line from your 0930 position to your EP position is your Course Made Good (CMG), you actually did this course.

Exercise 12 – Position - DR and EP page 18 in Questions and Answers Booklet
Answers 12 – Position - DR and EP page 46 in Questions and Answers Booklet

POSITION - RUNNING FIX

A running fix is a fix using two bearings and it doesn't matter how far the course line is from the bearing object, therefore it is used when you have no means of measuring the range.

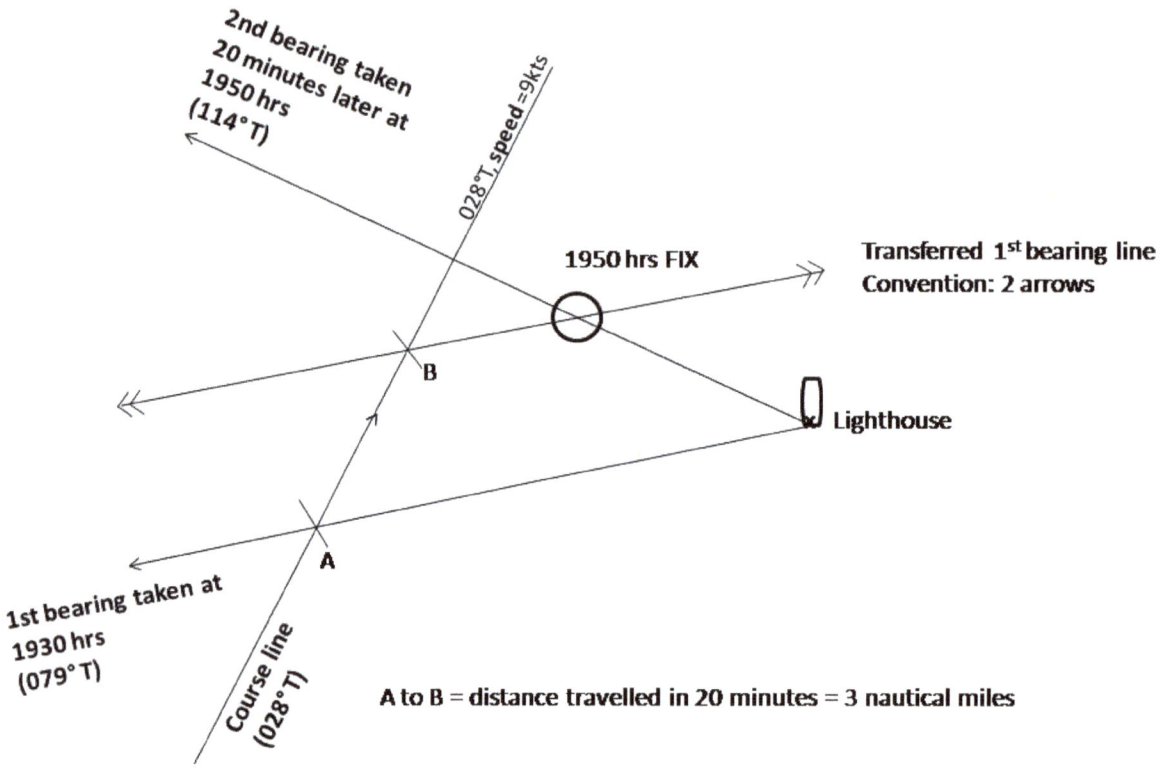

Step by step: how to plot your position using the running fix method:

Plot your course line. Label this line with your course and speed, in this example, 028°T at 9 knots.

This is plotted in the area you are in and the direction you are going. At the moment you do not know where, exactly, you are - so this line indicates direction and speed only, NOT position.

Take the first bearing of a known charted landmark (079°T), lay this bearing off on your chart (ensure it is TRUE) and note the time (1930hrs) on your chart. You are on this bearing line somewhere at 1930hrs. This must cross your course line. (Some people prefer to lay off the first bearing line on the chart to start, so they ensure the course line crosses this bearing line. It does not matter where your course line is, providing it is in the right direction and crosses the first bearing line.)

For a period of time you continue on the same course (028°T).

Take a second bearing from the same landmark (now at 114° T in our example), note the time (1950hrs) and lay off on your chart (TRUE), this also crosses your course line.

From your first bearing line, along your course line (A), mark the distance travelled in the time period between bearings (A to B). The time period in this example is twenty minutes (convert to decimal = 0.33hr) speed is 9kts and distance 3 nm. (9kts x 0.33 = 3nm).

On your chart, transfer the first bearing line (079°) to the distance covered in twenty minutes (B).

Draw this line parallel to your first bearing (use your parallel rule or bi-rola). This line is marked with double arrows at each end to denote its meaning (transferred bearing line).

The point where the transferred first bearing line intersects the second bearing line is your FIX.

The accuracy of the running fix depends on the accuracy of the estimate of the vessel's movement between A and B. (The movement made good between the two observed bearings or position lines.) Your fix places you approximately four nautical miles off the lighthouse bearing 114°T.

Exercise 13 – Position - Running Fix page 19 in Questions and Answers Booklet
Answers 13 – Position - Running Fix page 46 in Questions and Answers Booklet

DOUBLE THE ANGLE OFF THE BOW

This calculation takes advantage of the properties of an isosceles triangle. An isosceles triangle has two sides of equal length and consequently, it has two internal angles that are also equal. This rule is used when the second bearing between the bow of your boat and the target is double the angle of the first bearing.

How to perform 'double the angle off the bow' on board: See Figure 1 (below) for a complete depiction of what double the angle off the bow refers to. Your first angle off the bow needs to be between 020° to 045° (less than 020° can reduce accuracy). So how do you measure this?

FIGURE 1 – DOUBLE THE ANGLE OFF THE BOW

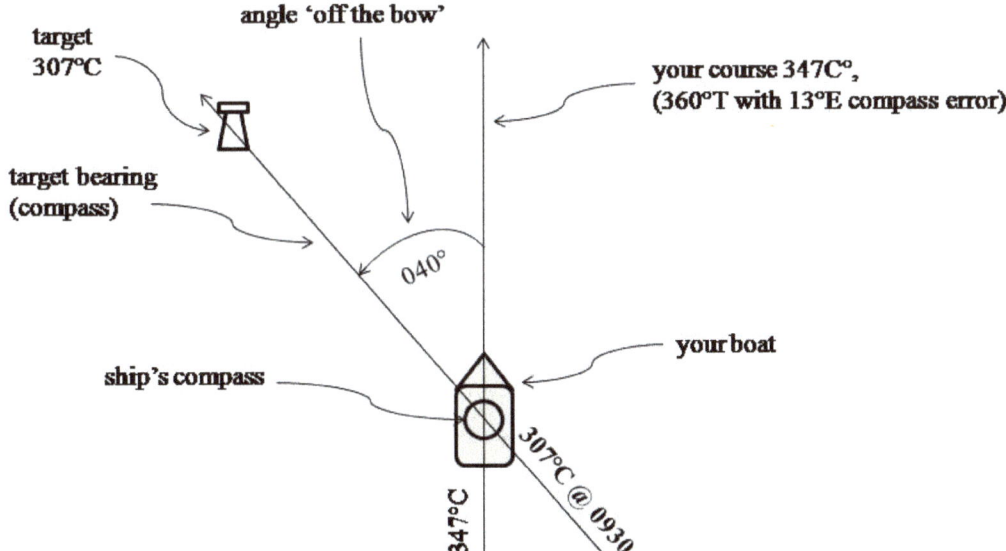

In this example the angle off the bow is a red bearing, i.e. Red 040° (Red-because it is on our port side). This is determined by reading your compass course (347°C), then reading the target's compass bearing (307°C). The difference between the two is the target's angle 'off the bow', i.e. 347°C - 307°C = Red 040°

Step by step: how to calculate distance off, using double the angle off the bow method:

Take note of the compass course you are steering. In our example, the course steered is 347°C (see Figure 2).

With your hand-bearing compass, or by sighting over your ship's compass, take a compass bearing of the chosen target (a lighthouse makes a good target).

Record this bearing, your log reading and the time. For example, Course = 347°C, bearing to Target (e.g. Nobby's Head Lighthouse) = 307°C, Time = 0930hrs, Log reading = 0.

The difference between course steered and the target's bearing is the target's angle off the bow. Study Figures 1 and 2.

Angle off the bow = 347°C - 307°C = 040°

As the target is on our port side, we can call this angle RED 040°.

If our first angle off the bow = RED 040°, then doubling this angle will give us RED 080°.

The compass reading required for the second bearing line to the target will equal the course steered minus the double the angle off the bow.

See Figure 2 below.

347°C - 080° = 267°C

As you are proceeding along the chosen course (347°C), keep an eye on the target's bearing.

When the same target (Nobby's Head Lighthouse) bears 267°C, note down (again) the time and distance run (from the log).

Course steered = 347°C, target bearing = 267°C, distance run = 5nm, time of second bearing = 1030hrs.

The number of sea miles covered (A-B) (assuming no current or leeway) equals the distance the vessel is from the target (B-C). So you can say, 'At 1030hrs we are 5nm from Nobby's Head Lighthouse, which is on a bearing line of 267°C.'

FIGURE 2 - DOUBLE THE ANGLE OFF THE BOW

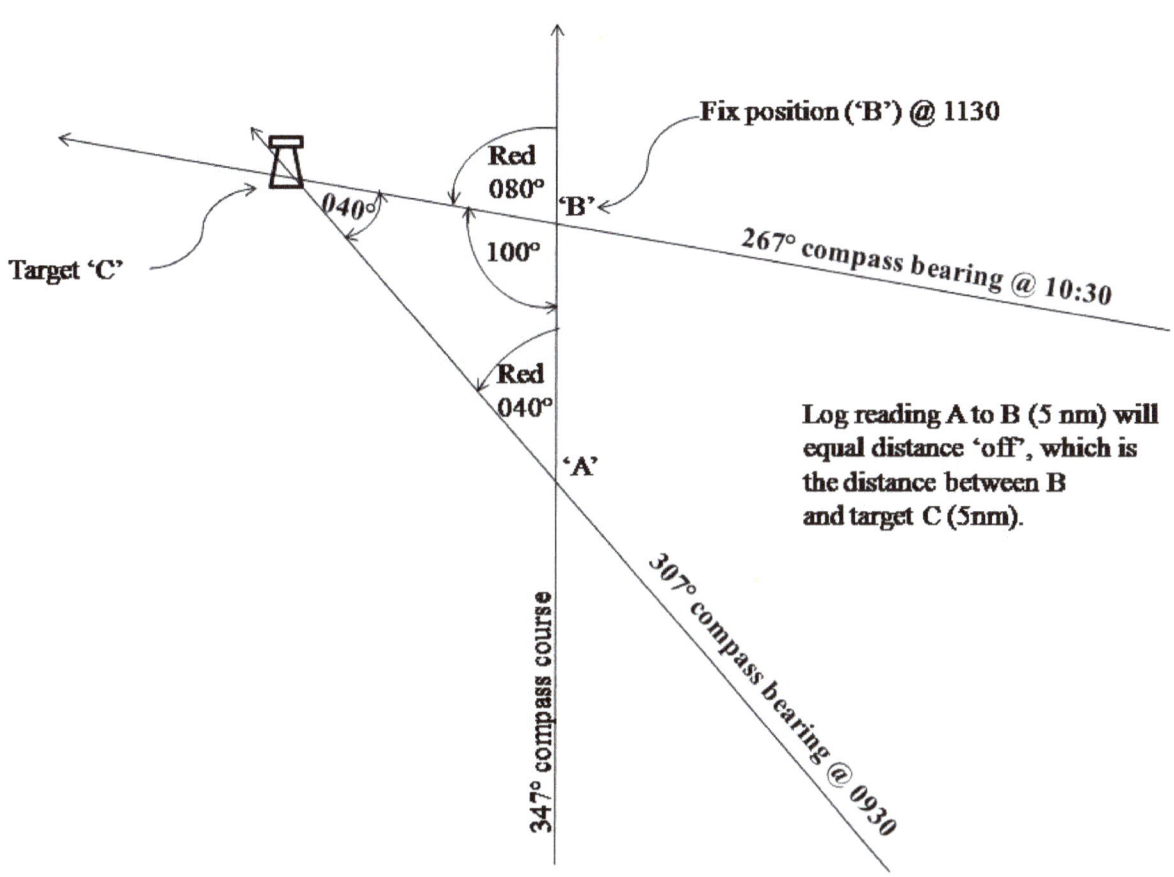

When you get the chance, have a go; it's actually quite simple and straightforward.

Another useful method is to guess 045° off the bow using your arm. Swing your arm from pointing at the bow to pointing abeam of your boat. Half of this swing (090°/2) is 45°. When the target is 045° off the bow, note the time and log reading, double the angle off the bow will be 090° or abeam.

When target is abeam, note the time and log reading. As before, the distance run will equal your distance off the target.

This method is easier, but it is not predictive, i.e. you may have to avoid a danger that is lying off a headland. By using an initial angle off the bow less than 045° (e.g. 030°), you can predict your clearance off the headline on arrival. By using 045° as your initial angle, by the time 090° (abeam) comes up, you could be in the danger zone!

Remember: to be able to plot the fixed position on a chart, convert all bearings to TRUE. We have used a total Compass error for the above example of 13°E. We have to add 13°E to all the Compass bearings to obtain the True bearing for the chart work.

The Isosceles Triangle - how does it help us?

Refer to Figure 2. A straight line (our course) = 180°. We cut that line with the double angle of 080°, therefore 180° - 080° = 100° remaining.

This 100° forms the angle at the top of our isosceles triangle.

All triangles have three internal corner angles. The value of all three angles added together always equals 180°.

In our example, we have 100°+ 40° = 140°. We know triangles have a total of 180° internally, therefore the remaining angle must = 40°. There it is: our isosceles triangle!

We have a base line of a triangle, A to C and the two remaining sides (A to B and B to C) are equal in length because we have an isosceles triangle with two equal internal angles.

If we know the length of one side (our course covered, A to B) from our log reading, we then know the length of the side B to C.

A to B = 5 nautical miles, therefore B to C = 5 nautical miles.

We are 5 nautical miles from the target at 1030hrs.

Exercise 14 – Position - Double the Angle off the Bow page 19 in Questions and Answers Booklet
Answers 14 – Position - Double the Angle off the Bow page 47 in Questions and Answers Booklet

THE TRANSIT BEARING

When two charted objects come into line they are in transit. We've already seen how a transit can be used to calculate Ship's Compass Deviation. A transit bearing can also be used to obtain a fix in conjunction with another position line. The pictures below illustrate a fix with a range (with the transit line) and the second picture shows a transit bearing and a sounding. A transit in conjunction with a sounding is not as accurate as a bearing and a range).

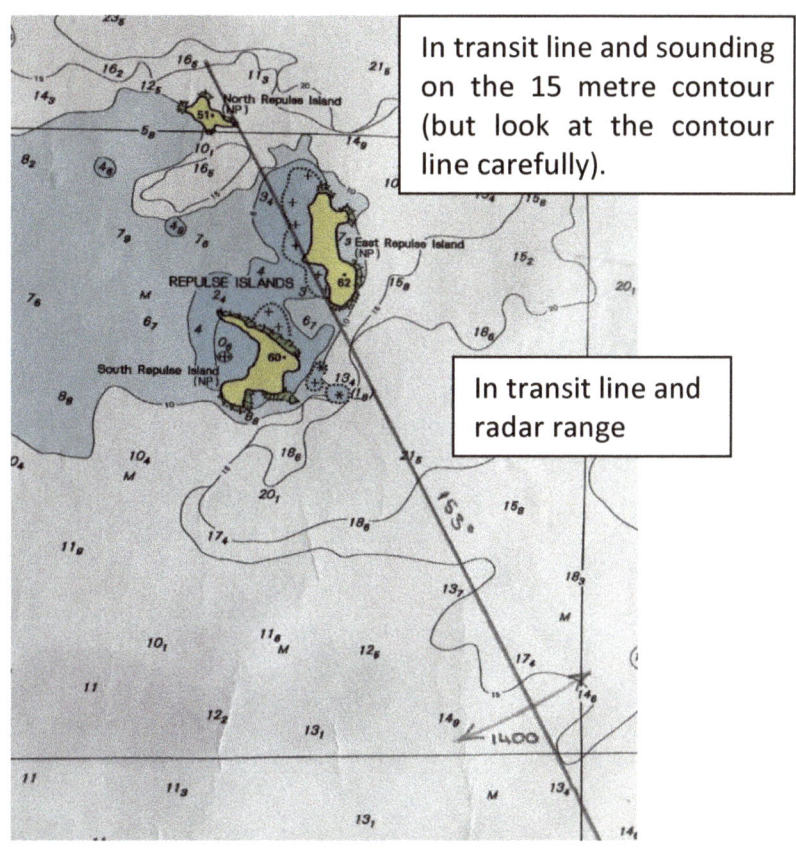

In transit line and sounding on the 15 metre contour (but look at the contour line carefully).

In transit line and radar range

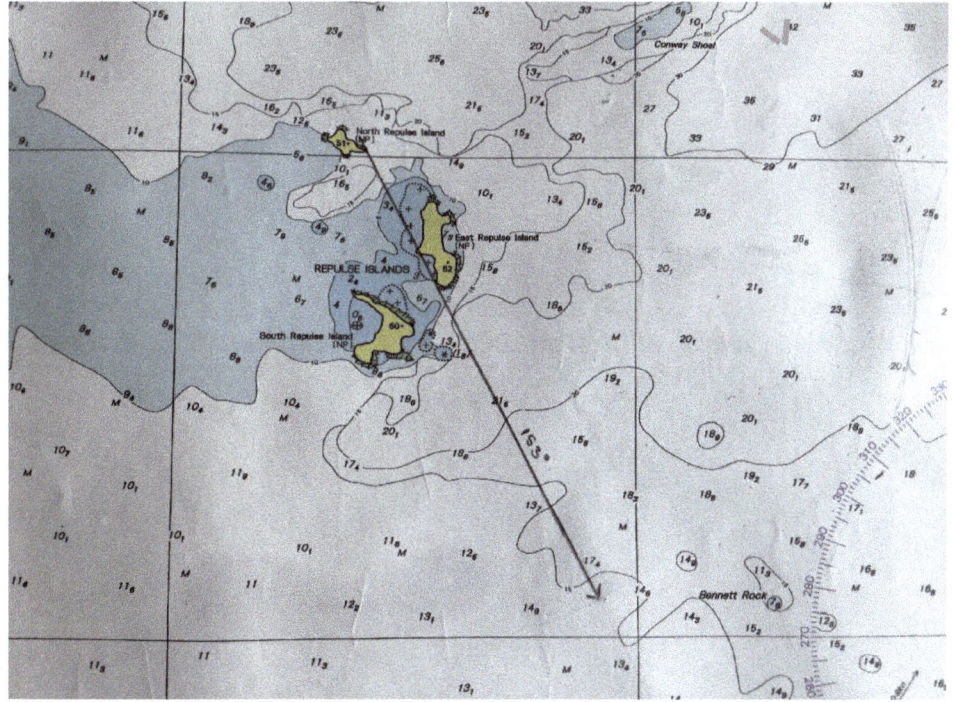

The transit bearing crosses the 15 metre contour line in several places. Tide heights need to be applied as well – this is not as accurate as the transit with a radar range fix.

Exercise 15 – Position - Transits page 19 in Questions and Answers Booklet
Answers 15 – Position - Transits page 47 in Questions and Answers Booklet

SET AND DRIFT

Counteracting Set and Drift

At 0900 You are in position: 20° 50.00' S   149° 10.00' E

Your destination is: 20° 50. 00' S   149° 00.00' E

You are steering 270°T at 5 knots and the known set and drift rate is 180°T and 2 knots.

(We'll plot this over an hour, if you were to calculate this over a thirty-minute period, your drift rate would be 1 knot, but in that case, you must remember to use half-an-hour throughout the entire work, e.g. speed, distance, etc.).

Plot your position and call this A

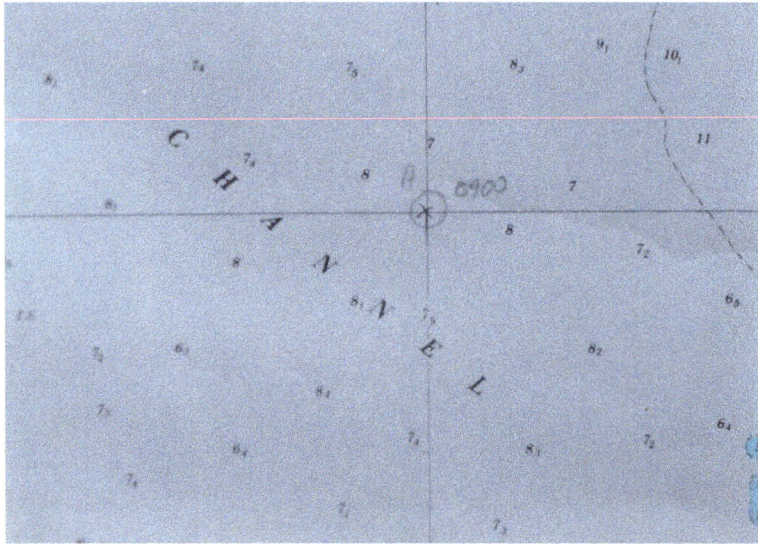

1. You want to reach point B which is at: 20° 50. 00' S   149° 00.00' E

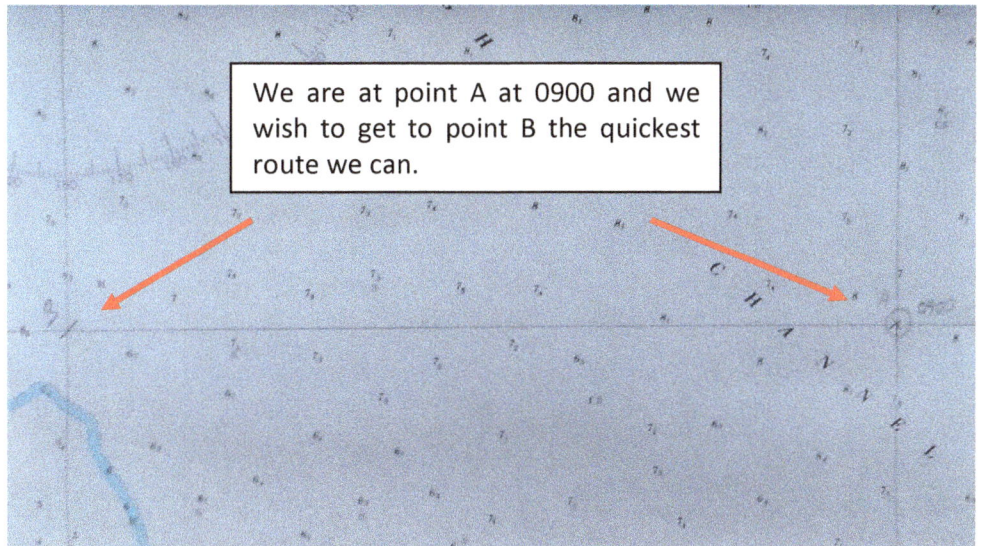

We are at point A at 0900 and we wish to get to point B the quickest route we can.

2. From A draw in the set and drift vector. Two nautical miles south (measure 2 nautical miles using the latitude scale adjacent to your work and simply follow the longitude line) - Mark this C.

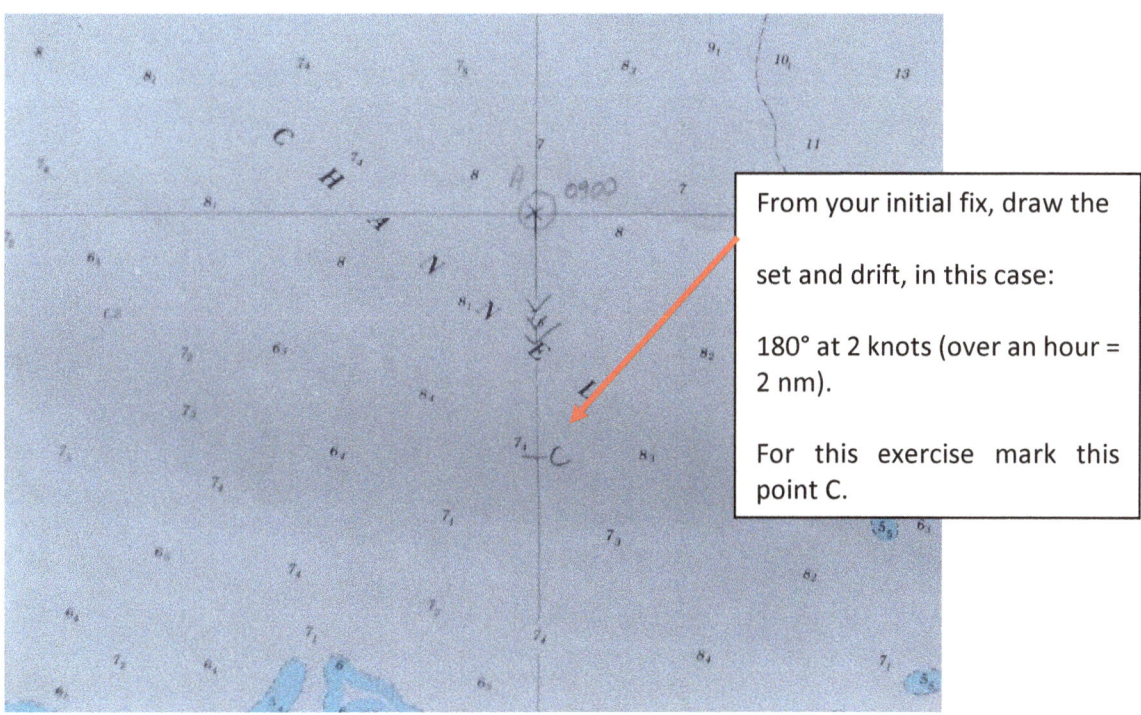

From your initial fix, draw the set and drift, in this case:

180° at 2 knots (over an hour = 2 nm).

For this exercise mark this point C.

3. From C measure the distance, through the water, you cover in 1 hour @ 5 knots = 5 nm
Mark that 5 nm line (from C) on the AB line and that point is called D.

©Jackie Parry   www.sistershiptraining.com   91

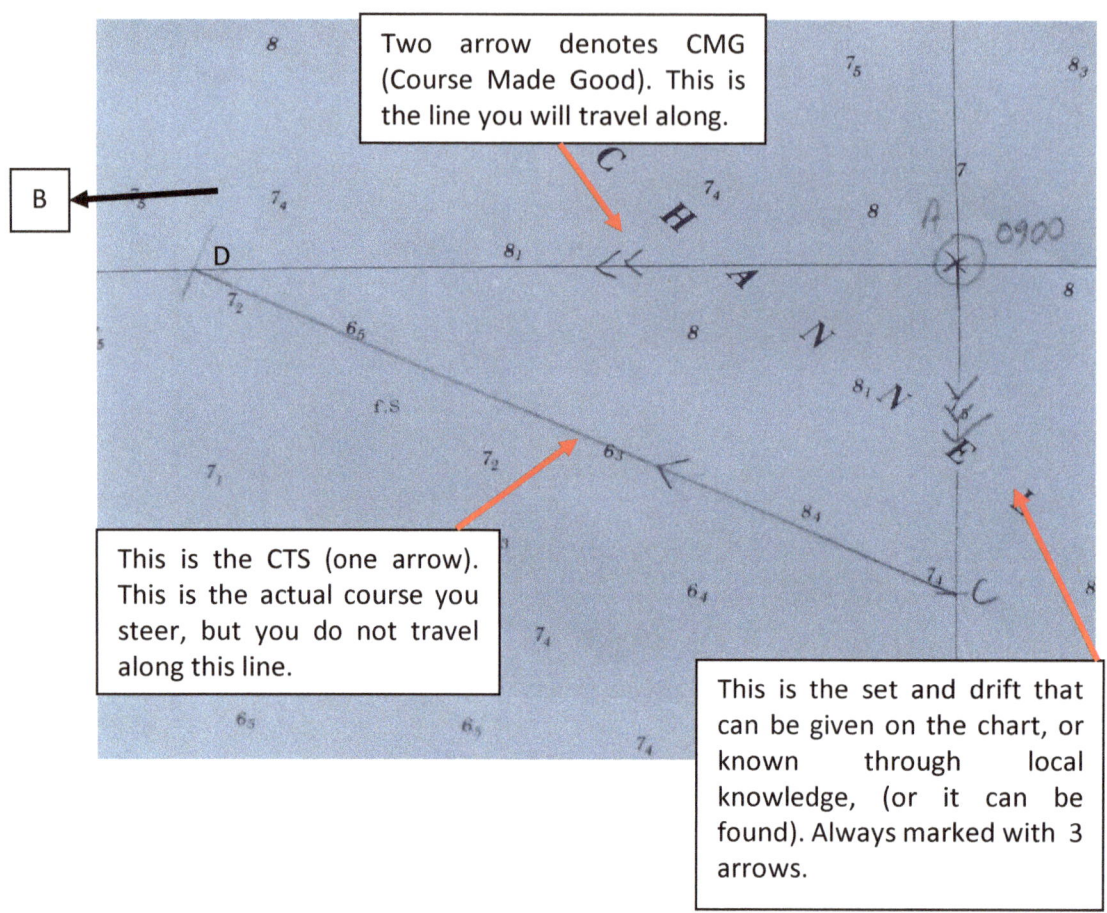

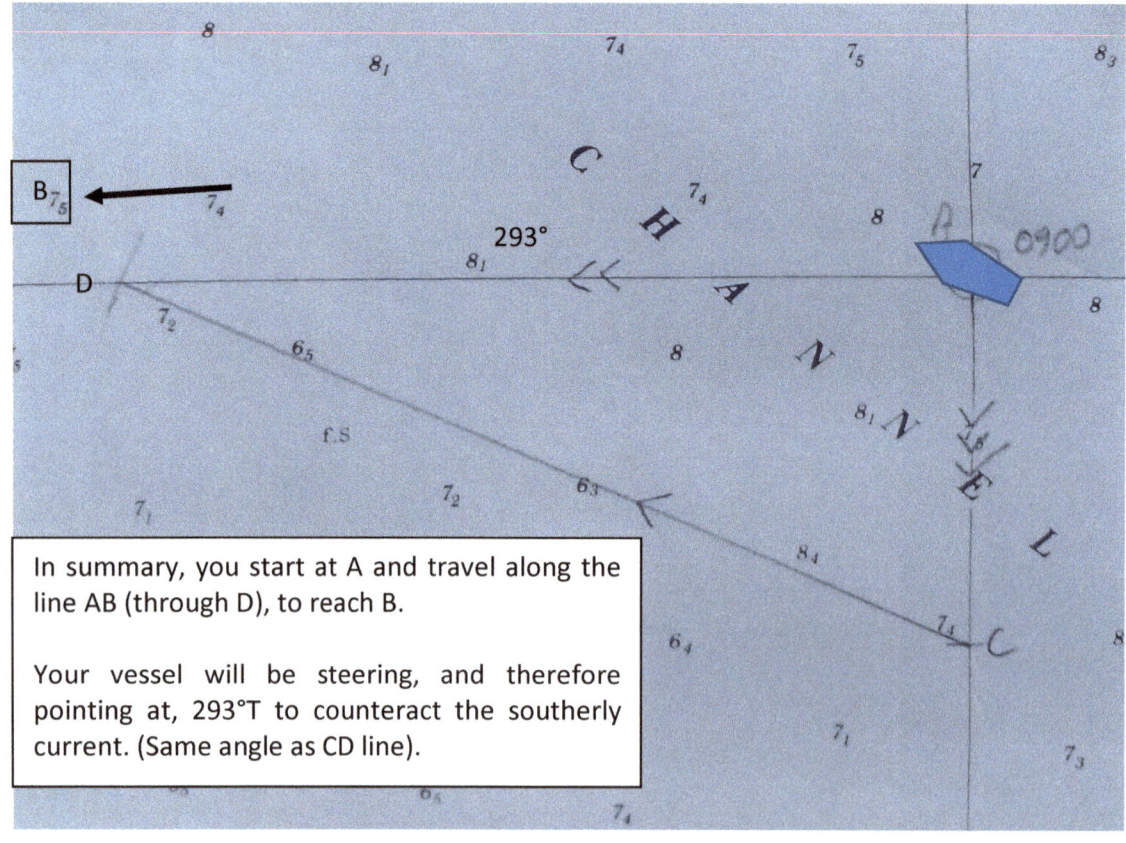

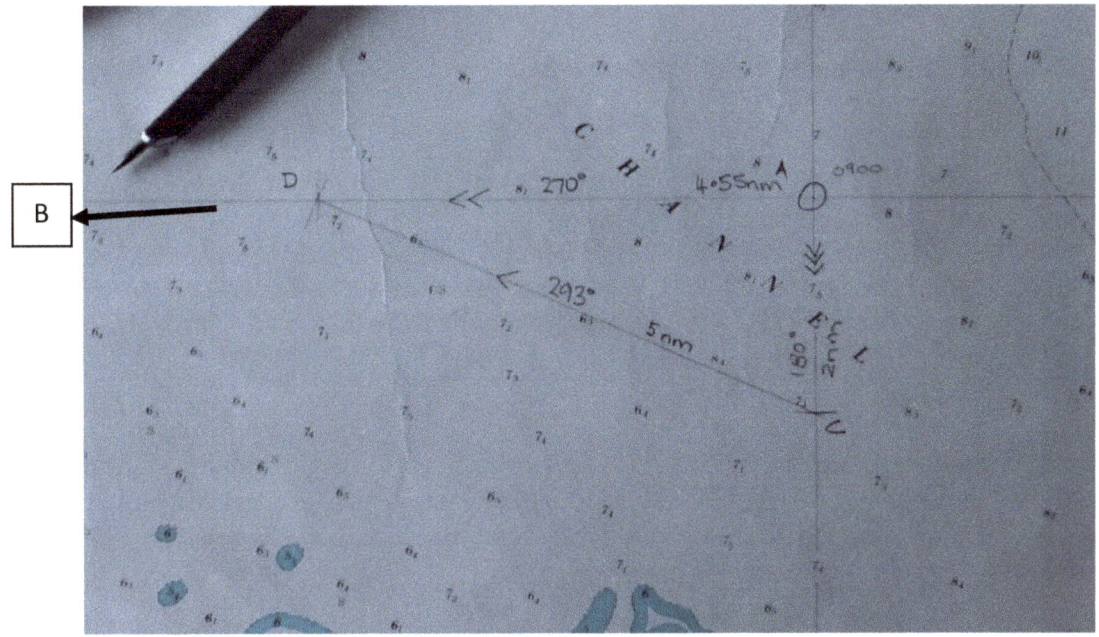

CD= the course you actually steer (CTS) = 293°T (instead of 270°T, to counteract the southerly current).

AD is the Speed Made Good, what speed you actually did = 4.55 knots (the current slows you down slightly).

Distance A to D = 4.55nm   Time = 1 hour
D= 4.55 nm   S = D / T =   S= 4.55 / 1 = 4.55 knots

Imagine sitting on A but you are facing 293°T – a boat doesn't necessarily go in the direction she is pointing.

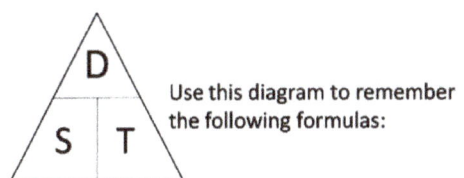

Use this diagram to remember the following formulas:

D = S x T
S = D / T
T = D / S

If reaching B was a rescue operation, you could calculate your ETA at B.

You now know your Speed Made Good, which is the speed you do against the current = 4.55 knots.

Use the Speed, Distance, Time formula

Time = Distance (AB) / Speed (4.55 knots)

Time = 9.4 / 4.55 = 2.066
That is 2 hours and 4 mins (remember to change the decimals of an hour to minutes)

We were at point A at 0900, our ETA at point B will be 1104.

Exercise 16 – Position – Three Bearing Fix with Set and Drift page 20 in Questions and Answers Booklet
Answers 16 – Position – Three Bearing Fix with Set and Drift page 47 in Questions and Answers Booklet

LEEWAY

We have so far calculated the current effects (above).

Understanding the effect the wind has on your vessel comes from experience. Different vessel structures have different windage effects. This is your vessel's leeway.

To counteract the leeway, in the example below the CTS (Course To Steer) is approximately 072°T. If your vessel is required to steer 072°T with a southerly wind that you expect to cause 4° leeway (determined through your experience on your vessel), then the vessel's track will be 076°T (072° + 4°). In other words, you have to steer this vessel 4° into the wind to make allowance for leeway that is caused.

When counteracting set and drift on your chart, always lay off the set of the known current first to determine the course to steer (CTS), and then apply leeway. As a matter of course, most helmsmen/women automatically steer to counteract these effects, if they can see their target. In the ocean, you have to calculate these compensations.

To understand Leeway, let's look at a Set & Drift calculation with Leeway applied:

As a reminder: Current will push you in a certain direction (called 'set') and over a period of time, the current will move you a distance (called 'drift'). To counteract set and drift, you need to know the speed and direction of the current. (You could do this by taking a good fix position and comparing that position to your DR position. The difference between your good fix and DR position will be the set and drift).

Finding the Course to Steer (CTS) allowing for a known current:

The diagram below shows the vessel at A.
From A the vessel wishes to get to point B.
A to C shows the set and drift quantities of the current in one hour.
A to B is the course to make good (CMG), (you actually travel along the line AB).
A to D is the speed made good.
C to D is the speed of the vessel through the water.

We've constructed Set and Drift vectors and we can see our CTS (course to steer) is the line CD. We are experiencing a 4° leeway from the southerly wind. Therefore, if our CTS is 072° (to allow for set and drift), with the leeway you need to steer into the wind and your CTS becomes 076°.

Constructing the triangle from Current and Wind to determine Course to Steer (CTS), allowing for known current and leeway.

Scale:
1′ latitude = approx 15.7 mm

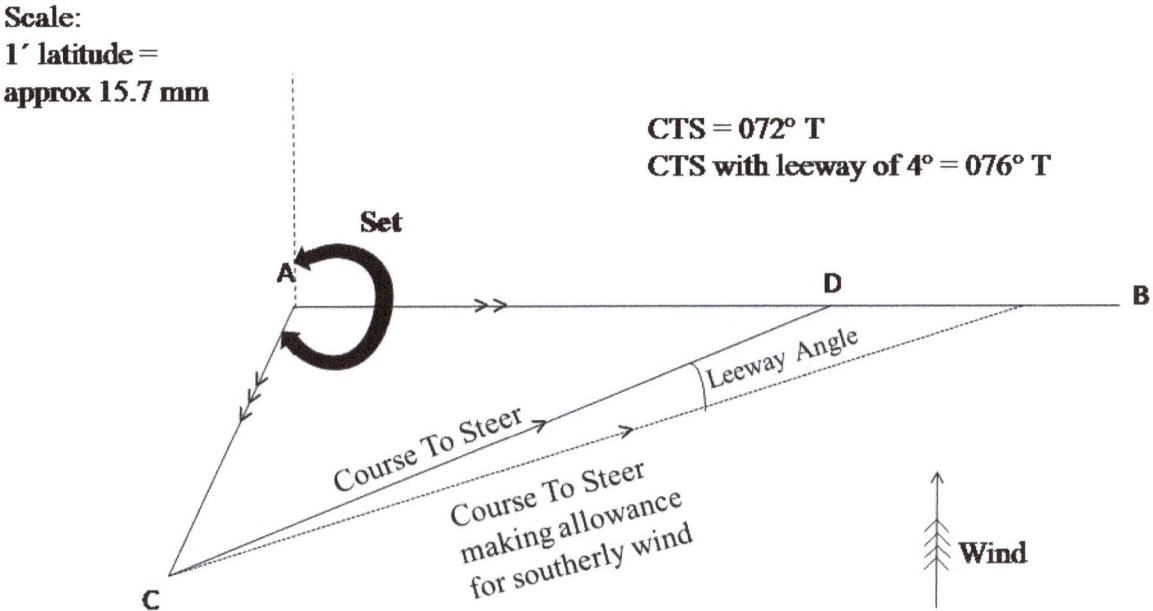

CTS = 072° T
CTS with leeway of 4° = 076° T

Due to the current, even though you are doing 6 knots through the water you are only doing 4.5 knots over the ground.

The current is effectively slowing you down by 1.5 knots.

From A, the vessel wants to make good a course of 090° TRUE, in order to reach point B.
The known current is set at 190°T at 2.2 knots. The vessel's speed is 6 knots.

We are looking at the Leeway in this exercise, but here's a reminder of how to find the Course To Steer – step by step:

On your chart, lay off the course to make good, which is AB.

Draw a vector triangle over a one hour period. This will help you calculate how to steer your boat along the A to B line. To do this, plot one hour of current (the set and the drift) from A and label this as C.

From C as the starting point, lay off the distance the ship will travel through the water in one hour, (6 nm measured off the latitude scale, 1′ = 1 nm). The line should start at C and end on the original AB line, mark this as D.

The direction CD is the True course to steer from A, in order to counteract the current.

The distance AD is the distance you will cover in one hour, that is the actual distance made good (DMG) in one hour, and is therefore your speed made good (SMG), i.e. you cover 4.5 nm in one hour, therefore 4.5 knots is your speed. (Your GPS would say 4.5 knots due to the actions of the current; this is the actual speed over ground you will achieve, even though you are doing 6 knots through the water.)

©Jackie Parry   www.sistershiptraining.com

The distance AB (7.1 nm) is divided by the speed made good AD (4.5 knots) to find the ETA.

Time = D/S
Time = 7.1/4.5 = 1.58 hours   0.58 x 60 = 35 minutes = 1 hour 35 minutes

Therefore, if the ETD (Estimated Time of Departure) = 11:00, then ETA = 12:35

Doesn't all this make the GPS a wonderful invention? For those cruising under wind vanes or electronic steering, it is interesting to see and understand why your ship's compass reads different to your GPS.

Exercise 17 – Leeway page 21 in Questions and Answers Booklet
Answers 17 – Leeway page 49 in Questions and Answers Booklet

Terminology Reminder

Course To Steer
This is the True course to steer with allowance for set, drift and leeway. This CTS has been calculated on your chart in True. To steer by Compass you must convert the True course to Compass course. We do this by applying Variation and Deviation. (See 'Compass' earlier in this section.)

(CMG) Course Made Good (True)
This is the actual course over the ground between two observed positions.

Distance & Speed
This is related to the vessel's movement through the water and is usually established from the ship's log.

(DMG) Distance Made Good
This is the measurement between two observed fixed positions, measured 'over the ground' not through the water. The effective distance you actually covered.

(SMG) Speed Made Good
This is related to the measurement between two positions, measured 'over the ground' not through the water, i.e. the effective speed obtained.

Set
This is the direction towards which a current and/or tidal stream flows.

Drift
This is the distance covered in a given time due to the movement of a current and/or tidal stream.

Rate Of Drift
This is the speed of the current and/or tidal stream, i.e. the distance, in nautical miles, the current covers in one hour.

Drift Angle
This is the angular difference between the track through the water and the track over the ground, caused by the current or tidal stream.

Leeway
This is the effect of the wind blowing the vessel to leeward. It depends on the wind's strength and direction, type of vessel and its draught. This is generally estimated from experience.

Leeway Angle
This is the angular difference between the ship's heading and the track through the water. Observe your wake compared to the fore and aft line of your vessel.

Position Line
This is a line on the chart on which the vessel lies or has lain. It may be straight for bearings or curved for ranges (see Radar).

Sextant
We sometimes break up long sea journeys by taking star sights. It is good practice and very satisfying to find your position by the stars. It also provides the confidence to know you can get home if all else

fails. Practice celestial navigation prior to your voyage and take all your books and equipment on board. A celestial computer is a great aid and speeds up the whole process, however they are prone to inherent failures of electronic equipment (usually a flat battery and loss of data).

SECTION SUMMARY

You have learned how to plot your position using Deduced Reckoning and Estimated Position. You have constructed vectors to counteract Set and Drift and established the set and drift effect. You can re-calculate your course and speed taking into account the Set and Drift. You've also learned several different methods of position fixing without electronic charts or a GPS.

Congratulations you are well on the way to becoming a good marine navigator!

FURTHER INFORMATION

Publications

Sailing Directions (Pilots) – These are written directions, describing the routes to be taken by boats and ships during coastal navigation, and port approaches. These should be read together with your charts. They are published by the Hydrographer of the Navy or by Local Government.

The same as charts, they must be kept up to date by the latest supplement and Notice to Mariners.
http://www.hydro.gov.au/prodserv/important-info/chart-related-info.htm

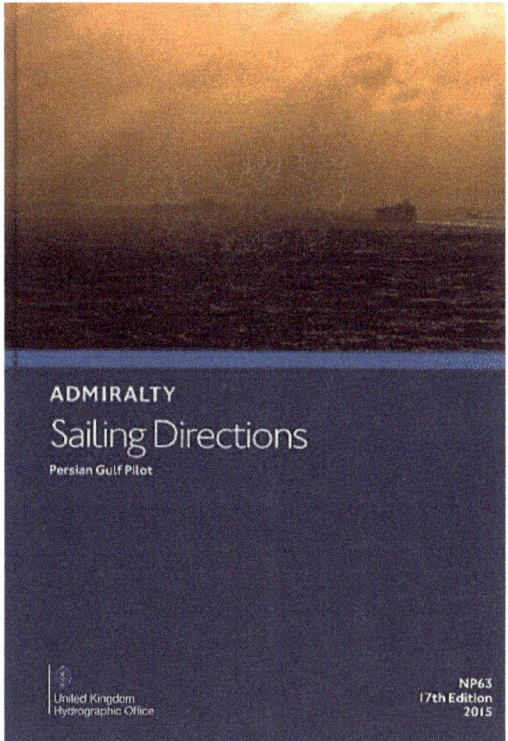

Lucas and other authors provide useful cruising guides for recreational sailors. But they often do not cover the depth of information (or provide a way to update the information) like the Sailing Directions.

Admiralty List of Lights and Fog Signals: ADMIRALTY List of Lights and Fog Signals provides coverage of over 85,000 light structures including lighthouses, lightships, lit floating marks, fog signals and other lights of navigational significance.

Each volume of List of Lights and Fog Signals offers:
- Descriptions of the characteristics of lights and fog signals, together with the equivalent foreign language light descriptions, to help bridge crews with identification.
- Tables to assist in the calculation of geographical and luminous ranges of lights.
- Details for all lights listed including the international number, location and/or name, geographical position, characteristics and intensity, elevation in metres, range in sea miles and description of structure.
- Published in 14 regional volumes (A-P) for simplicity and ease of handling.
- Available from the Hydrographic office and provide details of all official navigational lights.
- This is corrected from Australian Notices to Mariners issued fortnightly.
- A number and a position (latitude and longitude) is provided for each light. This is also available digitally.

Tide Tables: Published annually by the Hydrographic Office covering all Australian Ports, Papua New Guinea and Solomon Islands. Locally published tables are published by State Governments and often give other useful information. This covers tidal predictions, the weather, fishing guide, etc.
http://www.hydro.gov.au/prodserv/publications/antt.htm

Notices To Mariners: Issued by the RAN Hydrographic Service.
http://www.hydro.gov.au/n2m/about-notices.htm#relate
They contain corrections for the following:
- Charts
- Sailing Directions (Pilots)
- List of Lights
- Admiralty List of Radio Signals
- Chart Catalogues

©Jackie Parry

Mariner's Handbook for Australian Waters AHP20 and AHP24 Chart and Publication Maintenance Handbook. Hydrographic Office
http://www.hydro.gov.au/prodserv/publications/ash.htm

In Australian waters charts can be identified using 2 catalogue sheets.
- Northern sheet covers from Port Clinton in Queensland to N.W. Cape in Western Australia. (Including Papua New Guinea and the Solomon Islands.)
- The Southern sheet covers the rest of Australia including Tasmania.

The sheets give the Chart Number, Title, Scale and Current Edition Date.

On the back of each sheet are various miscellaneous charts and publications.
Their numbers are:	Southern Aus 5001
			Northern Aus 5000
			Solomon Islands SLB 1001

http://www.hydro.gov.au/prodserv/paper/standard-aci.htm

The catalogue charts should not be used for navigation but are invaluable for planning a voyage and ordering charts and publications required.

SALIENT POINT LATITUDES - CHART NO. AUS 252

Anchorsmith Island	20°37.0'S
Blacksmith Island	20°38.1'S
Dumbell Island	20°10.5'S
East Repulse Island	20°36.0'S
Edward Island	20°15.1'S
Mount Arthur	20°30.8'S
Pioneer Point	20°14.0'S
Platypus Rock	20°31.5'S
Shaw Island	20°28.3'S
Silversmith Island	20°35.4'S
Thomas Island	20°32.9'S

COASTAL NAVIGATION

QUESTIONS & ANSWERS

JACKIE & NOEL PARRY

EXERCISE 1: TIME CALCULATIONS

Time Calculations – Convert these minutes into decimals of an hour

a) 30 minutes

_____

b) 54 minutes

_____

c) 1 hour 30 minutes

_____

d) 15 minutes

_____

e) 40 minutes

_____

f) 22 minutes

_____

g) 1 hour 15 minutes

_____

h) 5 minutes

_____

i) 39 minutes

_____

TIP: It is good practice to write out the entire formula for every calculation. If you make an error it is easy to find by going back through your work. Also, you are less likely to miss a step.

EXERCISE 2: TIME CALCULATIONS

Time Calculations – Convert these decimalised minutes into regular minutes

a) 0.45 hours

_____

b) 1.5 hours

_____

c) 0.6 hours

_____

d) 0.8 hours

_____

e) 0.75 hours

_____

f) 0.5 hours

_____

g) 0.2 hours

_____

h) .10 hours

_____

i) .18 hours

_____

j) .24 hours

_____

TIP: Mercator charts are in degrees, minutes, and decimals of a minute and a GPS can be set the same way. To reduce errors, set your GPS to match your charts.

EXERCISE 3: SPEED, DISTANCE, TIME

1. Find the distance travelled in 15 minutes if your speed was:

a) 20 knots

_____

b) 40 knots

_____

c) 10 knots

_____

d) 8 knots

_____

e) 4 knots

_____

f) 6 knots

___

g) 15.5 knots

___

h) 12.4 knots

___

2. How long will it take you to reach your next waypoint if you had 3.5 nautical miles to go and your speed was:

a) 12 knots

___

b) 16 knots

___

c) 20 knots

___

d) 4 knots

___

e) 15 knots

___

f) 6.5 knots

___

g) 12.4 knots

___

h) 5 knots

___

3. At 1549 your vessel is sailing at 6.5 knots, how many nautical miles will you have travelled by 1600?

___

4. You are travelling at 6 knots, how many nautical miles will you travel in:

a) 0.4 hours

___

b) 15 minutes

c) 1 hour 25 minutes

d) 1.5 hours

e) 2 ¾ hours

f) 0.8 hours

g) 4.2 hours

h) 2 hours 15 minutes

5. You have travelled 8.7 nautical miles in 45 minutes. How many knots, on average, were you doing during this time?

6. What is your speed if you travelled 6 miles in:

a) 26 minutes

b) 40 minutes

c) 1.5 hours

d) 10 minutes

e) 1 hour

©Jackie Parry

f) 1 hour 45 minutes

___

g) 50 minutes

___

h) 75 minutes

___

7. How long would it take you to travel 12 nautical miles if your speed was:

a) 15 knots

___

b) 3 knots

___

c) 9 knots

___

d) 12 knots

___

e) 20 knots

___

f) 4 knots

___

g) 4.5 knots

___

h) 17 knots

TIP: Think about your speed questions. Do the above questions produce a speed that is referring to your speed through the water or speed over the ground? It is speed through the water so a current will affect your speed over the ground and consequently the time taken to reach the required distance over the ground.

EXERCISE 4: CHART SYMBOLS

1) Identify the following lights

a)

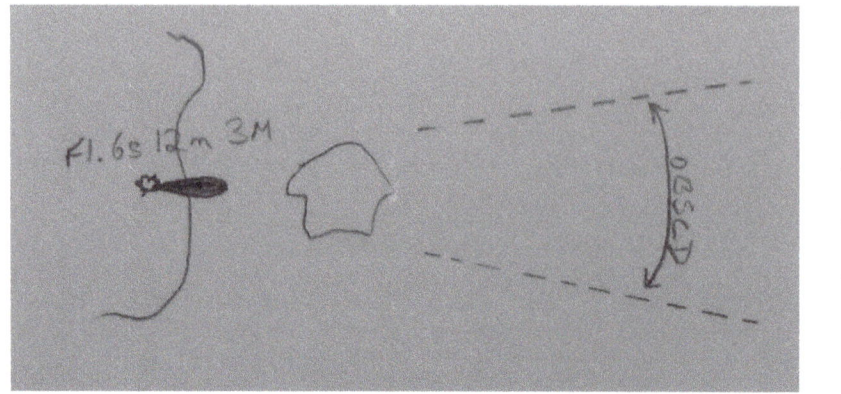

b)

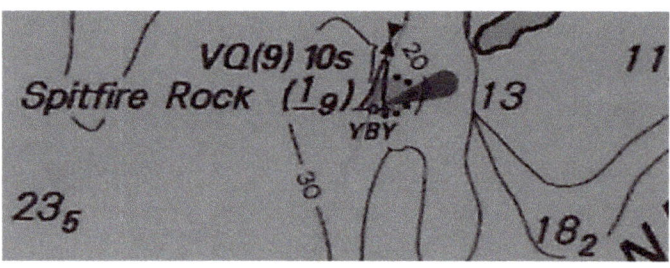

c) Iso

_____

d) Oc

_____

Identify the following chart symbols

 Mast(s)

⊛ 4_6 Wk ⊛ 4_6 Obstn	
⊡ 4_6 Wk ⊡ 4_6 Obstn	
✳ ($\underline{1}_6$)	
🪨 ($\underline{1}_6$)	
✤	
✢	
⊛ 4_8 R	
✢ (4_8)	

♯	
20	

2) Identify the following Nature of Seabed symbols:

a) G _____

b) St _____

c) Sh _____

d) Co _____

e) S _____

f) M _____

g) Wd _____

h) Si _____

i) R _____

3) Identify the tidal stream and currents symbols shown:

a)

⎯⎯⎯ 4 kn ⎯→ _____

b)

(spiral symbols) _____

c)

⎯⎯⎯ 2.5 kn ⎯→ _____

d)

(wave symbols) _____

©Jackie Parry

EXERCISE 5: POSITION PRACTICE

1) Find the geographical position of the following features:

a) Pentecost Island (288) _____

b) Dent Island (158) _____

c) Workington Island (91) _____

d) Coppersmith Rock Light _____

e) Thomas Island (179) _____

f) Mansell Island (170) _____

g) Hook Island, Hook Peak (456) _____

EXERCISE 6: DISTANCE

1) Measure the straight-line distance in nautical miles:

a) Haselwood Island-north peak (135) to Whitsunday Craig (353) _____

b) Ladysmith Island (121) to Shaw Island-Mount Arthur (250) _____

c) South Repulse Island (60) to Pentecost (288) _____

d) Grimston Point (on the mainland) to Baird Point (top) (Hook Island) _____

EXERCISE 7 DIRECTION

1) Measure the direction:

a) From E. Repulse Island (62) to Cape Conway tip _____

b) From E. Repulse Island (62) to Silversmith Island (74) _____

c) From CID Island (215) to North Molle Island (nth) (124) _____

d) From CID Island (167) to Pine Island (100) _____

2) Draw (layoff) a bearing from South Repulse Island (60) in a direction 210°T for a distance of 6.8 nm and find the latitude and longitude of this point.

___

EXERCISE 8: COMPASS TO TRUE AND TRUE TO COMPASS

1) Complete the table (Including Total Error).

TRUE	100°			154°	225°	007°				179°
VARIATION	12°E	6°E	13°W				3°W		6°W	8°E
MAGNETIC				164°	214°	358°		208°		
DEVIATION	2°W	6°E			4°W	3°E	6°E		1°E	
COMPASS		214°	065°	160°			016°	212°	320°	182°
ERROR		12°E	5°W			12°E		3°W		

2) if the Variation is 10°W and the total error is 14°W, what is the Deviation?

T

V   10°W

M

D

C

Error   14°W

3) What is the total Compass error if the Variation is 8°E and the Deviation is 4°W

___
___

4) What is the True bearing of a lighthouse if a bearing of 280° is taken with a hand bearing compass and the Variation is 4°W

___
___

5) Calculate the Compass course to steer if the Compass error is 15°E and the True course is 060°

___
___

©Jackie Parry

Answer the following three questions using Variation: 6°E and use this deviation card:

COMPASS	DEVIATION	MAGNETIC
160°	7°W	153°
180°	5°W	174
200°	2°W	188°
220°	1°E	220°
240°	3°E	242°
260°	5°E	275°
280°	7°E	285°

6) What is the True course (using the above Deviation card) if the Compass course steered is:

a) 249°C

b) 208°C

c) 231°C

d) 259°C

e) 179°C

7) Find the Compass (using the Deviation card above) course given:

a) 178°T

b) 222°T

c) 241°T

d) 190°T

e) 254°M

8) Find the compass course (using the Deviation card above) to steer if the required true course is:

a) 225°T

b) 196°T

c) 181°T

d) 248°T

e) 281°T

9) Complete the table (this question does not apply to the above Deviation card)

TRUE	104°	**229°**	**073°**	143°	215°	004°	**013°**	**204°**	**327°**	182°
VARIATION	10°E	**9°E**	17°W	**26°W**	**8°E**	**7°E**	1°W	**7°W**	3°W	4°E
MAGNETIC	**094°**	**220°**	**090°**	169°	207°	357°	**014°**	211°	**330°**	**178°**
DEVIATION	6°W	6°E	**15°E**	**11°E**	7°W	**4°E**	3°E	**2°W**	7°E	**2°W**
COMPASS	**100°**	214°	075°	158°	**214°**	**353°**	011°	213°	323°	180°
ERROR	**4°E**	15°E	2°W	**15°W**	**1°E**	11°E	**2°E**	9°W	**4°E**	**2°E**

10) Complete the following table:

True	105°	221°	**123°**	156°	222°	009°	348°	**205°**	**012°**	183°
Variation	15°E	**6°E**	12°W	**10°W**	**6°W**	2°W	3°E	5°W	5°E	
Magnetic	**090°**	215°	135°	166°	216°	357°	**345°**	210°	007°	

EXERCISE 9: THREE BEARING FIX

1) Hook Peak (456) bears 258° T

   Mosstrooper Peak (216) (Border Island) bears 186° T

   Petrel Islet (middle) bears 153° T

What is your position?

_____

EXERCISE 10: RADAR RANGE FIX

You are north east of Esk Island, and have taken these radar ranges. Fix your position:

South tip Border Island: 2.3 nm

Petrel Islet (west tip): 3.5 nm

Southern Tip of Deloraine Island: 3.5 nm

_____

EXERCISE 11: BEARINGS

1) Your vessel is steering 127°T and you observe a lighthouse bearing Red 69°. What is its true bearing?

_____

2) Your vessel is steering 324°T and you observe a lighthouse bearing 061°Rel. What is its true bearing?

_____

_____

3) You observe a vessel bearing Green 32° while your ship's head is 062°T. What is the target's true bearing?

_____

_____

4) You observe an object bearing Red 70°. Your vessel is steering 010°T. What is the target's true bearing?

_____

_____

5) You observe a vessel bearing 231°T. Your vessel is steering 312°T. Give the relative bearing of the other vessel.

_____

_____

6) You observe the lighthouse on the western side of Dent I bearing 350°T at 2.6 nm. Give your position in latitude and longitude.

_____

7) You observe Cid Island (215) bearing 136°T and South Molle Island (177) bearing 179°T. What should the bearing of North Molle Island (233) be? And what is your position?

_____

8) What is the course to steer (T) from the position in the Answer above to 20°03.00'S 148°48.5'E? What is the distance? And how long would it take to this position if you are sailing at 4 knots?

_____

_____

9) Your vessel is steering a course of 225°T. Assuming the top of your answer sheet to be the True North, draw the following, and include the true bearings or courses.

a) A vessel bearing Red 45°, steering a reciprocal course to your own.

b) A buoy on your port quarter.

c) A vessel bearing 045° Rel. and heading South East.

d) A vessel bearing 180° Rel. and going the same way as you.

e) A vessel steering 310°T has a light bearing 068° Rel. Give the true bearing of the light.

_____

_____

10) A vessel steering 112°T has a light bearing Red 74°. Give the true bearing of the light.

_____

_____

11) You are uncertain of the intentions of another vessel. You want to point out to your Skipper where the vessel is. Your course is 138°T with the other vessel bearing 123°T, which direction do you tell the Skipper to look.

_____

_____

12) You intend anchoring at: 20°32.9'S 148°43'E, and currently you are at 20°40.00'S 148°53.2'E.

a) What true course would you steer (given no current or leeway)?_____

b) If sailing at 6 knots how long would it take you to arrive? _____

13) You take the following radar ranges. Fix your vessel's position in latitude and longitude.

South Tip Triangle Island: 2.1 nm

The north tip of Dead Dog Island: 1.91 nm

South Tip Mansell Island: 2.1 nm

_____

14) Long Island Peak (269) bears 228°T and the light on the western side of Dent Island bears 137°T. What distance should you be from Pine Island (NE tip)?

_____

15) What is the course from the position in Question 13 to 20°35'S 149°00'E? And the distance?

_____

EXERCISE 12: POSITION – DR and EP

1) At 1000 hours you take the following bearings (and have converted them to True).

Dolphin Point (Hayman Island)	42° T
Hook Peak (456) (Hook Island)	116°T
Bird Island Light (most western light)	150°T

You then steered a course of 175°T at 4.1 knots until 1242.
Calculate: (a) the distance travelled, and
(b) the DR position at 1242.

_____
_____

2) At 0900 hours you observed these radar ranges:

North tip of Dungurra Island   2.6nm
Craig Point on WhitSunday Island   1.8nm
South tip Teague Island   2.65nm

You steered a course of 059° at 5 knots. At what time was Workington Island (91) abeam on port side?

_____

_____

EXERCISE 13: POSITION – RUNNING FIX

1) A vessel is steering 310°T at 5 knots. At 1100 hours East Repulse Island (62) is observed bearing 275°T. At 1142 hours it bears 247°T. Assuming there is no set or drift between bearings, find the position at 1142.

_____

EXERCISE 14: POSITION – DOUBLE THE ANGLE OFF THE BOW

1) A ship steering 058°T observes a single light at 0600 which bears 035° relative. At 0636 the light bears 070° relative. Ship's speed 10 knots. What is the true bearing and distance of the light at 0636?

_____

_____

EXERCISE 15: POSITION – TRANSITS

1) At 1200 Pioneer Point (on the mainland) and the north tip of North Molle Island are in transit bearing at 246°T. A radar range has been taken from the northern most tip of North Molle Island of 3nm. What is your position?

_____

2) You are just south of Dumbell Island and in 30 metres depth. Workington Island and Pallion point on Haselwood Island bear 126° T in transit. What is your position?

_____

EXERCISE 16: POSITION – THREE BEARING FIX WITH SET AND DRIFT

1) Depart from the Entrance Light to Port of Airlie: 20° 15.5'S 148° 43.6'E at 1100 hours. (Fl.G.2s)

   With a planned course of 359°C so as to clear East of Double Cone Island by 1 nm (approx.). Speed through the water is 5.5 knots. Deviation for the Ship's compass course of 359°C is 2°W.

   At 1200 hours a 3-bearing fix with a handheld compass is determined using:

   - Hook Island (405): 057°C
   - Eastern most tip of Double Cone Island: 322°C
   - Mount Merkara (373), (approx. 2 nm east of Port Airlie) bears 174°C

   Determine:
   a) DR Position

   _____

   b) Fix position (A) at 1200 hours (3 bearing fix)

   _____

   c) Course Made Good (CMG)

   _____

   d) Speed Made Good (SMG)

   _____

   e) Set experienced

   _____

   f) Drift experienced

   _____

2) Plot Way Point (B) at 1.5 nm NW off Dolphin Point (Hayman Island) and bears 120°T from the same point (with a given Deviation of 3°W).

   Using the set, drift, and boat speed (through the water) of Question 1 above, (starting at your 3 bearing fix in the first part of the question) determine the:

   a) Course To Steer (CTS), given 3°W Deviation

   _____

   b) SMG

   _____

c) ETA way point (B)

_____

d) What is the Compass bearing of 120°T?

_____

3) Plot Way Point C where Double Cone Island (104) bears 253°T and at a range of 1 nm off the eastern most tip of the Island.

From Fixed Position (A) in Question 1 (3 bearing fix) @1200, (using the same set and drift experienced at (A) in question 1). What is the:

a) CTS (Compass), with a given Deviation: 6°W

_____

b) SMG

_____

c) ETA at Way Point C

_____

d) What is the Compass bearing of 253°T with a given Deviation: 4°E?

_____

EXERCISE 17: LEEWAY

1) You want your vessel to make good a course of 053°T. There is a strong SE wind blowing and you estimate leeway to be about 8°. What course should you steer?

_____

2) You want to make good a course if 130°. There is a strong SW wind blowing and you estimate leeway to be about 10°. What course should you steer?

_____

REVISION

1) Draw a diagram of the Earth and show the North Pole, South Pole, Equator, Greenwich Meridian

2) Define a nautical mile.

_____

_____

3) Define Latitude and Longitude

_____

_____

4) Convert the seconds into decimals of minutes:

a) 35°31'18" _____

b) 123°49'36" _____

c) 118°32'06" _____

d) 68°01'12" _____

e) 179°59'54" _____

5) Plot the following position on your chart: 20° 20.00' S 149°05.00'E
   a) In what direction is SE Working Island from you and how far?

   _____

   b) In what direction are the following from you:

   Perseverance Island (92):_____

   Pentecost Island (288): _____

   Teague Island (87): _____

6) What are the positions of the following on your chart?

   a) North tip Deloraine Island:_____

   b) Grimston Point: _____

   c) Dent Island Light: _____

   d) Cid Island Light: _____

7) Name the four cardinal points and what is the degree measurement of each?

   _____

   _____

   _____

   _____

8) Imagine you are standing on the Equator. The North Pole is on your right and the South Pole on your left, in which direction in degrees are you facing? And is this the True direction?

_____

_____

9) Is the longitude or latitude scale used for measuring distances, explain your answer?

_____

_____

_____

_____

10) Plot the following position on your chart: 20° 22.1'S 148° 54.6'E

What symbols are in in this immediate area, why do they mean?

_____

_____

11) Plot the following position on your chart: 20° 07.00'S 149°04.00E

In what directions are the following from you in True?
Pinnacle Point:____ _____

Whitsunday Cairn (380): _____

Petrel Islet (Middle): _____

Mosstrooper Peak (216): _____

12) What is the latitude and longitude of each of the following points:

   a) Ireby Island   _____

   b) Pinnacle Point   _____

   c) Pioneer Rocks   _____

   d) Coppersmith Rocks   _____

   e) Sidney Island   _____

13) What is the True Bearing of a lighthouse if the variation is 14°E and the bearing 121°M is taken with a hand bearing compass?

   _____

   _____

   _____

14) What is the course to steer if the True course is 052°T and the variation is 9°E and Deviation is 4°W?

   _____

   _____

   _____

15) The True course is 315° on the chart. What is the magnetic course to steer, allowing for a variation of 4°W?

   _____

   _____

   _____

16) The True course is 120°. If the variation is 2°E, what is the Magnetic course?

_____

_____

_____

17) You steer a Magnetic course of 182°. Variation is 4°E. What is the True Course to plot on your chart?

_____

_____

_____

18)

Compass Course	060°C	Compass Course	064°C
Deviation	6°E	Deviation	3°W
Magnetic Course	M	Magnetic Course	M
Variation	13°W	Variation	2°W
True Course	T	True Course	T
True Bearing	328°T	True Bearing	124°T
Variation	4°E	Variation	6°W
Magnetic Bearing	M	Magnetic Bearing	M
Deviation	6°W	Deviation	4°E
Compass Bearing	C	Compass Bearing	C

Compass Course	C	Compass Course	357°C
Deviation	3°W	Deviation	
Magnetic Bearing	247°M	Magnetic Course	001°M
Variation		Variation	
True Bearing	256°T	True Course	347°T

©Jackie Parry

Compass Bearing	C	True Course	000°T
Deviation	6°E	Variation	13°E
Magnetic Bearing	161°M	Magnetic Course	M
Variation	10°E	Deviation	6°W
True Bearing	T	Compass Course	C

True Bearing	T	True Course	172°T
Variation	7°W	Variation	
Magnetic Bearing	003°M	Magnetic Course	176°M
Deviation		Deviation	
Compass Bearing	358°C	Compass Course	175°C

Compass Bearing	070°C	True Course	180°T
Deviation		Variation	
Magnetic Bearing	M	Magnetic Course	M
Variation	6°W	Deviation	2°W
True Bearing	066°T	Compass Course	176°C

Compass Course	090°C	Compass Course	043°C
Deviation		Deviation	4°W
Magnetic Course	087°M	Magnetic Course	M
Variation	11°E	Variation	11°E
True Course	T	True Course	T

Compass Course	C	Compass Course	C
Deviation	3°E	Deviation	4°W
Magnetic Course	M	Magnetic Course	340°M
Variation	13°E	Variation	17°E
True Course	T	True Course	T

19) DEDUCED RECKONING
   a) At 0900 hours in position 20° 10'S 149°00'E you steer a course of 031°C for 1 hour 20 minutes at 5.5 knots.
      Compass Deviation for that course is 16°W
      What is your DR position at 1020hrs?

   _____

   b) At 1200hrs in the fixed position 20°45.0'S 148°50'E you steer 000° T at 5 knots.
      a. What is your DR position at 1300hrs?

   _____

   c) You notice on the chart the ebb and flood arrows closest to your DR area, what is your estimated position knowing you have been sailing on maximum ebb current? (Use symbols closest to you that could put you in danger).

   _____

20) THREE BEARING FIX
   You are on a vessel using the ship's compass with a pelorus (sighting telescope attached) to enable you to take bearings using the ship's compass.

At 0915 hours NW tip of Anchorsmith Island (36) is in transit with NW tip of Blacksmith Island (NP).

Mount Arthur (250) on Shaw Island bears 323°C, Silversmith Island (74) bears 069°C.

Deviation for the course you are on is given as 10°E

What are the True Bearings:

a) Of the transit _____

b) Bearing to Mount Arthur (250) _____

c) Silversmith Island bearing (74) _____

d) What is your fix position at 0915hrs _____

21) RUNNING FIX (TRANSFERRED BEARING LINE)

On the same vessel as Qu.20.

At 1430hrs on a course of 300°C (Deviation 16°E) at a speed of 6 knots, a bearing of 354°C is taken of the west cardinal mark on Platypus Rock.

At 1500hrs a second bearing, using the same compass, of 082° C is taken.

a) What is your True course? _____

What are the True bearings of:

b) The first bearing _____

c) The second bearing _____

d) What is the distance covered between the bearings _____

e) What is your fixed position at 1500hrs _____

COASTAL NAVIGATION

Answers Section

EXERCISE 1: TIME CALCULATIONS – ANSWERS

1. Time calculations – convert these minutes to decimals of an hour

a) 30 minutes: 30 / 60 = 0.5 hours

b) 54 minutes: 54 / 60 = 0.9 hours

c) 1 hour 30 minutes: 30 / 60 = 0.5 minutes, therefore = 1.5 hours

d) 15 minutes: 15 / 60 = 0.25 hours

e) 40 minutes: 40 / 60 = 0.7 hours (rounded up from 0.66)

f) 22 minutes: 22/ 60 = 0.4 hours (rounded up from 0.37)

g) 1 hour 15 minutes: 15 /60 = 0.25, therefore, = 1.25 hours

h) 5 minutes: 5 / 60 = 0.083 (but we'll round up), therefore, = 0.1 hours

i) 39 minutes: 39 / 60 = 0.65
(0.6 is accurate enough for calculations involving degrees) = 0.6 hours

EXERCISE 2: TIME CALCULATIONS – ANSWERS
Convert decimalised minutes into regular minutes.

By the same method of converting seconds to decimals of minute we can determine minutes as a decimal of an hour.

This is commonly used for calculating speed, distance and time.

a) 0.45 hours
0.45 x 60 = 27 minutes

TIP: be careful – do not confuse .45 with 45 minutes, it is a decimal.
Remember the decimal 0.5 is one half of a whole. E.g. 0.5 hours is 30 minutes.

b) 1.5 hours
1.5 x 60 = 90 minutes, which is the same as 1 hour 30 minutes.

TIP: You should be able to instantly recognise that 0.5 of an hour is 30 minutes, and the answer is quickly calculated = 1 hour 30 minutes.

c) 0.6 hours
0.6 x 60 = 36 minutes

TIP: Again, you know that 0.5 is 30 minutes, so you instantly know that your answer (for 0.6) will be a little more than 30 minutes)

d) 0.8 hours
0.8 x 60 = 48 minutes

e) 0.75 hours
0.75 x 60 = 45 minutes

TIP: We know that 0.75 is three-quarters of one whole (1), and we know that 45 minutes is three-quarters of an hour.

f) 0.5 hours
0.5 x 60 = 30 minutes

g) 0.2 hours
0.2 x 60 = 12 minutes

h) .10 hours
.10 x 60 = 6 minutes

i) .18 hours
.18 x 60 = 10.8 minutes, therefore 11 minutes is fine for sailing boat calculations

j) .24 hours
.24 x 60 = 14.4 minutes, therefore = approximately 14 minutes

EXERCISE 3: SPEED, DISTANCE, TIME – ANSWERS

1. Find the distance travelled in 15 minutes if your speed was:

a) 20 knots
Decimalise the minutes
15 / 60 = 0.25
D = S x T
D = 20 x 0.25
Distance travelled in 15 minutes at 20 knots = 5 nautical miles

TIP: We know 15 minutes is one quarter of an hour. Therefore, travelling for one hour at 20 knots we would cover 20 nm. It's easy to see that in one quarter of that time we will travel 5 nm.

b) 40 knots
D = S x T
D = 40 x 0.25
Distance = 10 nautical miles

TIP: One quarter of 40 is 10.

c) 10 knots
D = S x T
D = 10 x 0.25
Distance = 2.5 nautical miles

©Jackie Parry

d) 8 knots
D = S x T
D = 8 x 0.25
Distance = 2 nautical miles

e) 4 knots
D = S x T
D = 4 x 0.25
Distance = 1 nautical mile

f) 6 knots
D = S x T
D = 6 x 0.25
Distance = 1.5 nautical miles

g) 15.5 knots
D = S x T
D = 15.5 x 0.25
Distance = 3.875 nautical miles (round up to 3.9)

h) 12.4 knots
D = S x T
D = 12.4 x 0.25
Distance = 3.1 nautical miles

2) How long will it take you to reach your next waypoint if you had 3.5 nautical miles to go and your speed was:

T = D / S

a) 12 knots
T = D / S
T = 3.5 / 12
Time = 0.3
Convert decimalised minutes to actual minutes
0.3 x 60 = 18 minutes

b) 16 knots
T = D / S
T = 3.5 / 16
Time = 0.2
0.2 x 60 = 13 minutes

c) 20 knots
T = D / S
T = 3.5 / 20
Time = 0.175
0.175 x 60 = 10.5 minutes (10 minutes and 30 seconds)

d) 4 knots
T = D / S
T = 3.5 / 4
Time = 0.875
0.875 x 60 = 52.5 minutes

e) 15 knots
T = D / S
T = 3.5 / 15
T = 0.23
0.23 x 60 = 14 minutes

f) 6.5 knots
T = D / S
T = 3.5 / 6.5
T = 0.54
0.54 x 60 = 32 minutes

g) 12.4 knots
T = D / S
T = 3.5 / 12.4
T = 0.28
0.28 x 60 = 17 minutes

h) 5 knots
T = D / S
T = 3.5 / 5
T = 0.7
0.7 x 60 = 42 minutes

3. At 1549 your vessel is sailing at 6.5 knots, how many nautical miles will you travel by 1600. Answer to two decimal places.

D = S x T
6.5 x 11 mins
Decimalise minutes = 11 / 60 = 0.183
6.5 x 0.183 = 1.19 nm

4. You are travelling at 6 knots, how many nautical miles will you travel in:

D = S x T

a) 0.4 hours
D = S x T   D = 6 x 0.4
Distance = 2.4 nautical miles

b) 15 minutes
Turn minutes into decimals first
15 / 60 = 0.25
D = S x T   D = 6 x 0.25   Distance = 1.5 nautical miles

c) 1 hour 25 minutes
= 1 + 25/60 hrs
(Turn minutes into decimals first)
25 / 60 = 0.42, therefore, Time = 1.42hrs
D = S x T
D = 6 x 1.42
Distance = 8.52 nautical miles

d) 1.5 hours
D = S x T
D = 6 x 1.5
Distance = 9 nautical miles

e) 2 ¾ hours
= 2 hours 45 minutes
= 2 hours (45 / 60)
= 2.75 hrs
As we know, ¾ of an hour is 45 minutes (without having to do the above calculation)
D= S X T
D= 6 x 2.75
Distance = 16.5 nautical miles

f) 0.8 hours
D = S x T
D = 6 x 0.8
Distance = 4.8 nautical miles

g) 4.2 hours
D = S x T
D = 6 x 4.2
Distance = 25.2 nautical miles

h) 2 hours 15 minutes
Decimalise minutes first
2 hours 15 (15 / 60) = 2.25
D = S x T
D = 6 x 2.25
Distance = 13.5 nautical miles

5. You have travelled 8.7 nautical miles in 45 minutes. How many knots, on average, where you doing during this time?
We are trying to find speed. So use the formula
S = D / T
The time is in minutes so first decimalise the minutes
45 / 60 = 0.75
S = D / T
S = 8.7 / 0.75
Speed = 11.6 knots

6. What is your speed if you travelled 6 miles in:

S = D / T

a) 26 minutes
Convert minutes: 26 / 60 = 0.43
S = D / T
S = 6 / 0.43
Speed = 14 knots.

b) 40 minutes
Convert minutes: 40 / 60 = 0.66
S = D / T
S = 6 / 0.66
Speed = 9.10 knots

c) 1.5 hours
S = D / T
S = 6 / 1.5
Speed = 4 knots

d) 10 minutes
Convert minutes: 10 / 60 = 0.17
S = D / T
S = 6 / 0.17
Speed = 35

e) 1 hour
S = D / T
S = 6 / 1
Speed = 6 knots

f) 1 hour 45 minutes
Convert minutes: 45 / 60 = 0.75
S = D / T
S = 6 / 1.75 (don't forget to include the hour)
Speed = 3.43 knots

g) 50 minutes
Convert minutes: 50 / 60 = 0.83
S = D / T
S = 6 / 0.83
Speed = 7.23 knots

h) 75 minutes
Convert minutes: 75 minutes is 1 hour 15 minutes
15 / 60 = 0.25
So we have 1.25 hrs
S = D / T
S = 6 / 1.25   Speed = 4.8 knots

©Jackie Parry

7. How long would it take you to travel 12 nautical miles if your speed was:

T = D / S

a) 15 knots
T = D / S
T = 12 / 15
Time = 0.8
Convert to minutes: 0.8 x 60
Time = 48 minutes

b) 3 knots
T = D / S
T = 12 / 3
Time = 4 hours

c) 9 knots
T = D / S
T = 12 / 9
T = 1.33 hrs
Convert .33 hrs to minutes: .33 x 60 = 19.8 (let's say 20 minutes)
Time = 1 hour 20 minutes

d) 12 knots
T = D / S
T = 12 / 12
Time = 1 hour

e) 20 knots
T = D / S
T = 12 / 20
T = 0.6
Convert: 0.6 x 60 =
Time 36 minutes

f) 4 knots
T = D / S
T = 12 / 4
Time = 3 hours

g) 4.5 knots
T = D / S
T = 12 / 4.5
T = 2.67 hrs = 2 hrs + (0.67 X 60) minutes = 2 hrs 40 minutes
We've just converted .67 to minutes: .67 x 60 = 40 minutes
Time = 2 hours 40 minutes

h) 17 knots
T = D / S
T = 12 / 17   T = .71   Convert: .71 x 60 = 42   Time = 42 minutes

EXERCISE 4: CHART SYMBOLS EXERCISE 4 - ANSWERS

1)

   a) All-round light with obscured sector (Flashing every 6 seconds, 12 metres high, visibility 3 nautical miles)

   b) Westerly Cardinal Marker (Keep West Of Me) Very Quick Flash 9 times every 10 seconds. Yellow Black Yellow stripes

   c) Isophase - a light which has dark and light periods of equal length.

   d) Occulting - An *occulting light* is a rhythmic *light* in which the duration of *light* in each period is longer than the total duration of darkness.

   e)

┼┼┼	Wreck, least depth unknown but usually deeper than 20 metres.
⊥	Visible wreck.
┼┼┼ Mast(s)	Wreck of which the mast(s) only are visible at chart datum.
4₆ Wk 4₆ Obstn	Wreck or obstruction, least depth known obtained by sounding only.
4₆ Wk 4₆ Obstn	Wreck or obstruction, least depth known, swept by wire drag or diver.

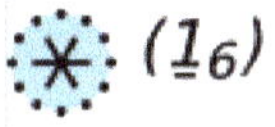

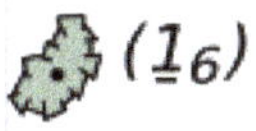

✳ (1_6) 🪨 (1_6)	Rock which covers and un-covers, height above chart datum. (In this example the rock is visible 1.6 metres <u>above</u> chart datum.)
✣	Rock awash at the level of chart datum.
✢	Underwater rock of unknown depth, dangerous to surface navigation.
(4_8) R ✢ (4_8)	Underwater rock of known depth, dangerous to surface navigation.
♯	Remains of a wreck, or other foul area, non-dangerous to navigation but to be avoided by vessels anchoring, trawling etc.
 ⸺ (20)	Wreck over which the exact depth is unknown, but considered to have a safe clearance to the depth shown.

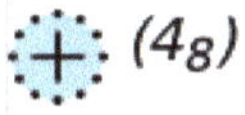

2.

a) G   Gravel

b) St   Stones

c) Sh   Shells

d) Co   Coral

e) S   Sand

f) M   Mud

g) Wd   Weed

h) Si   Silt

i) R   Rock

3)

   a) Ebb tide stream

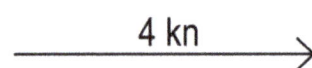

   b) Eddies

   c) Flood tide stream with rate

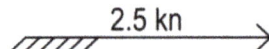

   d) Overfalls, tide rips, races

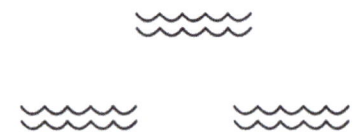

©Jackie Parry

EXERCISE 5: POSITION PRACTICE - ANSWERS

1) Find the geographical position:

a) Pentecost Island (288)   20° 23.81'S 149° 01.8'E

b) Dent Island (158)   20° 20.95'S 148° 55.9'E

c) Workington Island (91)   20° 16.1'S 149° 07.3'E

d) Coppersmith Rock Light   20° 35.9'S 149° 07.05'E

e) Thomas Island (179)   20° 32.85'S 149° 06.8'E

f) Mansell Island (170)   20° 28.3'S 149° 07.6'E

g) Hook Island, Hook Peak (456) 20° 05.85'S 148° 55.81'E

EXERCISE 6: DISTANCE - ANSWERS

1) Measure the straight-line distance in Sea Miles:

   a) Haselwood Island-north peak (135) to Whitsunday Craig (353) = 5.29 nm
   b) Ladysmith Island (121) to Shaw Island-Mount Arthur (250)= 8.5 nm
   c) South Repulse Island (60) to Pentecost (288)= 15.69 nm
   d) Grimston Point on the mainland (north) to Baird Point (top of point on West side of Hook Island) = 12.72nm

EXERCISE 7: DIRECTION/BEARINGS - ANSWERS

1) Measure the direction in True:

   a) From E. Repulse Island (62) to Cape Conway tip   35° T

   b) From E. Repulse Island (62) to Silversmith Island (74)   86° T

   c) From CID Island (215) to North Molle Island (nth) (124)   295° T

   d) From CID Island (167) to Pine Island (100)   193° T

2) Lat: 20° 42.65'S Long: 148° 48.85'E

EXERCISE 8: COMPASS TO TRUE AND TRUE TO COMPASS - ANSWERS

1) Compass to True and True to Compass and Total Error

TRUE	100°	226°	060°	154°	225°	007°	019°	209°	315°	179°
VARIATION	12°E	6°E	13°W	10°W	11°E	9°E	3°W	1°E	6°W	8°E
MAGNETIC	88°	220°	073°	164°	214°	358°	022°	208°	321°	171°
DEVIATION	2°W	6°E	8°E	4°E	4°W	3°E	6°E	4°W	1°E	11°W
COMPASS	090°	214°	065°	160°	218°	355°	016°	212°	320°	182°
T. ERROR	10°E	12°E	5°W	6°W	7°E	12°E	3°E	3°W	5°W	3°W

2) If the Variation is 10°W and the total error is 14°W, what is the Deviation?

T
V   10°W
M
D   4°W
C
Error   14°W

3) What is the total Compass error if the Variation is 8°E and the Deviation is 4°W

8 – 4 = 4° E
We know it will be East as we take the largest number's suffix.
4°E

4) What is the True bearing of a lighthouse if a bearing of 280° is taken with a hand bearing compass and the Variation is 4°W

T= 276°
V= 4°W
M=280° (compass bearing, no deviation)

5) Calculate the Compass course to steer if the Compass error is 15°E and the True course is 060°
Answer, East compass least, therefore we subtract:

060° - 15°E = 045°

Answer the following three questions using Variation of 6°E and using this deviation card (below)

COMPASS	DEVIATION	MAGNETIC
160°	7°W	153°
180°	5°W	174
200°	2°W	188°
220°	1°E	220°
240°	3°E	242°
260°	5°E	275°
280°	7°E	285°

6) Find the true course if the compass course is:
(a) 249°C
(b) 208°C
(c) 231°C
(d) 249°C
(e) 179°C

C	249°	208°	231°	259°	179°
D	4°E	1°W	2°E	5°E	5°W
M	253°	207°	233°	264°	174°
V	6°E	6°E	6°E	6°E	6°E
T	259°	213°	239°	270°	180°

7) Find the True course given:
(a) 178°T
(b) 222°T
(c) 241°T
(d) 190°T
(e) 254°M

C	177°	215°	233°	185°	250°
D	5°W	1°E	2°E	1°W	4°E
M	172°	216°	235°	184°	254°
V	6°E	6°E	6°E	6°E	6°E
T	178°	222°	241°	190°	260°

8)
Find the compass course to steer if the required true course is:
(a) 225°T
(b) 196°T
(c) 181°T
(d) 248°T
(e) 281°T

Write it out:

C	218°	193°	180°	239°	270°
D	1°E	3°W	5°W	3°E	5°E
M	219°	190°	175°	242°	275°
V	6°E	6°E	6°E	6°E	6°E
T	225°	196°	181°	248°	281°

9) Complete the table

TRUE	104°	229°	073°	143°	215°	004°	013°	204°	327°	182°
VARIATION	10°E	9°E	17°W	26°W	8°E	7°E	1°W	7°W	3°W	4°E
MAGNETIC	094°	220°	090°	169°	207°	357°	014°	211°	330°	178°
DEVIATION	6°W	6°E	15°E	11°E	7°W	4°E	3°E	2°W	7°E	2°W
COMPASS	100°	214°	075°	158°	214°	353°	011°	213°	323°	180°
ERROR	4°E	15°E	2°W	15°W	1°E	11°E	2°E	9°W	4°E	2°E

©Jackie Parry

10)

True	105°	221°	123°	156°	222°	009°	348°	213°	002°	183°
Variation	15°E	6°E	12°W	10°W	6°E	12°E	2°W	3°E	5°W	5°E
Magnetic	090°	215°	135°	166°	216°	357°	350°	210°	007°	178°

EXERCISE 9: THREE BEARING FIX – ANSWER

1) Hook Peak (456) bears 258° T

   Mosstrooper Peak (216) (Border Island) bears 186° T

   Petrel Islet (middle) bears 153° T

   Position: 20° 04.4'S 149°03.03'E

EXERCISE 10: RADAR RANGE FIX - ANSWER

You are north east of Esk Island, and have taken these radar ranges. Fix your position:

South tip Border Island: 2.3 nm

Petrel Islet (east tip): 3.5 nm

Southern Tip of Deloraine Island: 3.5 nm

Position: 20° 13.05'S 149°03.43'E

EXERCISE 11: BEARINGS - ANSWER

1)   127°T - Red 69°
   True Bearing 058°T

2)   324°T + 061°Rel
   True Bearing 385°T
   -360°
   True Bearing 025°T

3)   062°T + Green 32°
   True Bearing 094°T

4)   010°T - Red 070° = -60
   True Bearing   = 60 + 360°
   = 300°T

5)   312°T (your vessel)
          True Course 231° (other vessel)
          Vessel bears Red 081°: (312 – 231 = 081°)
          Vessel bears 279°Rel.: (360-81)

6) 20°24.7'S 148°56.2'E

7) 208°T Position: 20° 11.61'S 148° 50.8'E

8) 346°T Distance: 8.89 nm, time taken 2 hours 12 minutes

9)
a)

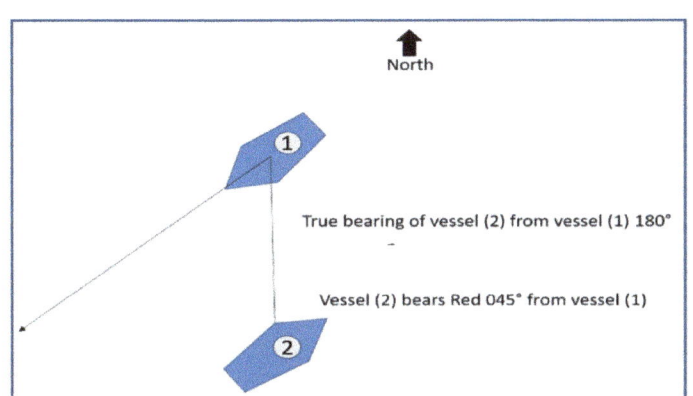

(b)

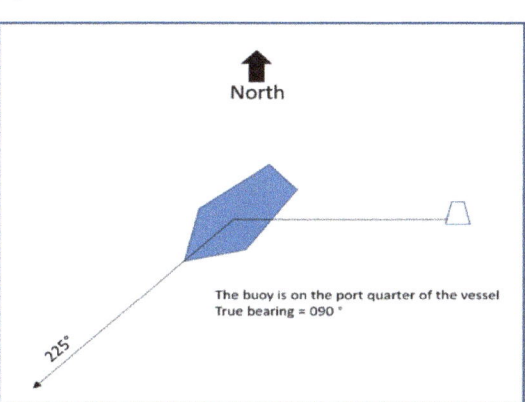

c)

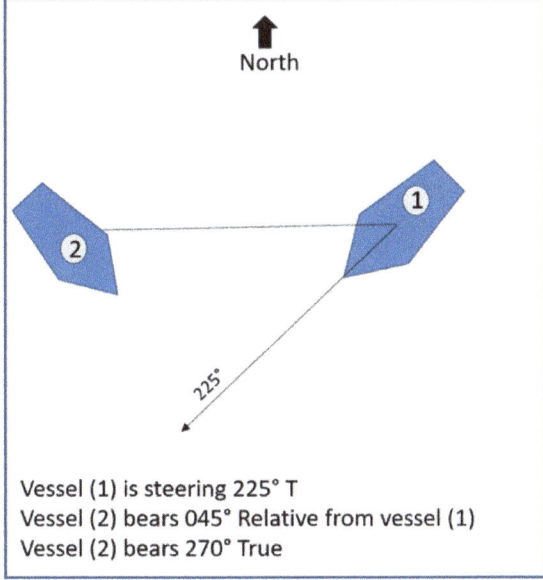

d)

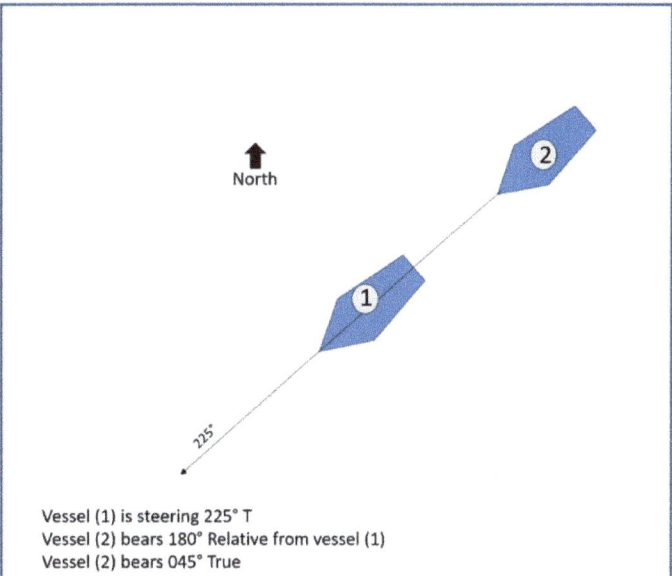

e) 310°T   068°Rel = 378 - 360

      018°T = True bearing of light is 018°

10) Vessel steering 112°, light bearing Red 074°
   True bearing = 112 – 074 = 038°T

11) 138°T - 123°T = Inform the skipper to look 15° Red

12) Steer 307.5°T at 6 knots – covering 11.9 nm will take a little under 2 hours.

13) 20° 31.00'S 149° 08.45'E

14) 1.82 nm

15) Course 243°T Distance = 8.82 nm

EXERCISE 12: DR AND EP - ANSWERS

1. Distance = 11.1 nm

   DR position = 20° 14.88'S 148° 52.34'E

2. ETA at Workington Island (91) Abeam, port side = 1015 after having travelled 6.3nm

EXERCISE 13: RUNNING FIX - ANSWER
20° 34.4'S 148° 57.2'E

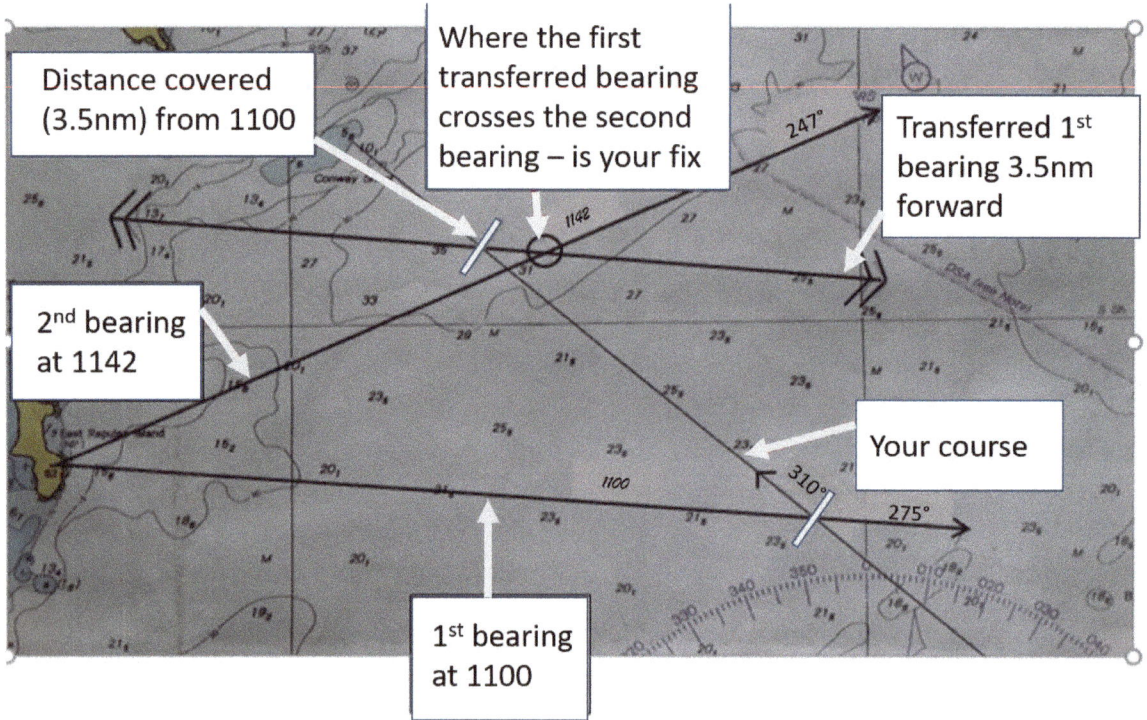

D= S x T = 5 x 0.7 (42 mins /60)
= 3.5 nm

EXERCISE 14: POSITION – DOUBLE THE ANGLE OFF THE BOW - ANSWERS

Time between bearings = 36 minutes (0.6 hrs)

Distance run = 10 x 0.6 nm

= 6 nm

True course = 058°T

Relative bearing = 070° Rel

Therefore the true bearing = 128°T

At 0636 the light bears 128°T at distance 6 nautical miles.

EXERCISE 15: POSITION – TRANSIT BEARINGS - ANSWERS
1) 20° 11. 6'S   148° 51.5'E
2) 20° 11.2'S 149°00.61'E

EXERCISE 16: POSITION – THREE BEARING FIX WITH SET AND DRIFT - ANSWERS

1) Convert Compass bearings and course to True. Remember we need to apply Variation and Deviation for the compass course, as you are using the ship's compass. But only apply Variation for the handheld compass bearings, as we assume no Deviation for handheld compass bearings.

	Course	Hook Island	Double Cone Island	Mt Merkara
C	359°C	057°C	322°C	174°C
D	2°W	-	-	-
M	357°M	057°M	322°M	174°M
V	8°E	8°E	8°E	8°E
T	005°T	065°T	330°T	182°T

a) Fix Position (A) = 20° 10.4'S 148° 46.05'E
b) 20° 10'S 148° 44.15'E
c) CMG = 024°T
d) SMG = 5.6 knots
e) Set = 103°T
f) Drift Rate: 1.8 knots

2)

a) CTS = 011° T   006°C

    T 011°
    V 8°E
    M 003°
    D 3°W
    C 006°

b) SMG = 5.75 knots
c) ETA at Waypoint (B) = 1348 hours

Time of voyage = Distance (A to B) / Speed = 10.35 nm / 5.75 knots = 1.8 hours

.8 x 60 = 48 mins = 1 hour 48 minutes. ETA is therefore 1348.

d) 117°T

T 120°
V 8°E
M 112°
D 3°W
C 115°

3) a) CTS = 339°C
b) SMG 4.4 knots
c) 1308

Distance A to C = 4.95 nm

Time = Distance / Speed = 4.95 / 4.3 = 1.15 hours

.15 x 60 = 9 mins. Therefore Time = 1 hour 9 minutes.

ETA = 1309 hours

d) C 241°
D 4°E
M 245°
V 8°E
T 253°

EXERCISE 17: POSITION – LEEWAY – ANSWERS

1) You want your vessel to make good a course of 053°T. There is a strong SE wind blowing and you estimate leeway to be about 8°. What course should you steer?

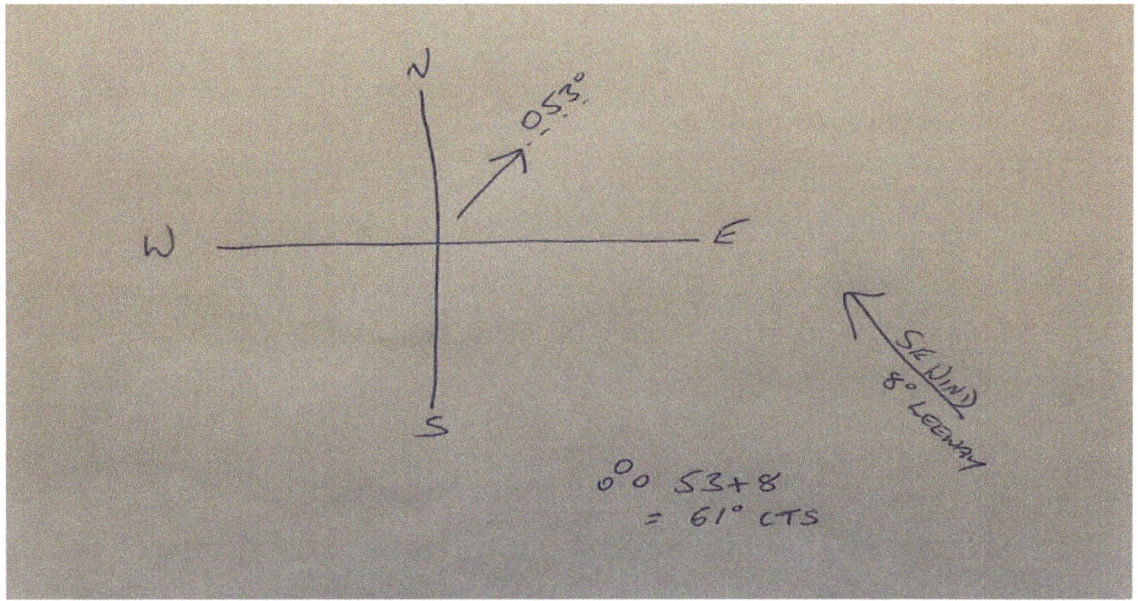

2) You want to make good a course if 130°. There is a strong SW wind blowing and you estimate leeway to be about 10°. What course should you steer?

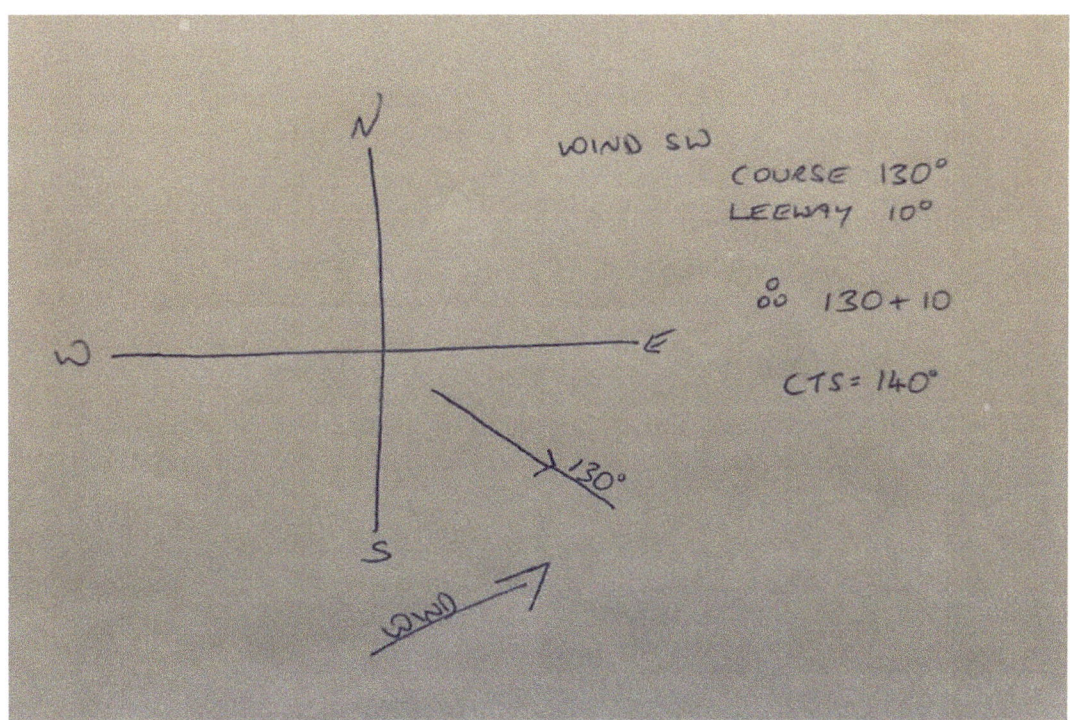

REVISION - ANSWERS

1) Define a nautical mile.

The Nautical Mile is the length of one minute of latitude.

2)

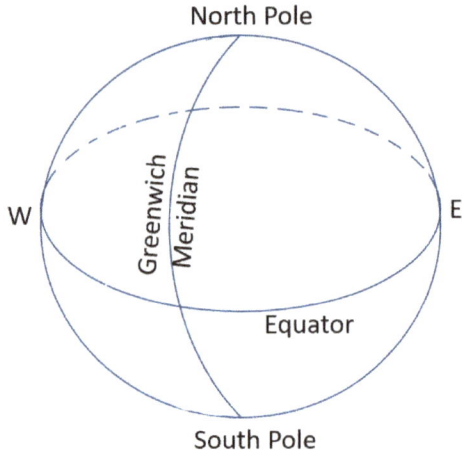

3) Describe Latitude and Longitude

Latitude: The north-south position of a location on the globe. Locations in the Northern Hemisphere are identified by northern latitudes (above the Equator). Southern Hemisphere locations are on southern latitudes (below the Equator).

The Equator = 0° latitude, North Pole = 90° North and South Pole = 90° South.

Longitudes run from the geographical North Pole to the geographical South Pole, intersecting the Equator. They meet at both Poles, and specify the East and West position of a location.

Half of a longitudinal circle is known as a Meridian. Meridians are perpendicular to every latitude.

4) Conversion into degrees, minutes and decimals of minutes

    a) 35°31.3'
    b) 123°49.6'
    c) 118°32.1'
    d) 68°01.2'
    e) 179°59.9'

5) Plot the following position on your chart: 20° 20.00' S 149°05.00'E

    a)   In what direction is SE Working Island from you and how far? 033°T and 4.38 nm

b) In what direction are the following from you:
   Perseverance Island (92): 256°T

   Pentecost Island (288): 219°T

   Teague Island (87): 334.5°T

4) What are the positions of the following on your chart?

   d) North tip Deloraine Island: 20° 09.35'S 149° 04.4'E

   e) Grimston Point: 20° 10.61'S   148° 40.6'E

   f) Dent Island Light: 20° 22.15'S 148° 55.7'E

   g) Cid Island Light: 20° 16.4'S 148° 54.5'E

5) Name the four cardinal points and what is the degree measurement of each?
   North 000° (360°), East 090°, South 180°, West 270°.

6) You would be looking True West.

9) Distance is measured on the latitude scale because the Mercator projection used for charts creates a distorting elongation of the longitude scale.

10) Ebb flood steam and Flood tide stream with rate of flow

11) Plot the following position on your chart: 20° 07.00'S 149°04.00E

In what directions are the following from you in True?

   Pinnacle Point: 300°T

   Whitsunday Cairn (380): 240°T

   Petrel Islet: 150°T

   Mosstrooper Peak (216): 212°T

12)
   (a) Ireby I.   20°13.7' S 149°08.6' E

   (b) Pinnacle Pt. Light 20°03.7' S 148°57.9' E

   (c) Pioneer Rks.   20°13.7' S 148°45.4' E

   (d) Coppersmith Rk.   20°36' S 149°07' E

   (e) Sidney I.   20°27' S 149°00.5' E

13) T 135°
    V 14°E
    M 121°

14) T 052°
    V 9°E
    M 043°
    D 4°W
    C 047°

15) T 315°
    V 4°W
    M 319°

16) T 120°
    V 2°E
    M 118°

17) T 186°
    V 4°E
    M 182°

18)

Compass Course	060°C	Compass Course	064°C
Deviation	6°E	Deviation	3°W
Magnetic Course	66°M	Magnetic Course	61° M
Variation	13°W	Variation	2°W
True Course	53° T	True Course	59° T
True Bearing	328°T	True Bearing	124°T
Variation	4°E	Variation	6°W
Magnetic Bearing	324° M	Magnetic Bearing	130° M
Deviation	6°W	Deviation	4°E
Compass Bearing	330° C	Compass Bearing	126° C

Compass Course	250°	C	Compass Course		357°C
Deviation	3°W		Deviation		4°E
Magnetic Bearing	247°M		Magnetic Course		001°M
Variation	009°E		Variation		14°W
True Bearing	256°T		True Course		347°T

Compass Bearing	155°	C	True Course		000°T
Deviation	6°E		Variation		13°E
Magnetic Bearing	161°M		Magnetic Course	047°	M
Variation	10°E		Deviation		6°W
True Bearing	171°	T	Compass Course	053°	C

True Bearing	356°	T	True Course		172°T
Variation	7°W		Variation		4°W
Magnetic Bearing	003°M		Magnetic Course		176°M
Deviation	005°E		Deviation		001° E
Compass Bearing	358°C		Compass Course		175°C

Compass Bearing	070°C		True Course		180°T
Deviation	2°E		Variation		6°E
Magnetic Bearing	072°M		Magnetic Course		174°M
Variation	6°W		Deviation		2°W
True Bearing	066°T		Compass Course		176°C

Compass Course	090°C	Compass Course	043°C
Deviation	003°W	Deviation	4°W
Magnetic Course	087°M	Magnetic Course	039°M
Variation	11°E	Variation	11°E
True Course	098° T	True Course	050°T
True Bearing	237°T	True Bearing	097°T

Compass Course	232°C	Compass Course	344°C
Deviation	3°E	Deviation	4°W
Magnetic Course	235°M	Magnetic Course	340°M
Variation	13°E	Variation	17°E
True Course	248°T	True Course	357°T
True Bearing	317°T	True Bearing	020°T

19)
Distance = Speed x Time

= 5.5 knots x 1 hr 20 minutes
= 5.5 x 1.33hrs (20 mins = 20/60 = 0.33)
= 7.315 nm

True Course = 023°T

C 031°
D 16°W
M 015°
V 8°E
T 023°T

DR at 1020hrs = 20°03.3'S 149° 03.05'E

(a) DR Position at 1300hrs = 20°40'S 148° 50'E

(b) EP Position at 1300hrs = 20°39.05' 148° 02.5'E

20) THREE BEARING FIX – REVISION ANSWERS
   a) 223°T   b) 341°T   c) 087°T   d) 20°35.3'S 149°05.3'E

21) RUNNING FIX (TRANSFERRED BEARING LINE) REVISION ANSWERS
   a) 324°T b) 018°T   c) 106°T   d) 3nm e) 20°30.5'S 148° 59.8'E

C	082°	354°	300°
D	16°E	16°E	16°E
M	098°	010°	316°
V	8°E	8°E	8°E
T	106°	018°	324°

SALIENT POINTS

Airlie Beach	20°16.1' S
Anchorsmith Island	20°37.0' S
Baird Point (Hook Island)	20°07.0' S
Bird I.	20°05.4' S
Blacksmith Island	20°38.1' S
Border I.	20°09.8' S
Cape Conway	20°32.2' S
Cid Island	20°15.9' S
Coppersmith Rock	20°36.0' S
Craig Point	20°19.0' S
Dead Dog Island	20°32.8' S
Dent Island	20°21.1' S
Deloraine Island	20°09.5' S
Dolphin Point	20°02.3' S
Double Cone Island	20°06.0' S
Dumbell Island	20°10.5'S
Dungurra Island	20°22.0' S
East Repulse Island	20°36.0'S
Edward Island	20°15.1'S
Esk Island	20°14.0' S
Grimston Point (Mainland)	20°10.7' S
Haselwood Island (North Peak)	20°16.0' S
Hayman Island	20°03.1' S
Hook Island	20°07.0' S
Hook Peak	20°06.0' S
Ireby Island	20°13.8' S
Ladysmith Island	20°39.2' S
Long Island Peak	20°22.6' S

Mainland – Airlie Beach	20°16.1' S
Mainland Grimston Point	20°10.7' S
Mansell Island	20°28.3' S
Mosstrooper Peak	20°09.5' S
Mount Arthur	20°30.8'S
Mount Merkara	20°15.0' S
North Molle Island	20°14.0' S
Pentecost Island	20°23.9' S
Perseverance Island	20°21.3' S
Petrel Islet	20°11.9' S
Pine Island	20°23.1' S
Pinnacle Point	20°03.8' S
Pioneer Point	20°14.0' S
Platypus Rock	20°31.5' S
Port of Airlie	20°16.2' S
Shaw Island	20°28.3' S
Shaw Peak	20°28.3' S
Sidney Island	20°27.0' S
Silversmith Island	20°35.4' S
South Molle Island	20°16.0' S
South Repulse Island	20°37.0' S
Teague Island	20°18.1' S
Thomas Island	20°32.9' S
Triangle Island	20°29.5' S
Whitsunday Cairn	20°10.2' S
Whitsunday Craig	20°18.4' S
Whitsunday Island	20°16.0' S
Workington Island	20°16.3' S

www.ingramcontent.com/pod-product-compliance
Lightning Source LLC
Chambersburg PA
CBHW042301010526
44111CB00047B/2959